The
SAMARITAN'S
DILEMMA

The SAMARITAN'S DILEMMA

Should Government Help Your Neighbor?

DEBORAH STONE

NATION
BOOKS

A Member of the Perseus Books Group

Published by Nation Books, A Member of the Perseus Books Group
116 East 16th Street, 8th Floor
New York, NY 10003

Nation Books is a co-publishing venture of the Nation Institute and the
Perseus Books Group

Books published by Nation Books are available at special discounts for
bulk purchases in the United States by corporations, institutions, and
other organizations. For more information, please contact the Special
Markets Department at Perseus Books Group, 2300 Chestnut Street,
Suite 200, Philadelphia, PA 19103, or call (800) 810-4145, ext. 5000,
or e-mail special.markets@perseusbooks.com.

Designed by Brent Wilcox
Text set in 11 point Adobe Caslon

Library of Congress Cataloging-in-Publication Data
Stone, Deborah A.
   The Samaritan's dilemma : should government help your neighbor? /
Deborah Stone.
      p.   cm.
   ISBN 978-1-56858-354-9
   1. Altruism.   2. Compassion.   3. Self-interest.   4. Social ethics.
5. Political ethics.   6. Public welfare—Moral and ethical aspects—
United States.   I. Title.
HM1146.S76 2008
177'.7—dc22
                                                      2008007045

10 9 8 7 6 5 4 3 2 1

To
Stephen Arthur Stone
1917–2002 and beyond

CONTENTS

Introduction

While I was working on this book, my hairdresser asked what it was about. I told her it's about people who help others and try to do good for their communities, and why we need more of that generosity in politics. "Oh," Becca stopped me cold. "I was with you when you said it's about people who try to do good, and if that's what it's about, I'd like to read it. But if it's about politics, no, I'm sorry, I won't read it."

For those of us who care deeply about politics, Becca's dismissal ought to set off alarms. At the same time, though, her reaction offers the most important clue to the problems that worry us—growing apathy, declining political participation, decaying democracy. In order to get people like Becca to care about politics, we need to reconnect government with helping people and doing good.

Becca is not alone. While teaching at Rutgers University, Tobi Walker asked her students for adjectives to describe how they thought people regard community service and politics. For community service, the students listed "altruistic, caring,

1

helping, selfless, giving, individualistic, and one-on-one." For politics: "dirty, corrupt, ambitious, crooked, dishonest, compromising, slow."[1] Like Saul Steinberg's drawing of the world as seen from New York, Walker's students mapped how Americans have come to view altruism and politics. Standing in the midst of politics, they see altruism as a far-off continent, barely visible at the edge of the horizon. This is the map that decades of civics lessons about the virtues of self-interest have put in citizens' heads. For many people, politics seems not only remote from their daily lives but abhorrent to their personal values. They do not see that they and government have a shared purpose.

I was in college when I discovered that democracy can be a humanitarian endeavor. At age twelve, I had decided to go into medicine, because being a doctor seemed like goodness personified, the surest way to help people. But then I took Introduction to Government, where I met the likes of Plato, Aristotle, Hobbes, Rousseau, Marx, and Tocqueville. I was hooked. To contemplate government and design it to yield up justice, freedom, and human welfare—it didn't get any more noble than that.

Those of us who studied politics in the sixties came of age in a bubble of postwar optimism, almost euphoria, about democracy's potential to cure the world's ills. I hoped I could make a much bigger difference by healing whole communities than by treating one person at a time. Just as I was leaving graduate school, a new field of public policy emerged, and, happily, I landed a job teaching in one of the first programs. The field sought to apply social science to help government improve citizens' lives. Public policy was diagnosis and treatment for society at large, so I felt as though I had gotten to be a doctor after all.

But not for long. Starting in the late seventies, public policy was overtaken by economists—Milton Friedman and his chilly acolytes from the University of Chicago—who believed that the unbridled pursuit of self-interest is the source of all things good. Political science, imitating economics, was overtaken by rational-choice theorists. Their model citizen was a robot that knows only one thing: how to maximize its gain. Sometime in the eighties, politics went off the rails, hijacked by corporations and Wall Street. By now, the people who practice politics, the people who study politics, and the media people who narrate politics to the rest of us rarely speak about helping, caring, or doing good. They talk mostly about who's doing bad and who's in it for what selfish reasons.

For three decades, economists, social scientists, conservatives, and free-market ideologues have had us believing that self-interest makes the world go 'round, that greed is good, that personal ambition is a social virtue, and that anybody who thinks politics ought to foster kindness and compassion is charmingly naive. They warn us that help is harmful, that it undermines ambition and makes people dependent and helpless, and that if we really want to help, we should curb our compassion and withhold our help to "toughen them up." A *New Yorker* cartoon in 1999 captured the spirit of the times: a man lounging in his plush armchair lowers the newspaper long enough to tell his son, clutching his own sheet of paper, "Daddy's way of helping you with your homework is not to help you."

There's nothing wrong with striving for goals, but the cult of self-interest has become an attack on help, and particularly on government help. Once help is removed from government's portfolio, politics feels empty, if not venal. A government that purports to help by not helping violates our moral sense and does violence to the way we live. Even the child at his father's knees can recognize Orwellian doublespeak.

The merchants of self-interest have divorced us from what we know in our pores: we care *about* other people and devote a lot of time and effort to caring *for* them. We live our daily lives by helping and being helped, and we think helping those who need help is the first and last moral duty. We'd just as soon not need help, and we certainly don't want to feel dependent on others. Yet our deepest satisfactions come from helping others and contributing to something larger than ourselves. We may not want to need help, but we need *to* help.

I wrote this book to challenge the attack on help and to reunite politics with doing good. I started from the intuition that what real people care about is not what social scientists by and large tell us we care about. We care most about relationships with other people. We want to love and be loved. We want to care and be cared for. Other people dwell in the core of our self-interest. Yes, we want to eat, survive, and be comfortable, maybe even luxuriously comfortable, but we want more. We want passion. We want to *care about* somebody and something. We want to make a difference. When the sun sets, we hope to have lived a life worth living. And if we have to have government, we want one that helps us lead a good life.

Democracy can work only if people want to participate in politics. They want to participate only if government can help them live out their dreams. Fortunately, it all goes around in a circle.

Caring about and helping others are the very qualities that make good democratic citizens.

My aim is not—most definitely not—to argue that social problems could be solved if only more people performed more acts of kindness. Nor do I propose that we can dispense with most government on the faith that altruism will guide citizens to serve the public good. Rather, I aim to show that altruism is a powerful, centripetal force in everyday life. It's what holds families, friends, and communities together. Altruism is a source of human motivation and energy that can be harnessed for the common good, if only intellectual and political leaders recognize and cultivate it. Moreover, government wins citizens' loyalty and elicits their efforts only by helping them be the generous and kind people they aspire to be.

I will tell a new story about politics with old-fashioned stories about how real people talk, think, and feel. I build this story not from statistics and abstract models of humanity, as so much of social science does, but from the voices of ordinary people talking about their everyday lives to interviewers, reporters, and, in some cases, me. The story may not strike you as scientific because I didn't even try to measure the attitudes and feelings I report, at least not in the conventional sense of counting to see how often something occurs. I didn't put people in laboratories or computer games, watch how they behave, and guess at their motives. Nor did I speculate about what evolution "designed" them to do. Nevertheless, I hope my story will strike you as authentic, because I did try to take the measure of people by finding out what's in their hearts. I measured with words instead of numbers, and counted by listening with an empathic ear.

If we hope to revive democracy and to fulfill its promise, we need to make the public square a place where real people want to gather. We have to start by knowing that these real people draw their life meaning from helping others, making a difference, and trying to do good.

1

The American Malaise

A few years ago, at the tail end of a harsh New Hampshire winter, our local newspaper carried a story headlined "Panhandler Concerns Residents." It seems that every day, a man stood at an intersection in the small town of Henniker holding a sign reading "Hungry." Many residents complained to the selectmen and asked them to do something about it. When the topic came up at the next selectmen's meeting, the chairman asked, "What are you going to do, arrest him and then give him a meal?"

Sixty years ago, that would have been precisely the response to a hungry vagrant in small-town New Hampshire. He would have been taken to the jail if there was one, to an inn or a private home if there wasn't, and there he'd be fed. Thirty years ago, a local official might even have helped him sign up for food stamps or welfare. But now, feeding a hungry man would seem to be trouble waiting to happen, for one of the other selectmen advised the townspeople, "The best way to avoid the problem is not to give out free food."[1]

Times have changed. To be sure, common morality still calls for feeding a hungry man, yet today, when I tell this story and ask audiences what they think the selectman meant, everyone seems to know. It's as if I'd asked a kindergarten class the color of the sky.

"If you give out free food, the man will just keep coming back for more."

"If you give him food, he'll become dependent."

"Other poor people will come to the town, knowing that there's free food."

"If you help him, you're just enabling him."

"Better to teach a man to fish."

These answers pretty well summarize the new conventional wisdom: "Help is harmful. Think twice before you do it, and do it with restraint." What's worse, these answers inform the minds and policies of our politicians and are written into the moral code of government. Taken together, they express the reigning public philosophy in post-Reagan America: Help is harmful. Giving has too many bad consequences. Compassion is often a form of self-indulgence—it makes us feel better but worsens the problem. Helping people enables them to slack off their personal effort. Sharing opens the door to freeloaders. Government should teach personal responsibility. Self-reliance is the best way to live.

But when someone tells us what's "the best way to avoid the problem," we ought to wonder exactly what problem we are trying to avoid, in Henniker or anywhere else. Is it that a hungry man is begging on our town streets, disturbing the residents, and making passers-by uncomfortable? Or is it that he's hungry? If he's hungry, perhaps we should feed him first and tend to his moral education later. Common morality still calls upon us to help a person in distress.

Americans are caught in a tension between these two views of help. In one view, too much help makes people passive and dependent. If they don't need to make any effort to get what they want or need, they won't. Only self-interest spurs people to work and contribute to society. Therefore, we should help our fellow citizens as little as possible so as to stoke their ambition and prod them to self-reliance. As good citizens, we should restrain our compassion, just as the Henniker selectman advised, and rethink our support for government helping programs. A nation that coddles its weak becomes a weak nation.

In the other view, the Good Samaritan stands as moral hero. His moral code is simple: Help When Help Is Needed. It's almost always wrong not to help. In everyday life, people help their friends and families, and they often help strangers. They help because they believe no one is truly independent and that help is usually helpful. Most of all, though, people help others because they care about others. "Care" is another way of saying that our interests are hopelessly intertwined and that anyone's self-interest includes the well-being of others. In this view, people want to help others, and they think government ought to help them do it. They think a community is only as strong as its weakest link.

Our deepest political struggles aren't over the mechanics of government or the details of policy but over the moral code we steer by. These two views of help are two moralities pulling in different directions. For thirty years or so, the country has gravitated toward the first view that help is usually harmful. In a great political upheaval, the political center moved rightward and turned the Good Samaritan's moral code inside out. Instead of

"Help When Help Is Needed," the national public philosophy proclaims, "Help Is Harmful."

The trouble with this dichotomy, you might object, is that it paints everything too starkly, too either-or. Plenty of people genuinely need help, but there are also plenty of con artists, slouches, and folks who just lack the self-confidence or the skills to help themselves. We have to make judgments about when someone really needs help. When they really need it, we should offer it, but when they don't, we should offer them tough love. Parents would raise incompetent children if they helped every time the child couldn't do something and asked for help. Teachers would fail if they always helped their students instead of letting them figure things out for themselves. Surely, you say, there's a middle ground where most reasonable people would agree that help can be harmful.

Indeed there is. When people lack the knowledge or skill to solve their own problems, "doing it for them" instead of allowing them to learn helps them only in the short run. And there are indeed many problems for which individuals would not need help if they had learned, or could learn, certain skills, or if they got up off their sofas. But these are not, by and the large, the kinds of problems at the heart of our political debates. The problems that get people pumped up about politics are ones that are beyond the capacity of individuals to solve themselves no matter how smart and skilled they are or could become and no matter how hard they try. Among these problems: health insurance; much if not most illness and injury; safe and affordable housing; steady work with sufficient pay and benefits to take care of a family; adequate retirement income; affordable higher education and effective primary education; broken, violent neighborhoods; transportation between where people live and where they work; and all the various forms of discrimination, in which people are treated on the basis of stereotypes, no matter what their merits.

A few years ago, Barbara Ehrenreich, a successful writer with a Ph.D., dove incognito into the low-wage workforce, cleaning lavish houses, serving up meals in a restaurant and a nursing home, and putting on a smile as a Wal-Mart "associate."[2] She resurfaced with a report so startling to people above water that it sold more than fifteen million copies worldwide, though all it said was what low-wage workers already know: No amount of effort in the jobs available to them will ever afford them a decent place to live, three square meals, or medical care. They can work full-time, they can work overtime, they can even work two or three jobs, but their jobs simply don't pay enough to keep them afloat. Their needs for help derive from structural problems in the American economy, not personal failures. The most fundamental problem is that a forty-hour-a-week job at the minimum wage does not pay enough to bring a family of three above the poverty line.[3] Period.

People at the bottom can grasp these basic economic facts without any training in economics. In the words of Cindy Franklin, a woman who worked but still had to avail herself of public assistance: "There are only so many good-paying jobs that exist in this society, and there are tons and tons of minimum wage jobs. As long as we expect people to work them, there are gonna be people who can't make it without help."[4]

Just as we make judgments in our personal lives about when individuals really need help and when they need to learn how to do for themselves, in public policy we have to make judgments about which categories of people genuinely need society's help. The unemployed? The aged? Kids? The working poor? All of them, or only some of them? The debate about whether help is harmful or helpful is really a debate about the *causes* of problems. Our willingness to help others turns on whether we think their need for help results from things over which they have control, or from systemic failures and factors outside their control.

The Samaritan's dilemma—to help or not to help—is not a question of finding the proper balance between help and tough love. At the level of government and public policy, it's no longer a matter of assessing people one by one, as a social worker might do. These are questions of public morality, of finding the right balance between social obligation and individual responsibility. Public morality, the nation's underlying philosophy about social responsibility, shapes everything else, most especially the way citizens think about the boundaries of community and the role of government. If "the boundaries of community" is too abstract for you, think, "Who is my neighbor?" If "the role of government" puts you to sleep, think about it this way: "How do I want to live together with other people?"

Thinking straight about our public philosophy is important because public philosophy is the deepest form of political power. It's more potent than having the votes to pass a bill in Congress and more potent even than having the clout to prevent a bill from coming up for a vote. It's more potent because it's invisible, because no one official or even group holds it, and because it influences the way we think without us ever noticing a jolt to the brain.

Imagine going to a Chinese restaurant with a group of friends. You're hungry and keen to get a meal stacked with the dishes you find most tasty. If you're not too hungry and a little bit curious about power dynamics, you might also pay attention to who seems to have the most influence over which dishes the group orders. The person who gets most of her first choices would seem to be the most powerful. She has decision-making power. But somewhere out of sight, the restaurant owner sits contentedly slurping her noodles, thinking that she has more power than any of you because she composed the menu. You and your friends can choose only from among the options she put before you. She has agenda-setting power. Before *she* gets too cocky, though, let me ask this question: who decided that the concoctions served up in Chinese restaurants in America—brown curly fungus, watery precursors of bamboo poles, tiny ears of corn nipped in their fetalhood, and fat fish with their eyeballs fixed on the diners—who decided that these are edible, let alone tasty and a desirable way for American friends and families to eat together and have fun? No one "decided" these matters, of course, but our collective ideas about cuisine—about what counts as food and what counts as tasty—shape all the other choices we make, and so hold imperceptible power over us. They direct us to one kind of restaurant rather than another. Our ideas about cuisine are akin to public philosophy. They set the framework for all our other choices. They direct us to some kinds of policies rather than others, while we mistakenly believe we are making our choices independently, from scratch, and aren't we so lucky to be free.

"Help When Help Is Needed" pretty well describes the American public philosophy after the Great Depression, especially the New Deal and the Great Society programs. Franklin Roosevelt's and Lyndon Johnson's public rhetoric promised to fix things that were wrong with society, and government was to be the Great Fixer. Conservative opposition to the New Deal remained as an undercurrent during the long years when Republicans were out of power, and even during the Eisenhower and Nixon administrations, which were both relatively liberal by today's standards. Both Eisenhower and Nixon accepted the basic principle that government should ensure economic security. Hard-line conservatives detested the equalizing aspects of the New Deal that increased taxes on the wealthy, forced them into a public pension scheme, and helped farmers and workers at their expense, but they were fighting a rearguard action. As Eisenhower wrote to his brother in 1954, "Should any political party attempt to abolish Social Security and eliminate labor laws and farm programs, you would not hear of that party again in our political history."[5]

With Ronald Reagan's presidency, the dominant public philosophy changed to "Help Is Harmful." Reagan shared the conservative antipathy to government in general, but he directed special venom toward welfare. He offered up welfare "chiselers" and "cheaters" as the cause of high taxes and, with subtly coded racial images, focused white working-class resentment on poor blacks.[6] Right-wing think tanks funded research and position papers that gave a scientific gloss to conservative ideology. Ultimately, as we'll see in the next chapter, conservative intellectuals successfully painted welfare as "handouts"—giving out free food to people who do nothing but ask, perhaps making no more effort than to hold up a sign reading "Hungry." With spurious science and devastatingly brilliant rhetorical devices, they were able to win over many liberals and make "Help Is Harmful" seem like common sense.

"Help Is Harmful" soon became the mainstream view of many liberal government helping programs and much of the Great Society and the New Deal. After welfare, the story of "Why It's Best Not to Give Out Free Food" was told over and over, with new hungry men as its antagonists and new programs as its targets. Social Security causes workers to spend freely without saving for retirement, confident that Social Security pensions will take care of them. And worse, mandatory Social Security reduces workers' pensions by forcing them to invest their money in low-performing U.S. Treasury notes instead of the stock market. Unemployment insurance makes workers lax about looking for work when they are laid off. Affirmative action teaches minorities and women that they don't need to work hard to get ahead, and so they don't, harming themselves and their children. Public education taxes parents and prevents them from using their money to find better schools for their children. Health insurance makes people feel as though medical care is free, and so they don't take good care of themselves or their children and they rack up medical bills with abandon, all at the expense of more responsible taxpayers. Lavish social services entice immigrants from other countries and enable them to live as parasites off hardworking Americans. Bilingual education handicaps their children, preventing them from learning English and assimilating. Foreign aid, like welfare, acts as a handout to satisfy people's needs, removing the incentive for developing countries to build their own productive economies.

"Why It's Best Not to Give Out Free Food" is our new public philosophy, our national story.

By now, the Help Is Harmful view claims broad popular allegiance. That's why so many people can answer my question about the Henniker selectman with such easy certainty. But as a guidance system for public life, Help Is Harmful violates our basic moral sense and our everyday experience.

This new moral code flouts ancient human beliefs. Our faith, whether Christian, Jewish, Muslim, or Buddhist, obliges us to watch out for the interests of others. Our upbringing as Americans of whatever faith—or none—teaches us the same obligation. We may have been raised on swashbuckling stories of rugged individualism, but we were also steeped in moral lessons like the Golden Rule and the Good Samaritan. We often celebrate our accomplishments as triumphs of personal achievement, but we know from daily experience that we get by only with help from our friends. The Help Is Harmful philosophy distorts our deepest beliefs and damages our integrity. It asks us to be citizens who are not the kind of human beings we admire or want to be.

Why do I think this? Just read the obituaries for the victims of September 11, the ones that ran every day for three months in the *New York Times*. In its short "Portraits of Grief," the *Times* broke with its tradition of formal obituaries for people of fame and great achievement. Instead, we saw ordinary people who led lives of dignity, hope, love, and kindness. We learned what they valued about their lives, and what their loved ones cherished about them. It wasn't self-reliance. It wasn't the pursuit of self-interest with a breezy faith that an invisible hand or divine justice would take care of everybody else. These obits for Everyman and Everywoman tell us that we treasure something else in ourselves and in the people we love. These people loved their families. They were kind. They were always ready to help someone else.

Stephen Dimino was a partner at Cantor Fitzgerald, but that fact gets a mere blip in his obituary. The family instead encapsulated his life with a story about his generosity. When he was nine and the family had gone into Manhattan to see *My Fair Lady* and have lunch at an Automat, young Stephen "spotted an old man sitting by himself who looked hungry. He brought his sandwich over to him. Then the rest of the Dimino family followed suit," his sister told the *Times*. A cousin, speaking of Stephen's generosity as an adult, added, "He was someone you'd want as your neighbor."[7]

Colleen Deloughery, a friend recalled, "stopped one day to talk to a homeless teenage mother living with her baby on the margins of a commuter station. After that, she started bringing things to the woman—a stroller, a carrier, clothes, food, milk."[8]

Abe Zelmanowitz stayed in the building with a quadriplegic friend rather than fleeing to save himself. His brother commented, "Had it been a casual acquaintance, he would have done the same thing. He could never turn his back on another human being."[9]

Telmo Alvear, a waiter at the Windows on the World, was supposed to have been on the night shift, but took the morning shift that day to help out a friend.[10]

Olabisi Shadie Layeni-Yee was one of many World Trade Center workers who had survived the 1993 bombing. That time, her mother watched and waited and prayed, and finally the call came. "Mom, I'm fine," Ms. Layeni-Yee had said. It had taken her so long to call because she had helped a pregnant woman walk down from the seventy-ninth floor.[11]

Brian Warner "was the good Samaritan who always stopped to help a stranded motorist change a flat tire. If a neighbor's driveway needed plowing, Mr. Warner was there. He spent hours on the phone talking friends and colleagues through computer problems. He was good at fixing human beings, too."[12]

Brian P. Monaghan Jr. was "the archetypal good kid, a 21-year-old who helped elderly women across streets and went to the store for neighbors who could not."[13]

Benjamin Suarez, a firefighter with Ladder Company 21, about to end his twenty-four-hour shift, called his wife to tell her he'd be late getting home to Brooklyn because "I have to help the people."[14]

Keith Glascoe, his father said of him, "was the sort who would stop and pick up a hurt animal in the street, take it to a doctor and pay for it."[15]

Sandra Campbell made a good living at Cantor Fitzgerald, but spent most of it on other people instead of vacations and clothes. She gave her mother $150 every month to pay for her blood pressure medications. "If I told her someone was in the hospital, she went," a friend said. "The people didn't even know her, and by the time she walked out the door, they knew her."[16]

Obituaries, you are probably thinking, are no place to find the unvarnished truth. Surely, we can't divine the human character from these tilted tributes born of grief. Or can we? I suggest we can divine something more important. Obituaries are not an unbiased record of human deeds, but they are a splendid mirror of our values. They document what sort of life we find praiseworthy and, in that, what kind of lives we aspire to lead ourselves.

What the September 11 obituaries document is a river of private morality running exactly counter to self-reliance and the pursuit of self-interest. They document many people who live their lives as the daily practice of simple generosities, and they document our reverence for people who live this way.

My favorite September 11 obituary is about someone who steadfastly rejected the Help Is Harmful philosophy. David Suarez was a consultant working on a project for Marsh and McLennan. He was also in the process of applying to MBA programs. Meanwhile, he volunteered in a soup kitchen and tutored high school students for their college entrance exams. Contrary to the advice of the Henniker selectman, he routinely gave to beggars. Once, his friends recounted to the *Times,* they found him "talking to some beggars outside a bar." The obituary goes on: "Mr. Suarez asked one of the beggars, who was in a wheelchair, 'What would it take to make you happy?'

"The man said, 'Give me $20.'

"Mr. Suarez gave him $20.

"The beggar got up, folded up his wheelchair, and walked off.

"Mr. Suarez was not angry. The episode did not make him jaded. . . . By his thinking, he would rather lose $20 here and there to an impostor than risk spurning someone who really needed his help."[17]

This is the kind of story that would make the Henniker selectman and his followers tisk knowingly, "See? Help is for suckers." But in their obituary for David, the Suarez family said in all but words, "This is the way we want to honor David's memory, because help is for heroes."

No recent social science idea has gripped the public imagination quite so firmly as Robert Putnam's haunting image of bowling alone. Putnam stirred up national angst by showing that Americans are joining fewer clubs and participating less in politics. The sense of community is evaporating like rain on the hot summer pavement, as people literally withdraw from group life. Putnam traced the cause of this withdrawal to the disappearance of the World War II generation—Tom Brokaw's "Greatest Generation"—and to the busyness of our lives and television's power to hold us in our living rooms. I trace this withdrawal to a deeper moral source: People who think of themselves as kind and compassionate hesitate to belong to a club of meanies. When people are told not to reach out to other people because help is harmful, they have to harden themselves and act mean when they would rather be kind. If citizens don't join groups, cooperate with each other, or participate in politics as much as we used to, it's likely because we can't get along with *ourselves*. The contradiction between our private and public moralities is too hard to bear.

Studies of young people's attitudes to politics lend some credence to this speculation. In one large survey by People for the American Way, youth aged fifteen to twenty-four equated good citizenship with being a good person, but few connected citizenship with the social or political sphere.[18] In another survey of youth, 94 percent believed "the most important thing I can do as a citizen is to help others." Yet of those eligible to vote, fewer than 32 percent had voted in the previous presidential election.[19] College students are more than twice as likely to do volunteer work (73 percent) as they are to vote (34 percent).[20] Young people don't connect the most elemental act of democratic politics—voting—with helping others. In fact, "they think about service and politics . . . as two distinct activities—one moral and one corrupt," in the words of a professor who teaches service-learning courses.[21] One tenth grader who volunteered actively in both a hospital and a local Special Olympics, put it this way: "I'm trying to be a good citizen, caring about people and *doing* something about it, rather than just caring." He went on to describe why he felt detached from politics: "It's almost as if politics has lost its meaning of helping, of doing what people want it to do."[22]

The American malaise, I propose, is the uncomfortable tug of our inner moral plumb line pulling against the public morality that has, temporarily at least, captured the machinery of government. Wendy Lesser, an editor and literary critic, opens an essay on philanthropy with a story that epitomizes this tug. She lives in Berkeley, a place where beggars abound. Like most Berkeley residents, she says, she's "long since developed a slight frown and quick shake of the head to shrug off all requests for spare change." (Perhaps you have your own version of this avoidance routine?) One day Lesser was walking with her two-and-a-half-year-old son when a woman politely asked, "Excuse me, ma'am, can you spare a quarter?" Lesser unthinkingly did her beggar routine and walked on. But then her son asked her what the woman wanted.

"'She wanted money,' I said.

"'*Why* did she want money?' he persisted.

"'Because she's poor.'

"'What's poor?'"

Horrified, Lesser realized that "what I had just done was to teach a small child to be hard-hearted. I was creating a monster of unthinking selfishness—or alternatively, I was presenting myself as a monster of selfishness in the eyes of an innocent, innately tenderhearted child."[23]

On a grand scale, American politicians have been building Lesser's beggar routine into the standard operating rules of government. And like Lesser, I suggest, we citizens are watching ourselves act according to a moral code that in our collective heart of hearts we find repugnant. Every once in a while, something happens that awakens our tenderhearted selves and makes us appear monstrous in our own eyes.

These little awakenings are happening every day, in the crannies of ordinary life where rules and laws push people to violate their most basic moral instincts. Medical care is one of the darkest crannies. In the mid-1980s, Dr. Robert Berenson, like most doctors, found himself practicing under managed-care rules that give doctors bonuses for holding down the costs of medical care, which of course means bonuses for withholding care from patients. This was a time when senior citizens were first encouraged by Medicare to enroll in managed-care plans.

One elderly woman enrolled in such a plan with Dr. Berenson as her primary-care doctor. Just after she landed in his bailiwick, she was diagnosed with inoperable cancer. She was a costly case, and to make matters worse, her supportive family actively pressed her interests. Dr. Berenson was acutely conscious that "her bills drained my bonus account." This attentiveness to his take-home pay was exactly the effect that the managed-care incentive system was supposed to have on doctors. But Dr. Berenson realized how the system also contorted him as a doctor and as a human being: "At a time when the doctor-patient relationship should be closest, concerned with the emotions surrounding death and dying, the HMO payment system introduced a divisive factor. I ended up resenting the seemingly unending medical needs of the patient and the continuing demands placed on me by her distraught family."[24]

Dr. Berenson's story perfectly diagrams the war between the two moralities. He represents a profession whose core value is helping—helping people who are sick and suffering, and helping their families cope with their powerlessness and grief. Suddenly, he finds himself practicing medicine in a system in which getting too close to patients and their families makes him an irresponsible doctor. A system in which abstract efficiency and bottom lines are more important than personal relationships. A system in which letting excess compassion drive his clinical decisions makes him a sort of outlaw who must be disciplined by financial penalties. A system in which there is *such a thing* as excess compassion. A system in which he is supposed to harden himself to the plight of others instead of empathizing and caring. For Dr. Berenson working under managed care, the moral imperatives of healing were turned inside out. The system put him in a double bind. If he acted virtuously by insurers' standards—which in this case were also his government's standards because the woman was insured by Medicare—then he would have to act badly by his profession's standards and his own lights.

Sometimes, when a public system traps people in a moral double bind, they violate the rules rather than their morals. A few days after Hurricane Katrina, two navy helicopter pilots deviated from their orders. Instead of returning to base after delivering supplies to other Gulf Coast military bases, they flew over New Orleans and rescued 110 people from rooftops. The hardest part, one of the pilots later said, was not deciding whether to divert to New Orleans without permission. The hardest part was "looking at a family of two on one roof and maybe a family of six on another roof and I would have to make a decision who to rescue." At the end of the day, the pilots were reprimanded. "We all want to be the guys who rescue people," their commander explained to the *New York Times*, "but they were told we have other missions we have to do right now and that is not the priority."[25]

This incident was only one of thousands in the aftermath of Katrina that revealed a colossal breakdown in the nation's system of help. The breakdown was not primarily a bureaucratic mess-up, though it was certainly that, and that is how the media played it. The breakdown stemmed from the same clash of moralities, the same rift in our philosophy of help. For the pilots, the Good Samaritan's moral code told them what to do: Help When Help Is Needed. For the commander, the navy's needs told him how his men should behave: Organizations need to set priorities and stay focused on their missions. If his men followed the Good Samaritan, they would harm the navy. Help Is Harmful.

This book is about what happened to public altruism and how we can reclaim it. Why is helping others the core of personal morality but "not the priority" for public officials or the laws that bind them? How is it that everyone "knows" it's wrong to feed a hungry man on a cold day in New Hampshire? How did we get to this topsy-turvy moral world from which mothers and doctors sometimes recoil and rescue pilots are sent to the brig? Or to put the question another way, why don't politics and government live by the same values we uphold as individuals? What happens to the Good Samaritan as he travels the road from private life to the public sphere?

The answer lies in a quiet revolution of ideas that changed the way Americans think about politics and government. Political revolutions always begin with revolutionary ideas—"All men are created equal" or "Our King has done us wrong," for example. The intellectual upheaval that dislodged the New Deal and the Great Society was driven by a profound change in the way we understand help and its relationship to individual freedom.

Americans have always had a complicated relationship to the idea of freedom. On the one hand, we long for a mythic image of our past, a society of villages and neighborhoods where people quietly cared for one another as a matter of course; where they raised each other's barns and jointly hammered up churches, meetinghouses, and schools; where families roamed from farm to farm, one day at a time, to get the haying done by sundown; where they watched out for each other's children, checked up on elderly widows, looked after the village idiot, shared kettles and tools with a neighbor who was without, and pledged the winter's wood supply to a minister they all needed. They depended on each other through and through, and understood individual free-dom to be the gift of communal solidarity.

On the other hand, we lionize self-reliance as the highest virtue. Ralph Waldo Emerson, writing in 1841, exactly the mo-ment when this blissful communal harmony was supposedly at its apogee, spat on the whole idea of help. "Your miscellaneous popular charities; the education at college of fools; the building of meeting-houses to the vain end to which many now stand; alms to sots; and the thousandfold Relief Societies;—though I confess with shame I sometimes succumb and give the dollar, it is a wicked dollar which by and by I shall have the manhood to withhold." Transforming charity and communal effort into something wicked is quite a feat, but Emerson's not through: "Don't tell me of my obligation to put all poor men in good situations. I grudge the dollar, the dime, the cent I give to such men as do not belong to me and to whom I do not belong."[26]

In our times, independence is back as the highest personal virtue. Self-reliance is once again the best way to live. Self-reliance, self-sufficiency, self-discipline, self-control, self-help, self-determination, self, self, self: these are the main entries in the contemporary American dictionary of virtues. The first duty of the good citizen is not to be dependent on others. He ought not go asking for help unless he's a child, an ancient mariner who's put in his time, or a disabled person who's not capable of taking care of himself. Somehow, a people who arrived on this continent thoroughly dependent on each other for food, shelter, and security—and on the Native Americans whose land they inhabited—now remember themselves as rugged individualists and self-made men. *Dependence* is the dirty word of American politics.

The trouble with our times, according to *Newsweek* columnist Robert Samuelson, is that people have become dependent on large institutions—government, business corporations, universities, medical systems, and school systems. People look to these institutions for everything from secure jobs to decent living standards, high-quality health care, racial harmony, a clean environment, safe cities, satisfying work, social justice, world order, and even personal fulfillment.

For Samuelson and the new political consensus he epitomizes, reliance on collective institutions is pathological, something wrong with "the nation's psyche." Like an uppity beggar or an addict in denial, Americans "deal with their dependence on large institutions" by cultivating an attitude of entitlement.[27] Exactly this kind of thinking led George W. Bush to cut back the Federal Emergency Management Agency (FEMA) shortly after he took office. Federal disaster assistance had become "an oversized entitlement program," his first head of FEMA explained to Congress in 2001.[28] That was before Hurricane Katrina bellowed that maybe government has some useful jobs to do after all.

By condemning citizens for seeking government help, this new conservative public philosophy undermines democracy. The entitlement diagnosis gets it exactly wrong. Mutual dependence is the essence of democracy. Democracy engages citizens with the hope that they can improve their lives by working together, and with the faith that they can accomplish more by working together than going it alone. Democracy requires its citizens to depend on each other, and on the schools, hospitals, universities, levees, and government institutions that they build and run together. In rejecting collective action, we've come a long way from our own democratic ideals, the ones we're trying to seed in Iraq, among other places.

Emerson made a crucial mistake when he set self-reliance as the chief virtue and rejected any obligation to help "such men as do not belong to me and to whom I do not belong." He confused two senses of "belonging." One suggests property and bondage: if a man's not my property, I'm not responsible for him. But that meaning of belonging is a red herring. No one wants to belong to anyone else in that sense, and we long ago banished that peculiar form of human belonging, at least in our laws. The other meaning of belonging is one we all cherish—membership. It means we can count on others to take us in and help us. It means we won't be left alone on the heath, like Lear, to howl at winter. Or as one welfare mother eloquently explained, she strives to dress her kids well "so they can go to school and look like they belong to somebody."[29]

We make Emerson's same mistake today when we confuse getting help with being dependent, beholden, and powerless. According to one contemporary voice of the Help Is Harmful revolution, help is "not the relation of free and equal citizens." Rather, it's "noblesse oblige," a phrase that manages to convey kindness and bondage in the same breath, for it describes feudal relations between noblemen and their serfs.[30] The lords weren't legally or morally obligated to help their serfs; when they did, help was a power trip. They boosted their own nobility by deigning to help those who had no claim to help.

Seeing help this way transforms personal bonds into bondage and makes gratitude a kind of resentment. No one wants to need help or, worse, feel helpless. But help is the way we live. We are born needing help, we die needing help, and we live out our days getting and giving help. Help and gratitude connect people. Without them, life would be terribly lonely. *Not* belonging is abject misery. Getting help and, better yet, being able to *count on* getting help make us part of the human family.

The Help Is Harmful view distorts the good side of help. Perhaps only a nation that once held people in bondage could run so scared from the idea of human bonding. We need to untwist our notion of personal freedom by acknowledging that dependence is the human condition. Genuine freedom can't be had by denying our individual limitations. Freedom comes from understanding them and working around them, and from building a community where bonds of loyalty compensate for the things we can't do ourselves.

"Help" is my shorthand for all the ways we feel and act for the benefit of others instead of ourselves. Philosophers and psychologists call it altruism, but most of us know help as a word we learned in infancy by being helped. Help includes all the ways we act when we mean to foster someone else's well-being. It stands for giving and serving. It stands for loyalty and love. It stands for raising children and taking care of the sick. It stands for doing what it takes to give dependent people their dignity. It stands for feeding the hungry, fighting poverty, and working for justice. It stands for kindness, great and small. Help, quite simply, is how we think, feel, and behave when we care for others.

Until fairly recently, philosophers thought that humans are moved by a variety of motives, some good, some bad. Now, according to modern social science, people are made of pure self-interest. To read most modern thinkers, you'd think the only question we ever ask ourselves is "What's in it for me?" With every choice we make, we aim to benefit ourselves. Even when we help others, we don't do it out of pure kindness. We help them either to make ourselves feel better (because their well-being contributes to our happiness) or to obligate them in case we ever need help. In this picture of human nature, people might behave *as if* they have other people's interests at heart, but altruism is always an illusion, nothing but a flattering self-portrait. Sure, the rare altruist might touch down here and there, like the rescuers of Jews during the Holocaust or the hero of *Hotel Rwanda*, but they are so rare they might as well be "a race of saints."[31]

If self-interest is the only motive we can count on, then it's really the only source of energy society can harness. People won't behave well or contribute to the common good unless they get personal rewards for it. Want people to recycle? Give them a refund for every can and bottle they return. With the right monetary incentives in place, people don't have to be socially minded to be good—they need only be mercenary. As long as they recycle, we don't care why. To coordinate individual behavior for the common good, leaders need only design incentives that appeal to self-interest. This picture of human nature is the basis for free-market philosophy.

Daily experience flies in the face of this picture. Taking care of each other is the way we live. We survive on everyday altruism. Altruism isn't the only human motive, and it may not even be the dominant one, but there's plenty of it to work with, and with the right leadership and policies, we can make more.

Two months after September 11, the *New York Times* celebrated a paramedic who had helped dig out the last two people pulled alive from the World Trade Center rubble. The man had somehow faded from the scene and the news, and the other rescuers who had worked alongside him that day wondered who this man was. All they knew was "a medic named Chuck." Chuck Sereika read about this mystery in the *Times,* and after a struggle with himself came forward. He said he hadn't wanted to appear in the press as a hero because he "didn't fit the mold." He told how he'd struggled with alcoholism for years, been in and out of rehabilitation, spent a few nights in jail, lost jobs and friends, and disappointed his family. For all we know, he might have been on welfare, too. But on September 11, Mr. Sereika put on his old medic uniform and went down there to help. He ordered oxygen and an IV and got them both going for one of the trapped men. Meanwhile, he could hear the rumble of 4 World Trade Center, but he kept on working. "I decided my life was not worth more than theirs," Mr. Sereika said. Later, he told the *Times,* "It's very easy for me to help other people. It comes naturally to me and to all paramedics. It's what we do. Taking care of myself, I'm not so good at."[32]

Mr. Sereika was the kind of down-and-outer that the Help Is Harmful school would spurn, to force him to take care of himself. Yet Mr. Sereika was just the man we needed on September 11. His story suggests that human motives are far more ambiguous and malleable than the pure self-interest our science teaches. The call to service called forth his better self. To help others, he put on his uniform and went back to work. Ralph Waldo Emerson might say that Mr. Sereika finally shaped up, showed up for work, and became self-reliant, but if that's what he did, it wasn't out of any ordinary self-interest. Mr. Sereika almost certainly didn't get paid. What got him back on the job was not an empty stomach but an empty heart. What got him there was the opportunity to take care of somebody else and connect with other people. For him at that moment, self-interest and altruism were one and the same.

Altruism, it turns out, is a motive we can count on. But we will learn how to strengthen and enlarge it only if we believe in it. For the most part, researchers who have studied altruism believe it all comes down to self-interest, so they try to encourage altruistic behavior, such as donating a kidney, by offering donors personal rewards. In this book, I listen to altruists as a believer in altruism. Instead of searching for their ulterior motives, I look for the meaning they themselves give to their altruism.

It turns out that helping others expands one's desire to help. Very often, after you help one homeless person, you want to help more. Helping others expands the sense of responsibility for others, too. Holding aside the question of whether help harms or helps the people we mean to help, by focusing on what help does to the helpers, we see something else. Helping others calls forth our altruistic selves and makes citizens who take responsibility for the problems of their community. There's another way to motivate people besides paying them rewards. Sometimes, asking for their help and then showing them why they are needed is a better way. If we guide our public life by the Good Samaritan's code, we rear good citizens and make a stronger community.

And that is the real message of the parable of the Good Samaritan. The plot is simple. The Good Samaritan came to the aid of a needy traveler on the road from Jerusalem to Jericho. The traveler had been robbed, beaten, and left for dead. A priest and a Levite—both his own countrymen—had seen him as they passed by but ignored him. A stranger, the man from Samaria, poured balm over the man's wounds and bandaged them, carried him to an inn, and gave the innkeeper money to care for him.

The story is so familiar, almost a universal folktale, that many people don't know its original context in the Christian Bible. In Luke's Gospel, the only place in the Bible where this story occurs, a lawyer asked Jesus what he must do to get into heaven or to inherit eternal life. Jesus, playing the Socratic teacher, asked the man what the law says, to which the lawyer replied (I'm paraphrasing here), "Love the Lord God with all your heart and love your neighbor as thyself." Right, said Jesus, just do this and you will live. In lawyerly fashion, though, the questioner wanted definitions and distinctions. He tossed the problem back to Jesus. "Who is my neighbor?" In other words, how do I know exactly whom I have to love as myself? In answer to *that* question Jesus told the story. Then he asked the lawyer, "Which one of these people behaved as a neighbor?"

The parable of the Good Samaritan, then, was the answer to two questions. The one we usually remember is "Who is my neighbor?" Answer: everyone. But the more important question was the one that got the whole story rolling: "What must I do to get into heaven?" Answer: help everyone.

One doesn't have to believe in an afterlife to accept the spiritual insight of the story. Simply take heaven as a metaphor for happiness and well-being. The parable tells us we should help others both because it helps them and because it helps us. Withholding help not only hurts them but also diminishes us. The story reminds us that *help* is a verb as well as a noun and that our actions make us who we are. The man from Samaria was a neighbor because of the way he acted, not because of his tribal identity.

The same insight holds for our collective selves—for the polity as well as the person. The character of our community is defined by our collective response to other people's troubles. Just as an individual asks, "What kind of person do I want to be?" we as citizens must ask ourselves what kind of community we want to be. What do we want government to do in our name for our fellow citizens? We should, I argue, hold ourselves collectively to the same standard we hold ourselves personally. We need to align our public morality with our inner moral compass.

The simple idea of helping others is a powerful moral value. It can reframe politics around a unifying moral vision.

2

Seven Bad Arguments Against Help

If it's virtuous for individuals to help their neighbors, why isn't a good government one that helps the neighbors, too?

Because:

> *"Government is not the solution to our problems, government is the problem."*
>
> —President Ronald Reagan in his first inaugural address[1]

Because:

> *"Compassion is a miserable basis for American politics."*
>
> —Political commentator Mickey Kaus[2]

Because:

> *"The [welfare] system hurts the very people it was designed to help."*
>
> —Marvin Olasky, intellectual mentor to Newt Gingrich and George W. Bush[3]

Because:

> *"Over the years, the entrepreneur has done more to serve people—to meet their material needs and raise their standard of living—than all the goodwill efforts sponsored by government, churches and philanthropic organizations put together."*
>
> —Conservative critic Dinesh D'Souza[4]

Because:

> *"Compassion is the province of families, neighbors and charitable institutions. Public compassion has brought us a national debt of $5.6 trillion, the injustice of racial quotas and chaos in the inner cities."*
>
> —Conservative columnist Don Feder[5]

Because:

> *"These are scary thoughts—they really are—that she [Hillary Clinton], or some Democrat, can take your money and they're going to use it for the common good."*
>
> —Rudy Giuliani,
> after a presidential candidates' debate in 2007[6]

Ronald Reagan assumed the presidency by denigrating the very government he led. His presidency was something of a Republican Restoration. He embodied the long-standing conservative frustration with the New Deal and its fundamental premises: that individuals cannot live as self-sufficient islands, that government should help citizens when problems are beyond the capacity of individuals, that no one in modern America should live in dire poverty, and that the wealthy have a moral obligation to contribute to the common good. Starting in the late 1960s, conservatives built a network of think tanks, foundations, and academic programs bent on attacking these ideas. They sought to eliminate altruism as one of government's guiding principles. With Reagan in the White House and the Republican Party in control of Congress, conservatives were able to begin translating their ideology into policy.

The think tanks funded research and position papers that gave a scientific gloss to conservative ideology. Most famously, the Manhattan Institute bankrolled political scientist Charles Murray to write *Losing Ground*, which used graphs, statistics, and imaginary characters to "prove" that government help for the needy destroys their ambition. Never mind that serious social scientists tore apart Murray's methods. His charming, folktale-like stories were brilliant rhetorical devices.[7] Ultimately, conservative intellectuals filled political discourse and social science with specious reasons that government should not help citizens (though helping businesses is another thing): Compassion destroys politics, people, and places. Public altruism wastes social resources. Help often harms people and communities instead of helping them. To make helping citizens government's responsibility, let alone its driving purpose, is to admit a destructive force into the heart of democracy.

These are wildly improbable ideas. They go against everyday morality, not to mention Jewish, Christian, and Muslim ethics. They contradict what most people think morality is: looking beyond self-interest to promote the welfare of others. It's a tough sell to persuade people, against an ancient grain, that altruism is dangerous or harmful. So instead, the intellectuals behind this great moral reversal present it in pragmatic terms, as if its facts and logic were unimpeachable. There are rational reasons, they claim, that helping harms and governing ourselves according to an ethic of altruism just doesn't work. They invoke the authority of science to prove that help is harmful. Ultimately, they insist, common morality must give way to hard reality: government help is ineffectual at best, and harmful at worst.

This great conservative moral revolution fits what economist Albert O. Hirschman called the perversity argument. Hirschman studied resistance to democratic reforms in several countries over several centuries and found that conservatives always criticized reforms on scientific grounds rather than on grounds of morality or justice. Conservatives almost always conceded the moral rightness of spreading economic and political power more broadly. But, they warned, proposed democratic reforms wouldn't work as the reformers hoped, and in fact would make things worse instead of better. Government programs meant to help people would hurt them instead.[8]

The perversity argument sidesteps the moral argument, which conservatives could never win. Instead of saying "It's wrong to help people," they say, "Liberal policies harm people, and everyone agrees, it's wrong to harm people." Today's conservatives make seven key arguments about how help harms. Ready, set, go.

One: Help Makes People Dependent

Marvin Olasky calculates that America's "compassion syndrome" has caused a "destruction of lives" equivalent to General Sherman's slaughter of twenty-five thousand former slaves. Political scientist Lawrence Mead figures that "racism *per se* was certainly harmful to blacks," but permissive government programs "have replaced the racist regime with one that is, in its own way, equally destructive."[9]

Granted some literary hyperbole, these statements reflect a fervent belief that help really does do violence to the people it is meant to benefit. Help works its ills insidiously. Like a virus that attacks the immune system, depriving the body of its ability to fight germs, help destroys people's motivation to strive. Without the will to fight, a person no longer tries.

Help saps motivation, because man is by nature irredeemably lazy. Charles Murray, intellectual godfather of the conservative backlash, put it this way: "Any of us, given a choice, will often take the easy way out even when we know that we will derive more satisfaction from the more troublesome choice." For Murray, this element of human nature explains why democratic governments pass more and more policies that "take the trouble out of things," policies such as Social Security, unemployment insurance, and aid to children. Since citizens are "endlessly willing to accept such measures" (that's human nature), democratically elected legislatures can't stop providing them. The majority of citizens always favor more help.[10]

To create a robust citizenry, Murray and his followers advised, government should alleviate only "extreme forms of suffering," but not interfere with moderate suffering. "Intermediate levels of deprivation . . . motivate all sorts of constructive choices, from getting up in the morning to go to work, to controlling bad habits like gambling, alcohol abuse, and overeating."[11]

Unfortunately, rued conservatives, liberal politicians believe that by providing social assistance, they are helping to meet people's needs, pure and simple. Not so, Murray argued in his stunningly influential book, *Losing Ground*. Help shapes people's psyches, beyond whatever physical needs the help satisfies. Without explicitly saying so, Murray likened social assistance to classical behavioral conditioning.

B. F. Skinner trained caged rats by giving them food whenever they did his bidding. If we train people (or rats) that they will receive whatever they need for the asking (or the lever pushing, in the rats' case), we're teaching them how to solve their problems by asking for help instead of doing for themselves. Welfare payments, unemployment insurance, food stamps, free medical insurance, and social assistance of every kind all train people to continue asking for help when they are needy, just as effectively as Skinner's conditioning trained rats to push a lever when they were hungry.

Recipients of help, Murray argued, will always interpret it as a reward for being needy and seeking help, just as rats interpret food as the consequence of pushing a lever. So inescapable is this result that Murray formulated it as an immutable scientific law, like the law of gravity. The "Law of Unintended Rewards" goes like this: "Any social transfer increases the net value of being in the condition that prompted the transfer."[12] In plain English: help makes being needy more profitable than not being needy. Help thus encourages people to remain in need of help. It does this by *rewarding* people for being in a position to need and get help, or by decreasing the suffering they experience while they are needy.

Imagine, Murray asked his readers, a middle-aged worker who has lost his job, wants desperately to work, but can find nothing. He gets unemployment insurance, and though he "hates every penny of it," it subtly changes his behavior and his attitude toward taking another job. It cushions his unemployment, and so might lead him to hold out a little longer for a better job or to refuse a job far away that would mean uprooting him from his home, his friends, and his family. "Unemployment Insurance has made the condition of unemployment more tolerable," Murray said, and thus has induced the man to choose unemployment over work. His unemployment is not completely involuntary.[13] Notice that we're not talking about a real person here. This unemployed man was a figment of Murray's imagination, and he does whatever Charles Murray imagined he would do. Murray didn't like what he imagined, but others might feel glad that unemployment insurance helps keep the man's home and family intact.

Murray conceded that help doesn't work this way for people who have absolutely no control over their situations. Giving medical insurance to paraplegics wouldn't "increase the value" of staying paralyzed because they have no choice in the matter. Giving Head Start programs to poor children wouldn't induce them to remain poor either, since they have no control over their families' income. But Murray thought there are very few such pure cases of genuine neediness, totally outside people's control. In fact, he seemed to be able to think of only these two—paralysis and childhood.

For Murray and others, help doesn't teach just any old kind of behavior—it teaches *bad* behavior. Help creates economic incentives to engage in exactly the behavior the helper seeks to end. (Remember the perversity argument? Here it is, full throttle.) If suffering and neediness result from personal choices (and that is the big "if" that underlies this whole line of thinking), then help encourages bad behavior because it rewards people for their poor choices. Murray believed all help is tainted by these purely economic incentives, no matter whether social norms condemn or approve the behavior.[14]

Conservatives apply the Law of Unintended Rewards to most social assistance programs and find, not surprisingly, that help almost always encourages bad behavior. Robert Rector of the Heritage Foundation, which has funded some of Murray's work, saw the law operating in the old welfare program Aid to Families with Dependent Children: "For 30 years, the welfare system has paid for non-work and non-marriage and has achieved massive increases in both." Heather MacDonald of the Manhattan Institute saw social assistance as the cause of New York City's "epidemic of illegitimacy": "Rather than penalizing such bad behavior, the city rewards it. Unwed mothers have priority for many benefits and get lavish day care centers in their high schools so as to make teen-child-bearing less onerous." To MacDonald, AIDS treatment for poor women, disability benefits for troubled children, and day care centers for teen mothers "normalize" self-destructive conduct. Furthermore, it's obvious that "if you insulate people from the consequences of their own self-destructive behavior, you're going to get a whole lot more of it."[15]

Helping people teaches them to rely on others only if individuals really could solve the kinds of problems for which we offer social aid. Few of us believe, for example, that helping sick people by giving them medical care keeps them sick and dependent, because we understand most illness to be outside the control of the individual. And most of us would be loath to withhold treatment for lung cancer in order to teach people not to smoke. Some of the most ardent conservatives admit scarcely any real barriers to success outside of a person's own character and effort. As we've seen, Charles Murray can think of none other than physical paralysis and infancy. James Payne, a Murray follower, admits there are cases of "extreme helplessness" that ought to trigger our sympathetic help. He offers three examples: "people in comas, babies, and the mentally incompetent."[16]

The social critics who propound this new behaviorism always depict help as a "reward" rather than "relief." To call help a reward is to conjure up an image of a bonus, a little extra *je ne sais quoi* that's nice to have but not essential. Images of rewards distract our attention from the very suffering that help is meant to relieve. Nowhere in these behaviorist portraits of how people respond to help is there any hint that they were hurting before help arrived or that they might have been wracked by hunger or devastated by some loss. No images of jobs lost because firms downsized, closed, or moved their operations overseas. No images of eyesight lost because glaucoma drugs are expensive and some people lack insurance. No images of income lost because a person had to quit a paying job to care for a severely disabled spouse or child.

If, instead, we imagine the recipients of our help as desperate and on the edge, or if we think of our help as critical food, water, medicine, or some kind of rescue from imminent danger, then we couldn't see help as harmful. We'd no doubt think that help enables people to go on living, to take care of themselves, and to do something productive besides. To believe help is harmful, you have to think of it as something people can do without. You have to have *already decided* that they don't really need it. And that is the big deception, the invidious moral claim at the heart of conservative logic.

Of course, it would be just as much a distortion to suggest that all help goes to people who are desperate as to claim that most help isn't really needed. That is why it's dangerous to base public policy on a one-dimensional view. The metaphor of help as a reward captures only one kind of help, help that isn't very important to the recipients. The metaphor is brilliant political framing. It changes our understanding of help from light to dark. Seen as a reward, help is nothing but payoffs to clever, lazy people who have learned to manipulate the levers of our sympathy. The metaphor makes us forget that help is the atom of social life, the reciprocity that extricates people from aloneness and binds them together.

The most pernicious trick of Murray's paradigm, though, is likening the human condition to a caged rat's life. Human recipients of help, the story goes, will invariably interpret it as a reward for being needy, just as a lab rat interprets its food as a reward for pressing a lever. But step outside the metaphor for a moment and ask yourself exactly why people who get help would interpret it as a reward for being needy.

When Dr. Skinner's rat is hungry, it is trapped in a cage—a situation behavioralists conveniently forget to mention. The rat has no other way to get food. It can't try foraging because it can't go anywhere. It's trapped in the cage, and no matter what it does, food won't come its way unless it performs exactly as its trainer wants. *Of course* it learns to press a lever as the only way of getting food. Let the rat out of the cage, and it will probably learn a lot of other ways of getting food, all of them more satisfying than begging. Only the rat's dependence on the trainer in the first place teaches it that asking for a gift—and continuing its dependence—is the best way to live.

If, metaphorically speaking, we let people out of their cages, if we give them a number of options for getting what they need, some more reliable and enjoyable than begging, then there's no reason to believe they will perceive help as a reward for their neediness, or that they'll come to depend on help as the only way to meet their needs. They will depend on mystical deposits of goodies such as unemployment checks or food stamps only if their situations leave them no other ways to solve their problems. In fact, under the old welfare system, before there were government-imposed time limits, most recipients escaped as fast they as they could. Almost half got off welfare within one year, and three-quarters left within two years. Only about 15 percent stayed on the rolls for five years. As ten years of time-limited welfare have proved, those people who stay on welfare for the long term are mentally or physically incapable of surviving on their own.[17]

Help doesn't trap people—cages do. Genuinely helpful public policy dismantles the cages.

Two: Entitlements Undermine Good Citizenship

Any kind of organized and regular help leads people to expect help and to feel that they deserve it. No matter whether the help comes from a public program such as Social Security or a private charity, help creates citizens with what conservatives have dubbed an entitlement mentality.

The trouble begins when government creates a legal right to help for specific needs, such as food, shelter, or medical care. People who meet the legal requirements for help, and even some who don't, will inevitably come to feel entitled to government help. "If one creates legal entitlements," says libertarian David Kelley, "one is promoting an entitlement mentality. There is no escape from this logic."[18]

Political scientist Lawrence Mead has explored this logic more than anybody, beginning with his first book about social policy, *Beyond Entitlement*. Because the poor can count on generous unemployment and welfare benefits, Mead reasons, they're unwilling to do the only jobs available to them. He acknowledges that most of the low-wage jobs available to them don't pay enough to live on, and that many of these jobs, besides paying poorly, are demeaning, injurious, unhealthy, or backbreaking. But given poor people's lack of education and skills, they have no right to expect better. There are plenty of jobs, Mead thinks, but workers often quit because "they are impatient with menial pay and working conditions and keep quitting in hopes of finding better." As a result, "Many unemployed, it appears, are no longer job-*seeking* in the traditional sense of accepting the best job they can get, however bad it is. Rather, they are job-*shopping*—seeking work but not accepting it unless it meets their conditions."[19]

"Job-shopping" is exactly what workers are supposed to do in classical labor-market theory, but Mead says unemployment among the disadvantaged should be seen for what it is: "a political act," one of the many kinds of "rebellious actions" that democratic political systems permit.[20] Not economic incentives, not rational behavior, but "resistance" accounts for high unemployment among black youths, or for the fact that fewer black women are willing to work as domestics than in the 1950s, before the civil rights revolution.[21] To overcome this resistance, "low-wage work apparently must be mandated, just as a draft has sometimes been necessary to staff the military."[22] Help is harmful, to believe Mead, because it permits—indeed actually helps—poor people to express their ambitions and assert their illegitimate economic aspirations. When middle-class people job shop and continually seek out something better, they're pursuing the American dream of self-improvement and upward mobility. Ambition and aspiration, it seems, are virtues for the middle class, but vices when they show up in poor people, and vices best not encouraged by government help.

Let's ignore for a moment the contradiction here: help, too freely offered, makes people passive, dependent, and helpless victims, yet it also makes them assertive and demanding. Let's ask ourselves this question instead: if a victim mentality is harmful because it renders people passive and helpless when they needn't be, why should an entitlement mentality be bad? After all, doesn't a sense of entitlement bolster people's initiative and drive?

There's only one way to make sense of the argument that an entitlement mentality is bad: rights to receive help teach people that seeking help is legitimate when it is really wrong; rights to help make people look to others instead of taking personal responsibility for solving their problems. If recipients don't deserve help, that is, if they don't deserve help according to general cultural norms, then the entitlement mentality puts people out of step with their culture. It makes them moral outlaws.

Like the metaphor of rewards, the entitlement critique rests on a prior belief that down-and-out people don't need help, and so don't deserve it. The supposed entitlement mentality works its effects on the human psyche only if we think people are lazy and conniving in the first place. Thus, the entitlement mentality isn't really a psychology of recipients—it's a philosophy of donors. The entitlement mentality is a potential donor's way of saying that many people don't deserve help and that most societal help is illegitimate.

The clamor about the entitlement mentality says as much about people who think they might be on the giving end of help as those who might be on the receiving end. Supposedly a condition of recipients, the entitlement mentality describes a long-standing fear on the part of donors that moral obligations to *give* might trigger somebody else's political demands to *take*. The entitlement mentality is a fear of the comfortable that they won't be able to limit their giving and that they will be coerced into depriving themselves.

The entitlement critique started with the poor, but many conservatives now think the entire population is at risk for the entitlement disease: liberals and conservatives, young and old, blacks and whites, able-bodied and disabled. Entitlements deprive the polity of a critical citizenry by giving citizens too much faith in bureaucracy, too much trust in government, and too much vested interest in the status quo. "Social Security and the twin medical entitlements [Medicare and Medicaid] have created a generation of seniors who aren't providing the political conservatism that the elderly typically contribute to a republic," bemoaned the *National Review*. In rather more inflammatory prose, another article blasted the elderly as "the beneficiaries of the most outrageous affirmative-action scam in the country."[23]

Affirmative action is a distinctly American locution for help, and it, too, incites conservative disdain. The phrase has come to mean help for racial and ethnic minorities and for women. It includes procedures for opening up jobs, schools, and elections to members of groups that were historically excluded by discriminatory rules. If the term weren't so stuffy and legalistic, it would be excellent shorthand for Good Samaritan ethics, because it conveys stepping forward to help someone instead of merely refraining from doing harm.

Affirmative action raises complex and troubling issues, and deserves to be carefully debated, but conservatives often short-circuit the debate with the perversity argument, claiming that preference policies harm their intended beneficiaries. Clarence Thomas, who says in his memoir that he unwittingly found himself the beneficiary of affirmative action at Yale Law School, worries that preference policies make people dependent on government. Blacks (or any other beneficiaries of affirmative action) might find themselves in a new kind of "enslavement, one which ultimately relied on the generosity—and the ever changing self-interests—of politicians and activists." This new dependency on government "might ultimately prove as diabolical as segregation, permanently condemning poor people to the lowest rungs of the socioeconomic ladder." Affirmative action, Thomas says, "cannabilizes" the values of hard work and self-help, destroying the very power that people need to thrive.[24]

Affirmative action in higher education draws special conservative ire, no doubt because admission to colleges and professional schools is the gateway into the elite. According to opponents, minority students, just knowing that they might get a little extra boost in college admissions, don't study as hard as they would if there were no affirmative action.[25] Here again is the basic logic of Help Is Harmful: help breeds laziness. But there's a more poisonous version for higher education. It goes like this: Students who are admitted to colleges and professional schools under affirmative action rules wind up over their heads, in schools for which they're not really qualified. They do poorly, get discouraged, and drop out. Affirmative action, the argument goes, prevents them from successfully graduating by keeping them out of a school for which they are better suited. The best way to help minority students is to let tests sort them into schools by ability, where they can all study in the insulated comfort of homogeneity.[26] The best way to help them is not to help.

Harming the people one means to help is bad enough, but affirmative action, some conservatives claim, also threatens democracy. "Such means are a threat to constitutional government," warned political scientist Harvey Mansfield Jr. With affirmative action policies, government imposes distributive results on citizens instead of accepting the consequences of free markets and free elections. Moreover, affirmative action supposedly eliminates the stimulus for minorities to work for their goals, as everyone else must. Government programs to help them gain electoral strength, such as the Voting Rights Act, remove their incentive to organize and fight for offices through the democratic process. No doubt, blacks benefit from having more of their own in office, Abigail Thernstrom wrote in her critique of the Voting Rights Act, but "this is an argument not for federal intervention but for black political organization."[27]

Every political scientist knows that the rules of the game advantage some groups and disadvantage others, but according to conservative logic, the disadvantaged are not supposed to try to change the rules. "How can [blacks] make themselves into first-class citizens?" Mansfield asked. "Not by affirmative action; not by receiving justice from others so much as by claiming their own places in the name of pride."[28]

Affirmative action is bad for democracy, conservatives argue, because it dilutes the quality of leadership in every sector. It interferes with the tough selection processes that sort people by ability and allow only the most talented to rise to the top. Affirmative action "entitles" people to good schools, good jobs, and leadership positions without them having to earn their way in. When disabled golfer Casey Martin asked for the right to ride a cart in pro tournaments, golfers and sportswriters everywhere forecast the end of true competition. No one, they worried, would be able to resist the easy way out.[29] The golf cart is a perfect metaphor for the conservative fear about help: helping citizens gives unfair advantages to some and enables them to rise above others who struggle unaided.

This argument would have some force if social life really were a meritocracy, but it isn't. Colleges and universities select some students on their academic accomplishments and promise, but they also give explicit preference to children of alumni and big donors, and implicit preference to students lucky enough to attend excellent high schools with a lot of financial resources and advanced placement courses. Employers, especially in the professional world, select and promote employees partly on the basis of ability, and partly on personal chemistry and networks. Seen in this light, the argument against affirmative action is one more justification for preserving elitism.

Government help, the entitlement argument goes, has made not only the poor but all Americans dependent, spoiled, and entitled. We expect too much from government. We want it to guarantee our jobs, boost our living standards, provide our health care, keep our environment clean, and protect us from danger. We want an end to business cycles, economic insecurity, poverty, and racism. Because we feel entitled, we make demands on government, businesses, and other institutions, but especially on government. We want it to solve these problems for us. We have become a nation of dependents.[30]

The entitlement argument is a stealth critique of democracy. The very citizen demands that conservatives consider symptoms of political disease appear in political science textbooks as characteristics of healthy democracies. In the 1950s and 1960s, American students learned that making demands on government is the essence of democracy. In undemocratic, totalitarian regimes, we were taught, demands go the other way, always from government to citizens. In the most influential post–World War II study of democratic citizenship, *The Civic Culture*, Gabriel Almond and Sidney Verba concluded, "If democracy involves high levels of actual participation in decisions, then the attitudes of a democratic citizenry should include the perception that they in fact can participate. *A democratic citizen speaks the language of demands.* Government officials accede to his demands because they fear some loss otherwise—the loss of his vote perhaps—or because they consider it legitimate that he make such demands."[31]

Fifty years after *The Civic Culture,* Robert Putnam praised voluntary associations as seeds of democracy precisely because they "allow individuals to express their interests and demands on government."[32] In democratic theory, the reason for citizens to participate in government is to make demands on it, to get it to help them lead better lives. The entitlement mentality *is* the democratic posture—or was, before the triumph of Reagan conservatism.

Civics education traditionally teaches students how to make demands on government: how to use their votes to support candidates who promise to help them, how to contact elected representatives for assistance, how to inform themselves about policy proposals and participate in legislative debates, how to band together with other like-minded citizens in interest groups and protest organizations. These are all modes of political participation allowed to corporations, industries, the wealthy, and the powerful. But conservatives criticize aid programs when they teach these same skills to the disadvantaged. For example, Heather MacDonald lambastes a New York City family shelter because it "has an informal program to help its mothers write to their political representatives in support of welfare, Medicaid, and child care." She wags at a city high school for teen mothers because it took the students to Washington "to lobby against welfare cuts." "Such a program sends precisely the wrong message to homeless mothers: that more government spending can rebuild their lives."[33] Maybe MacDonald is right that public spending isn't the full answer to young mothers' problems, but surely, some government action—raising the minimum wage or making health insurance affordable, for example—could help rebuild their lives.

Conservatives tend to regard demand as a virtue in the market but a sin in the political sphere, especially when committed by the poor. The economic citizen of the market—also known as the consumer—is virtuous when he is most demanding. In theory at least, the public good emerges when consumers demand high-quality goods at low prices and producers respond to consumers' signals. But in the conservative worldview, demand turns wrong when it becomes political demand, when citizens send signals to *government*. Then conservatives disparage demand as the "entitlement mentality."

Why this difference? In the classic economics textbook definition, consumer demand is the desire for a good or service backed up by "purchasing power"—that's "money" to most of us. Consumer demand, then, is equivalent to self-sufficiency. It's having enough money to purchase whatever you need, or whatever you want. Economics makes no moral distinction between wants and needs—all consumer demand is equally legitimate. Whatever a dollar wants, a dollar deserves.

Not so in politics, or at least not in the new conservative politics. The "entitlement mentality" is wrong because it signifies that people demand of society whatever they want or need *without* having the money to pay for it. Conservatives are troubled by the "entitlement mentality" because it means that people at the bottom define what they need and set the criteria for deservingness.

The entitlement critique harks back to nineteenth-century stan-dards of democracy, when only men of property could vote.

The campaign against the so-called entitlement mentality is deeply antidemocratic because it denies the legitimacy of col-lective action in politics. Citizens are supposed to make it on their own. Lawrence Mead tars the black civil rights move-ment as "dependency politics," because by seeking government protection from discrimination, blacks "*remained dependent* on the white man. . . . They continued to look to white society for the solution to their problems." Blacks, like everyone else, should work for their own success as individuals, but in the civil rights movement, they wanted whites to hand them suc-cess. As evidence of black entitlement, Mead offers Martin Luther King's metaphor of a promissory note in his "I Have a Dream" speech: "We have come to cash this check, a check that will give us upon demand the riches of freedom and the secu-rity of justice." When blacks have been "properly assertive," Mead admonishes, they have succeeded. What exactly counts as proper assertiveness in this individualistic view of politics? As examples, Mead offers that old canard of black artists and athletes who "work hard for success without expecting help from whites."[34]

If we accept this image of proper assertiveness, all collective efforts are ruled out. Individual achievement is the only proper way to assert one's desire for change, even for people whose goal is to be treated as an individual instead of stereotyped as a member of a group. How about the black baseball player who needs whites' help in order to gain admission to a league? How about the black entrepreneur who rallies a black business owners' association and the ACLU because she has to fight discriminatory lending and zoning practices before she can open her business? Through the concept of entitlement, conservatives have redefined the political. The very essence of politics—collective action in order to negotiate the terms of group and class relationships—no longer counts as legitimate. For the disadvantaged and the dispossessed, at least, collective action is the lazy way out of personal troubles.

Three: Help Robs People of Freedom and Dignity

American democracy makes three great promises to its citizens: freedom, independence, and equality. When government helps you or your neighbor, so this argument goes, it breaks these promises to both of you. "The relation of charitable giver and recipient is not the relation of free and equal citizens," Mickey Kaus wrote in a 1999 *New York Times* op-ed denouncing the "compassionate conservatism" that was the hallmark of George W. Bush's presidential campaign.[35]

No doubt the most influential voice in the conservative campaign against personal and public altruism was, and continues to be, Ayn Rand. Best known for two popular novels, *The Fountainhead* (1943) and *Atlas Shrugged* (1957), she is a conservative cult hero at the center of numerous institutes and admiration societies, including the Atlas Society for devotees of *Atlas Shrugged*. She died in 1982 but is still widely read. Prominent political figures such as Alan Greenspan and Clarence Thomas claim her as an intellectual influence. In

2007, the libertarian Cato Institute threw a daylong conference and banquet to celebrate the fiftieth anniversary of the publication of *Atlas Shrugged*.

A Russian emigrée to the United States whose father's business was confiscated during the Russian Revolution, Rand became a fierce defender of laissez-faire capitalism and individual self-sufficiency. Her writings resonated with the cold war anticommunist fervor, and like many political figures of the time, she sometimes equated altruism with socialism. Her sharpest philosophical statement defends the "virtue of selfishness." Altruism, she claimed, does violence to both people who receive help and people who help. When altruism is made into a social principle, it destroys society by sapping the vital creative forces of individualism. "I will remain faithful to the one commandment of my *code* which I have never broken: to pay my own way," swears Henry Rearden, one of *Atlas Shrugged*'s protagonists.[36] In Rand's cosmos, anyone who does not live by Rearden's code is a "moocher," and anyone who promotes redistribution to help the needy is a "looter." If everyone lived rightly, there would be no need for looting.

Rand dubbed organized public help as "collectivism," a term that deliberately reeked of Stalinism and stimulated American anticommunist juices. Her novels portray altruism as a philosophical weapon wielded by the weak and the mediocre to hold back the strong and the talented. In *The Fountainhead*, Ellsworth Toohey is an untalented journalist who espouses socialism because, as Rand writes his motives, if he can't get ahead on his own steam, at least he can restrain society's more talented competitors with moral coercion. Altruism, Rand thought, is how the unsuccessful guilt-trip the successful into slowing down to help them. With altruism, the weak can shackle the strong.

In *Atlas Shrugged,* in a chapter called "My Brother's Keeper," Rand composes a wickedly delicious mockery of altruism as a dialogue between a brother and sister. They are heirs to their father's national railroad company. The incompetent brother tells his far more competent sister that he wants to be president of the company. "Don't I have the right to demand any form of happiness I choose? Isn't that a debt which you owe me? Am I not your brother?" Finding no pity in his sister's face, he plunges his accusing dagger in deeper: "It's *your* sin if I suffer! It's your moral failure. I'm your brother, therefore I'm your responsibility, but you've failed to supply my wants, therefore you're guilty."[37] In this sibling spat Rand purports to show that the principle of altruism entitles losers to demand anything of winners and that it shames the truly virtuous (the talented, competent, and self-sufficient) into sacrificing themselves for their lesser brethren. The sister, by the way, doesn't succumb to her brother's nonsense, because she is a Rand heroine who lives for herself. But then, few people of any persuasion would be taken in by these rantings of a conniving, spoiled brat.

For Rand, anyone who believes in a moral obligation to help other people shows a lack of respect for them. "If a man accepts the ethics of altruism, he regards mankind as a herd of doomed beggars crying for someone's help." Merely believing that people need help degrades and demeans them by denying their capacity for self-sufficiency. Contemporary conservative critics of helping the poor echo Rand's idea. Simply assuming that the poor need to be helped is to "advertise the moral superiority of the compassion-givers," says Robert Samuelson. Helping the poor through big government programs "strips them of their self-esteem" (James Payne), "assigns their moral capacity to the environment" (Lawrence Mead), and "imperils their moral well-being" and "demoralizes" them (Gertrude Himmelfarb). Helping African Americans through affirmative action demeans them by assuming they are "severely handicapped" (Abigail Thernstrom and Stephan Thernstrom).[38]

Those are some of the supposed consequences of *believing* that people need help. *Actually* helping people damages them even more. Because many poor people already feel powerless, the argument goes, government aid programs only reinforce their feelings. The legal right to subsistence "infantilizes" the poor.[39] Social assistance "disassembles the personality" and feeds "defeatism."[40] By helping poor people, government affirms that they need help and sends a message that they are right to feel helpless. In effect, help psychologically cripples people, and the more dependable and effective the help, the worse its impact on the recipients' psychic independence.

Moreover, the argument continues, help is by its nature inegalitarian, because helpers have the power to do what others cannot do for themselves. Government help inevitably creates political inequalities. Although Mickey Kaus, like most conservatives, believes society should help those who are genuinely helpless, he thinks even this most worthy and righteous kind of help must necessarily be "condescending." Compassion, Kaus says, "carries the unmistakable implication of dependence and piteousness on the part of those on the receiving end of the sentiment."[41] Pity, condescension, grudging obligation, stigma, and disrespect are oppressive sentiments. Even if the recipients of help didn't feel dependent and unfree when they first sought help, the attitude of helpers would destroy their freedom and equality.

There's wisdom in the worry that help can be demeaning. But the reason help demeans, when it does, is not because help is inherently demeaning. When helpers start out believing that people who need help are inferior, they infuse their help with condescension, disrespect, and disgust. Help demeans only when the helpers believe those who need help are lesser creatures. This is exactly how conservatives have portrayed welfare. Our culture expects able-bodied people to work and to earn their living, Kaus says. When we give them aid, both they and we know that they don't deserve respect (or so Kaus thinks). Thus, welfare can never be respectful.[42]

Help doesn't have to cripple people or make them dependent. It doesn't have to subordinate or degrade them. It all depends on how it's done, in spirit and in deed. I learned this lesson when I was ten. I had spent the day down the street, playing at my friend Susan's house. School had been called off on account of a blizzard. When it came time to go home, the snow was higher than my waist, and I was afraid to walk home, afraid I'd not be able to lift my legs high enough. I was torn, for I knew I was old enough to walk home and was too proud to admit I was scared. Susan's mother must have intuited all this, because as I lingered in the front yard, trying to talk myself into bravery, Mrs. Pitt opened the door and called to me that the dog needed a walk so she might as well walk me home. Mrs. Pitt knew I was afraid, and I knew she knew. But she gave me cover and found a way to offer help without humiliating me. Only as I reflected on this incident years later did I realize something else. Mrs. Pitt might have thought to herself that I had no reason to be scared and that I could perfectly well get home safely on my own. But in order for her to help me and preserve my dignity as she did, she must have decided that I deserved help.

If we as citizens think our fellow citizens don't deserve help, then we will resent and condescend and punish at the same time as we gesture help. Help demeans only when, as Kaus recognizes, the dominant cultural norms *say* that people don't deserve the kind of help society offers. The claim that help always demeans reveals more about how conservatives feel about their fellow citizens than about the essential nature of help. Help degrades only in a culture that refuses to see anything between prosperity and an able body but an unwilling mind. Help destroys recipients' freedom and dignity only in a culture that makes self-reliance the apotheosis of virtue.

True, no one wants to need help, even apart from a culture of extreme self-reliance. Aging wouldn't be nearly so horrifying if it didn't bode waning independence. That is why raising the specter of humiliation and domination lurking behind all government help is such shrewd conservative framing. The suggestion preys on the natural human fear of being injured and helpless, the distaste for having to ask for help, and our revulsion toward being dependent on others. But dependence on each other is the human condition. Instead of fear-mongering, wise political leaders would help us live with our mutual dependence in the most satisfying ways.

Help's impact is all a matter of design and intent—whether we believe people deserve our help, how we offer our help, and whether we intend it to help them or to punish and humiliate them. When public helping programs are designed to empower people, they help, without subordinating or demoralizing their recipients. We can help in ways that give people voice, leverage, rights—and dignity.

Four: Help Enslaves the Helpers

Along with government duty to help citizens, Ayn Rand rejects any personal duty to help others. When altruism becomes a moral duty, she insists, it transforms the altruist into a means for other people's ends, a slave or a sacrificial animal. There are no unfortunate people in Rand's world, only "parasites, moochers, looters, brutes and thugs," and the misguided altruists who think they must sacrifice themselves to other people's failures. Rand's follower David Kelley puts the same point in polite American political language. The welfare state is a form of feudalism, he asserts, only now "it is no longer the feudal masters but the poor, the elderly, and the disabled who claim ownership rights in those who produce."[43]

The only rational ethical principle for human relationships, Rand believes, is free-market trade. The trader, not the altruist, embodies personal virtue: "A trader is a man who earns what he gets and does not give or take the underserved. He does not treat men as masters or slaves, but as independent equals. He does not switch to others the burden of his failures [translation: ask for help], and he does not mortgage his life into bondage to the failures of others [translation: help others for nothing in return]."[44]

Political philosopher Robert Nozick applies Ayn Rand's bondage motif to the idea of redistribution in general. Redistribution is another way of saying giving things to people, usually for the purpose of helping them, but Nozick focuses on the taking side of things, the donors rather than the recipients, and concluded that when government redistributes, it enslaves the donors. To redistribute, government must have a principle for deciding who gets what. We have to fill in the blank in "To each according to his _____." We might fill it with the recipients' needs, their achievements, moral worthiness, or past disadvantages, but whatever goes in the blank, it's a characteristic of the recipients. The sentence has no blank space for the donors' wishes. Yet whatever government redistributes has to come *from* somebody—from people who have a lot of it, or at least more of it than our principle says they should have. Thus, according to Nozick, redistribution always means taking from the Haves and giving to the Have-nots.

Organized redistribution, then, deprives Haves of the right to choose what to do with their possessions. In order to carry out any kind of redistribution, government must tax the Haves. It can tax their wages, their business profits, their savings and assets, their land, their personal effects, or whatever it chooses. But according to Nozick, "taxation on earnings from labor is *on a par with* forced labor": "Seizing the results of someone's labor is equivalent to seizing hours from him and directing him to carry on various activities. If people force you to do certain work, or unrewarded work, for a certain period of time, they decide what you are to do and what purposes your work is to serve apart from your decisions. This process whereby they take this decision from you makes them a *part-owner* of you; it gives them a property right in you."[45]

As staunch opponents of the welfare state, libertarians can claim to be compassionate and charitable because they do favor private generosity, so long as it remains voluntary. (Rand rejected even private generosity, and partly for that reason, she didn't consider herself a libertarian.) Benevolence, compassion, and generosity are still virtues in the libertarian moral universe, as long as "the donor [is] free to choose whether he wishes to contribute, and to whom, and subject to what conditions." Altruism isn't a "dangerous force," Richard Epstein allows, as long as it is limited to "daily voluntary interactions and kept out of the public sphere of politics." He has in mind things like loaning the neighbors milk, swapping babysitting, and watering the neighbors' plants and picking up their newspapers when they're away.[46]

For the sphere of politics, though, libertarians recommend a donor's-eye view of distributive justice: "From each as they choose, to each as they are chosen" goes Nozick's play on Marx. When government exercises its altruistic impulse, writes David Kelley, it coerces some citizens into being donors, and "to compel such service, even in a case of extreme need, is to impose a form of involuntary servitude." Whenever government treats help as a right for some citizens, it inevitably exploits other citizens to implement the right. Ayn Rand fumed about Medicare for just this reason. Of course, everyone agrees that it's desirable for the aged to have medical care, she said. But when citizens tell themselves that they're providing medical care "for the good of others," they lose sight of "the enslavement, and therefore, the destruction of medical science, the regimentation and disintegration of all medical practice, and the sacrifice of the professional integrity, the freedom, the careers, the ambitions, the achievements, the happiness, the *lives* of the very men who are to provide that 'desirable' goal—the doctors."[47]

In the libertarian view, the only way government can help some citizens is by selling others into slavery. Democratic governments may not legitimately help your neighbors, because to help them infringes on your freedom. If *you* want to help them, no one will stop you. You are free, and so are they, because each of you may help or not help, as you choose.

The libertarian picture of altruism as self-denial and servitude doesn't accord with the way most Americans live. People regularly help their neighbors and do it voluntarily. Not everyone, not all day every day, but enough that it's hard to believe so many people feel like sacrificial animals or slaves. In the remaining chapters, we'll see a radically different picture of altruism. When people help others, they almost always feel enriched rather than diminished. They rarely think or talk in terms of coercion. They say that helping others rewards them, enlarges them, connects them, teaches them, and strengthens them.

Most Americans want *government* to help their neighbors, too. Public opinion is slippery and notoriously hard to measure, but over decades of surveys, the public has consistently expressed its strong support for a vast array of government help.[48] At the top of the list: helping the needy. When asked about "the needy" or "the poor" or "people who cannot support themselves," large majorities consistently favor government help. Up until the early 1980s, when Reagan used his bully pulpit to turn citizens against government and the poor, well over 80 percent of people supported government help for the poor. Survey questions that use the word *welfare* elicit much less support, not surprising given all the negative publicity about welfare, but when opinion surveys ask about the *principle* of government helping the needy, Americans stand firmly behind it. In 1977, when welfare-crisis rhetoric was already at high pitch, 96 percent agreed that "it's not right to let people who need welfare go hungry." Even in 2007, after twenty-five years of antigovernment, anti-help rhetoric, almost 70 percent of Americans agreed that "it is the responsibility of government to take care of people who can't take care of themselves."[49]

Overwhelming majorities, upwards of 80 percent, support Social Security, even in periods of scare talk about baby boomers and empty coffers. Citizens want their government to help people find work, provide help with job-training support, maintain full employment, and to a lesser but still strong extent provide unemployment insurance to tide people over. They believe government should provide medical care for the needy and ensure that everyone has access to doctors and hospitals at an affordable cost. Overwhelmingly, they think government should take care of people "who cannot help their condition: the blind, disabled, the aged." By large majorities, they support government help with education, urban problems, regulation of business practices and working conditions, consumer protection, and environmental stewardship.[50]

Most citizens are willing to *pay for* government to help their neighbors, too. In a mid–1980s survey, a time when conservative anti-help fever was running high, huge majorities were satisfied with paying taxes for government helping programs: 81 percent were happy to pay for Social Security, 78 percent happy to pay for Medicaid, and even 65 percent, almost two-thirds, said they were satisfied to pay taxes for welfare. Asked whether they thought public spending on aid programs should be increased, decreased, or maintained, very strong majorities wished to see every program maintained or increased. The list included Medicare, Supplemental Security Income (a kind of disability insurance), Social Security, Medicaid, unemployment insurance, welfare (Aid to Families with Dependent Children), and food stamps. The least-popular program was food stamps, yet not quite a quarter of the respondents wanted to decrease it, and only 16 percent wished to decrease welfare. More than half said they would maintain both these relatively unpopular programs at their current levels.[51]

However we measure, most citizens want government to help others in their name, and do not consider themselves coerced into forced labor when government does. On the contrary, some people feel coerced into private charity because other institutions don't help their neighbors enough. Consider the man who was clocking forty hours at General Motors and another twenty at a supermarket. His wife was babysitting, shopping, and driving for a sick friend, he told an interviewer. "And she writes checks, even if they're small, because we live near the red all time. She has a heart full of charity. . . . Sometimes I wish she had a little less of that charity in her—and the same goes for me. We can't afford what we're giving! Maybe the church should do more and let us off the hook—or the government: a lot of people fall through the cracks."[52]

People like this couple suffer when they see others suffer, try their best to help, but feel powerless to stop people from slipping through the cracks while churches and government stand by. If government did more to help their neighbors, they wouldn't feel government was enslaving them, one suspects. They'd feel government was helping them be the good neighbors they want to be.

Asking government to help your neighbors is a lot like Ulysses asking his shipmates to tie him to the mast. Ulysses knew he wouldn't be able to resist the temptations of the beautiful Sirens awaiting him ahead, so before sailing into those dangerous waters, he put his wiser self in charge of his weaker self. He commanded his crew to bind him to the mast and ordered them not to obey him if he should later beg to be freed, as he knew he would, when the Sirens' songs reached his ears. When citizens ask their government to keep them safe or help the needy, they know that when the time comes to pay their share of the taxes or make whatever sacrifices they have to make, they will probably be tempted to wriggle out. Democracy is like a giant Ulysses stunt. Citizens pass laws during the calm, in careful deliberation about their principles, then bind themselves to abide by the rules that their better selves created. That's what the rule of law means and what the Constitution is all about.

Libertarians don't accept this fundamental notion at the heart of democracy. As Nozick saw it, whenever government redistributes according to a principle such as need, the principle decides who gains and who loses, not the people who start out wealthy in whatever resources government decides to redistribute. But that view forgets something important: in a democracy, citizens decide on governing principles through their elected representatives. "Principles" don't decide anything. To claim that government help coerces unwilling donors is like parachuting onto Ulysses' ship just as it's passing the Sirens, not having witnessed Ulysses' request, seeing him bound to the mast, and concluding that a mutinous crew enslaved its captain.

Five: When There's Not Enough for Everyone, We Can't Afford to Be Generous

After Hurricane Katrina, a pastor in Springfield, Vermont, suggested that the town ought to host a few refugee families. Some of the local charitable figures weren't so sure. The head of the local United Way said it was more critical to use scarce resources to help as many of the town's own as possible, rather than trying to help a small number of people from a disaster area. "We need to look to charity beginning at home," she admonished. The director of the local family center saw disaster looming in Springfield, with families caught in a squeeze between falling temperatures and rising fuel prices. "Families are either going to freeze or they're going to starve," she said. "Our needs here are incredible, and I'm scared what January will look like. Our resources are too little for too many needs."[53]

The two women spoke a modern version of an old classic. In 1798, Reverend Thomas Malthus published a very political book disguised as a treatise on demography. Its title was *An Essay on the Principle of Population*, and indeed my 1960s high school history course taught us about Malthus as if he deserved a posthumous Nobel Prize for discovering population control. His great contribution to intellectual history, we learned, was the insight that people multiply much faster than food, and, therefore, a society with unrestrained population growth cannot survive.

The book made Malthus famous, even in his own day, and it is still in print today.[54] Its real argument is much more devastating than the one I learned in high school. It's not so much a scientific treatise on population and hunger as a political tract on why helping the poor will only create more poverty and ultimately bring the English nation to ruin. Malthus was a brilliant polemicist, and in the *Essay* he established the strategy of the modern conservative argument about the place of altruism in public life. He packaged moral argument as science.

Malthus lifted social existence out of the sphere of politics and rooted it instead in natural science. From there, he pronounced social life to be subject to the laws of nature. Malthus's revision was an intellectual master move. Suddenly, poverty and suffering, benevolence and obligation, governance and policy were no longer matters of religion, morality, or politics. They were no longer problems for ordinary officials, politicians, or clergymen to tackle, nor were they proper topics for citizens to debate. Malthus thought it strange that anybody who had read Adam Smith and aspired to be a political economist "should still think that it is in the power of the justices of the peace, or even of the omnipotence of parliament, to alter by fiat the whole circumstances of a country."[55]

According to Malthus, all the answers to social questions were given by the laws of nature. And if human well-being was determined by natural forces beyond the control of man, then the only job for humans was to take notice of the natural laws and heed them. We might moralize all we want, we might yearn for noble sentiments in ourselves and our fellow men, we might rail against the unfairness of life, but nature's laws will never yield to our desires. Human morality must align itself with the law of nature. *That* was Malthus's main message.

The great law of nature that Malthus discovered was this: If all the plants and animals that come into existence were able to survive, they would soon expand enough to fill "millions of worlds." To avert the crisis of sheer room and food, nature wisely provides a built-in "check to population." Plants die, seeds can't germinate, animals starve or kill each other. Man, however, has foresight. Reason makes men think twice about procreating. But man doesn't always hear nature's advice. For him, misery is crucial to nature's plan. Starvation, malnutrition, and sickness ensure that the ratio of people to food doesn't get out of hand.

If Malthus sounds utterly Darwinian, there's a good reason. Malthus wrote his *Essay* some sixty years before Darwin wrote *The Origin of the Species.* Darwin, in his autobiography, said he got his inspiration for the mechanism of natural selection from Malthus. His early writings borrow Malthus's language of population increase, ratios, and checks. In the introduction to the last edition of *The Origin of the Species,* Darwin wrote that the "Struggle for Existence . . . is the doctrine of Malthus applied to the whole animal and vegetable kingdoms."[56] This is a curious attribution, as Malthus thought he was applying the laws of the vegetable and animal kingdoms to man. No matter, though. Malthus and Darwin were two peas in a pod.

Malthus's picture of what we now call a Darwinian universe doesn't seem terribly new, but in 1798, the idea that humans are trapped in a stingy world, consigned to the same miserable struggle as the plants and the animals, was shocking. In the Age of Enlightenment and the afterglow of the French Revolution, Europe was suffused with optimism and faith in the power of human reason to solve all problems. Men fancied themselves exempt from the mean life of other creatures.

Malthus's main purpose in the *Essay* was to puncture that optimism. Despite our capacities for reason and foresight, he insisted, humans cannot escape all the misery nature has in store for us. There is no way around the law of nature. "Necessity, that imperious, all-pervading law of nature, restrains [all living things] within the prescribed bounds. The race of plants and the race of animals shrink under this great restrictive law; and the race of man cannot by any efforts of reason escape from it."[57]

In prose so modern it could have come from Marvin Olasky or Lawrence Mead, Malthus warned that socially organized help is far more devastating than doing nothing: "It may be asserted, without danger of exaggeration, that the poor laws have destroyed many more lives than they have preserved."[58] Not only does natural science excuse the well-off from helping others as individuals, but the impossibility of improvement also excuses government from any obligation to help its least-fortunate citizens.

In the most haunting passage of the *Essay*, Malthus explained why a legal right to subsistence is a foolhardy human invention. A right to subsistence attempts to "reverse the laws of nature" with "laws that bind society to furnish employment and food to those who cannot get them in the regular market." A man who can't get subsistence from his parents or from a job, Malthus said, "has no claim of *right* to the smallest portion of food, and in fact, has no business to be where he is." Where this unfortunate man is, let's remember, is on government's doorstep, asking his fellow citizens for a morsel to keep him alive. And here is where Malthus held up nature as a moral model for our emulation:

> At nature's mighty feast there is no vacant cover for him [this hungry man whose labor society does not want]. She tells him to be gone and will quickly execute her own orders, if he does not work upon the compassion of some of her guests. If these guests get up and make room for him, other intruders immediately appear demanding the same favor. The report of a provision for all that come fills the hall with numerous claimants. The order and harmony of the feast is disturbed, the plenty that before reigned is changed into scarcity; and the happiness of the guests is destroyed by the spectacle of misery and dependence in every part of the hall. . . . The guests learn too late their error, in counteracting those strict orders to all intruders, issued by the great mistress of the feast, who, wishing that all her guests should have plenty, and knowing that she could not provide for unlimited numbers, humanely refused to admit fresh comers when her table was already full.[59]

What does this Parable of Nature's Mighty Feast teach us? That withholding help from the desperately needy is nature's law. That disobeying nature's law causes suffering. That reaching out to help desperately needy people is evil. ("The poor who were intended to be benefited suffer most cruelly from this inhuman deceit which is practiced upon them.")[60] That withholding help is not only "humane" but an exercise of moral fortitude on the part of those lucky enough to be comfortable. That giving in to our feelings of compassion inevitably brings disaster down around our ears.

Malthus wrote the script for the reluctant charity leaders of Springfield, Vermont: When there's not enough to go around, those already at the feast had better bolt the door. The rich, the strong, and the comfortable have no obligation to help the poor, the weak, and the miserable. Misery is part of nature's plan. To interfere with her plan is folly. "No improved form of government, no plans of emigration, no benevolent institutions, and no degree or direction of national industry can prevent the continued action of a great check to population in some form or other; we must submit to it as an inevitable law of nature."[61]

Almost two hundred years after Malthus, economist Amartya Sen noticed something odd. In any famine, some people eat quite well while others starve. Sen asked why. After meticulously studying famines in Southeast Asia and Africa, he found that none of them was caused by insufficient food or even a big drop in food supplies. In fact, some famines occurred after a country's total stock of food went up, not down. The great Bangladesh famine of 1974 happened in a year when rice production and wheat imports both peaked, and the districts within Bangladesh that suffered the worst effects of famine were those that experienced the greatest growth of food output.[62]

Sen concluded that famine happens not because there isn't enough food for all the people in a country or a region but because some people don't have claims on the community's food supply. They don't have land and resources to produce their own food, they don't have enough money or other assets to exchange for food, they can't get work that would earn them enough money to buy food, and no one helps them by making sure they get food. Sen called these different ways of obtaining food entitlements. An entitlement is a legitimate claim, one that fits with a community's laws and customs about how resources should change hands. Entitlements are legal claims that a society honors when a person exercises them. (Entitlement in Sen's sense is exactly the opposite of the contemporary American conservative usage, where it means a person's illegitimate desire to receive resources or help.)

Most people don't produce their own food. They get food by buying it, and they get money to buy it by selling their labor or by selling goods they make themselves. If the market for their labor or their goods collapses, they will starve for lack of purchasing power, regardless of how much food is available for purchase. In the Bengal famine of 1943, people died standing outside well-stocked food shops. They couldn't obtain food, even by force, because the state sent guards to protect the stores.[63] If, instead of sending the troops, the state had provided guaranteed work or had organized food relief, no one need have starved.

Sen's stunning insight was to see that nature rarely determines whether people starve—social arrangements do. Droughts may not be avoidable, but their human effects are eminently manageable. In the face of crop failures or any kind of natural food decline, social arrangements can eliminate starvation by making sure that everyone has entitlements to enough food. Socialist governments such as China were able to eliminate starvation *before* they were able to raise food supplies. How? They changed the entitlement system. They gave everyone guaranteed employment at wages that would afford enough food, and they provided social security for those who couldn't work. Even in the United States, where supermarkets always bulge, Sen observed, unemployment can sometimes rise sky-high and entire communities command few economic resources. Without public policies such as food stamps, unemployment insurance, and welfare, starvation would be widespread, though concentrated in pockets.

Amartya Sen roundly refuted Malthus by asking two simple questions: How did all of nature's mighty feast get stockpiled in that one banquet hall anyway? And why did some people receive invitations to the feast but others didn't? Sorry, Reverend Malthus, but you can't pin either of those things on nature. Between Mother Nature and human ingenuity, there's enough to keep everyone alive, as long as people have the will to help their neighbors.

Coincidentally, exactly two hundred years after Malthus first published *An Essay on the Principle of Population*, Sen won the Nobel Prize in Economics. Yet more intriguing, in 1933, the year of Sen's birth and almost fifty years before Sen would publish *Poverty and Famines*, President Franklin Roosevelt understood the political truth that Sen had yet to discover. In his first inaugural address, he outlined the "grim problem of existence" facing the nation. Then he offered hope in the form of human political arrangements: "Yet our distress comes from no failure of substance. . . . Nature still offers her bounty and human efforts have multiplied it. Plenty is at our doorstep, but a generous use of it languishes in the very sight of supply."[64]

Six: People Are Too Compassionate
for Their Own Good

In 1975, in an article called "The Samaritan's Dilemma," James Buchanan diagnosed the root cause of America's social troubles: "We may simply be too compassionate for our own well-being or for that of an orderly and productive society."[65] The diagnosis would be unremarkable—at the time, Buchanan's was only one voice in a growing conservative chorus—except that eleven years later, Buchanan was awarded the Nobel Prize in Economics for the same kind of work that inspired his odd interpretation of the Samaritan's dilemma.

For Buchanan, the Samaritan's dilemma is not whether to help. It's not, say, the terrible decision about which people to rescue from New Orleans rooftops if you're a helicopter pilot. Nor is it the awful bind of not being able to help one group of people without harming another—say, protecting Iraqis against insurgent violence without killing innocent civilians. Instead, the dilemma as Buchanan saw it was too many good Samaritans in our midst.

Buchanan reached his diagnosis by using the then-new tools of game theory and rational choice. He worked out abstract mathematical variations of a game in which two players named "A" and "B" try to get ahead. It's hard to imagine how either of them could get ahead, though, because all A and B can do in their stripped-down, colorless lives is choose a square in an imaginary grid. Each square contains numbers that represent imaginary payments they will receive from an imaginary, all-powerful Someone if they land in that square. A and B can't work hard or slack off. They can't dress smartly, keep up with the news, or check their stock portfolios. They can't pray or meditate, bowl or bird-watch, or do any of a million things that might make their lives interesting. They can't even talk with each other to share their thoughts, their hopes, and their dreams. They can't do any of these things because they're just ciphers, creations of Buchanan's mind, and he didn't imagine any possibilities for them except for moving into squares where Someone would make payoffs to each of them—according to rules Buchanan set.

Buchanan added one twist to make A and B more interesting to *us*, his readers. Like God, after creating his creatures, Buchanan named them. He called A "the Samaritan" and B "the parasite." And therein lies a tale.

The game in "The Samaritan's Dilemma" was a version of Prisoner's Dilemma, which has become the reigning model in economics and political science for understanding all human behavior. The game purports to explain not merely how two people might play poker, but how humans behave in all kinds of situations, never mind that it reduces life experience to the single matter of receiving more or less "payoff." So after describing how he thought A and B would make their moves, Buchanan explained to his readers that he was using the game to explain "much of the behavior that we observe in the modern world." Then he proposed this theory: "The hypothesis is that modern man has become incapable of making the choices that are required to prevent his exploitation by predators of his own species."[66]

Those "predators of his own species," lest you missed the point, are people who ask for help, and—one never knows—

might ask for more help after being helped once. They're parasites by assumption—Buchanan's assumption—only because he called them parasites, not because we know anything about their lives or their personalities. Poor B went straight from the alphabet to the shame stool without ever having lived.

But now, with some evocative names and a hypothesis to uphold, Buchanan starts to put some flesh and blood on A on B. He gives them thoughts and motives. The Samaritan has two choices. He may decide to "behave charitably" and give thirty dollars a month to the parasite, or he may decide to do nothing for the parasite. For his part, the parasite also has two choices. He could work, "in which case we may assume he earns an income, say one-fourth as large as that earned by the more capable Samaritan," or the parasite may "refuse to work."

At this point, Buchanan has become a fiction writer, creating characters, endowing them with emotions, motives, and livelihoods, and supposing how they will behave. Social scientists call these techniques "assumptions," but they are no more scientific than the novelist's craft. Nevertheless, Buchanan claimed that his "analysis lends substance to the cliché that modern man has 'gone soft.'" Take welfare, for example. If we understand it as a game between Samaritans and parasites, then we will see the problem. The Samaritan is at a disadvantage because "he may find himself seriously injured by the necessity of watching the parasite starve himself while refusing to work." The Samaritan, in other words, might be unable to withhold help because he can't bear to let another person suffer when he has the capacity to help.

For Buchanan, and for the many social scientists and self-styled compassionate conservatives who pursued his line of thinking, America's social troubles all stemmed from this one diagnosis: people are too compassionate. It hurts us to watch others suffer, we can't stand pain, and so we help. As a result, parasites exploit us, and ultimately drain and weaken society. Political leaders, Buchanan argued, should design charity programs to thwart this human weakness of natural compassion. For example, they should remove welfare-eligibility decisions from the social workers who meet face-to-face with clients and are likely to get "personally involved."

Compassionate conservatives follow Buchanan's calls for restrained compassion. Historian Gertrude Himmelfarb asks us to take a lesson from the Victorians, who understood that "it was sometimes necessary to feel bad in order to do good—to curb their own compassion and benevolent impulses in the best interests of those they were trying to serve." Tough love has become the vogue for child rearing and citizen rearing. "One has to be willing to let the person who needs aid suffer if he refuses to take the path of improvement," counsels James Payne. Or, as a FEMA spokesman explained why the agency was evicting people from its New Orleans trailer parks in the midst of an acute housing shortage, "We're very sensitive to the fact that this isn't an easy move. But it's a necessary move."[67]

Buchanan's article wouldn't merit so much time except that it reveals how ideologues can use specious science to undermine human hope and ordinary morality. Just as Malthus did, scientists in any culture can use their authority for political ends. And just as Malthus did, Buchanan used his academic podium to threaten us with annihilation if we don't heed his hard-hearted advice: "Unless equilibrium is established which imposes self-selected limits on Samaritan-like behavior, the rush toward species destruction may accelerate rather than diminish."[68]

Buchanan tapped into a universal human problem, but it's a different dilemma than the one he worried about. Almost everyone has the capacity to empathize, and empathy makes us vulnerable to claims on our help. Family and friends have moral and emotional claims on us—if they didn't, they wouldn't be family or friends. These ties are what make us members of a community and give us a sense of belonging. Most everyone wants a home, where, as Robert Frost said, "when you have to go there, they have to take you in." Most everyone wants a community that meets that test, too, one that provides the security of knowing that if you really need help, someone will be there to give it. Our image of the nightmare bureaucracy is the one whose employees have hard rules and harder hearts, and who will never soften because they don't ever have to look us in the eye.

Love and empathy do make us vulnerable to excessive claims on our help. Economist Nancy Folbre says we are "prisoners of love."[69] Sometimes we'd like to be insulated from demands on our time or resources. Sometimes people keep asking for help, again and again. Sometimes we don't want to help anymore but can't bring ourselves to say no. We feel duty-bound to help, either because of our relationship to the person on our doorstep or because our moral principles oblige us to help, or perhaps because, as Buchanan imagined, it hurts us too much to watch another suffer. But we can't have it both ways. If we want a home where they have to take us in, we must also make a home where we have to take them in.

In a good community, it *should* be hard to say no. And it should be impermissible to judge people parasites and refuse them help without first inquiring into their circumstances.

Seven: Markets are Better Helpers than Government

Charles Darwin observed hundreds of species to arrive at his theory of evolution. When he got around to considering humans in *The Descent of Man,* he noticed that helping the sick and the disabled was a peculiar human foible, albeit a noble one. "With savages, the weak in body or mind are soon eliminated; and those that survive commonly exhibit a vigorous state of health. We civilized men, on the other hand, do our utmost to check the process of elimination; we build asylums for the imbecile, the maimed and the sick; we institute poor laws; and our medical men exert their utmost skill to save everyone to the last moment. . . . Thus, the weak members of civilized societies propagate their kind." No one who has bred animals, Darwin surmised, could fail to see that "this must be highly injurious to the race of man. . . . [E]xcepting in the case of man himself, hardly anyone is so ignorant as to allow his worst animals to breed."[70]

Perhaps aware of the stir this thought might cause, Darwin quickly noted that we humans could not check our sympathy for the helpless "without deterioration in the noblest part of our nature." Then he added a regret: "We must therefore bear the undoubtedly bad effects of the weak surviving and propagating their kind."[71]

Nowadays, no one who has hopes for political leadership can say this kind of thing out loud. Yet the animal-breeder point of view is orthodoxy in economics. What common morality prevents us from doing to sick and injured people—*withholding help*—is perfectly acceptable, even desirable, in neoclassical economics as a way to treat debilitated firms and industries, or as a way to treat workers and families injured by plant closings, job export, technological obsolescence, or other economic forces. The market, economic theory holds, can create a much healthier economy if left to its own devices ("laissez faire") and not forced by government to prop up the weak. Indeed, economists often celebrate the market precisely because it is hard-nosed and un-sentimental and has no moral qualms. The market is a brilliant natural selector. It knows exactly who's been efficient and who's been wasteful.

Like Darwin's savages, a market-driven society thrives on its ability to let its weakest members go under. Markets are so much better than government, economist Charles Schultze once ex-ulted, because they have "the devil-take-the-hindmost approach" to individual loss and suffering. In the marketplace, people who suffer losses can't "stand in the way of change," as they can in pol-itics. They can't prevent changes that would lead to greater effi-ciency. By contrast, Schultze lamented, American government is hamstrung by losers. Government is incapable of taking a socially beneficial course of action that might inflict losses on even just a few people. Interest groups stand ready to stop government the moment they get wind of any pending decision that might be bad for them.[72]

Neoclassical economists are intellectual heirs to Thomas Malthus. He admired nature for its unsentimental fortitude. He counseled political leaders to stand back and let nature see to the good of the human species. Today's economic orthodoxy admires free markets for their unsentimental fortitude, and counsels leaders to let the market oversee our collective social well-being.

Economists since Malthus have been trying to find the natural laws that govern human life. The Law of Demand is economists' Law of Gravity.[73] It's a simple law: when price goes up, demand comes down. At first glance, the Law of Demand seems pretty innocuous: the higher the cost of anything, the less of it people will buy. But beneath this simple idea, the Law of Demand wields a powerful weapon. It renders help impossible. It's like a perverse Midas touch. Every time we try to help someone, the Law of Demand converts our help into harm.

Suppose, for example, we try to help low-wage workers by raising their wages or setting a minimum wage. The moment we do, the cost of labor goes up and employers will buy less of it. They'll hire fewer workers and lay off some current employees. Price goes up, demand comes down. Voilà! Instead of helping workers, we've hurt them.

Well, perhaps we've hurt some of them—the ones who get laid off or who don't get hired in the first place—but economists now think there's little evidence that raising the minimum wage causes unemployment.[74] Anyway, the rest are presumably better off thanks to their higher wages, but opponents of this kind of help usually fail to mention the workers who are now better paid, because they don't believe higher wages make *anybody* better off. By raising workers' wages, neoclassical economists are quick to say, we also raise the cost of the goods and services they produce. Higher prices harm all workers, the unemployed and the ones who keep working at higher wages, because they're all consumers, too. Higher prices mean they can now afford fewer goods and services.

The Law of Demand converts help into harm by shifting our attention from our earner selves to our consumer selves. Wage increases, industry subsidies, tariffs—all these forms of help are aimed at producers. Insofar as these measures give workers more money or save their jobs, such policies certainly help them. Only when economic analysis switches the focus to consumers do we, citizens who are *both* consumers and producers, see harm. Then we see higher prices. The focus on consumers shoves higher wages and secure jobs outside our range of vision.

In a democracy, it's the job of leaders to keep in mind that everybody is *both* a consumer and an earner (or a dependent of one), and to strike a fair balance between helping people in both roles. How do we find that balance point? Neoclassical economics has always has an answer: The correct balance point is where the market puts it. The balance point between hurting the fewest people and benefiting the most is exactly where the economy is now, and exactly where it will be at every moment in the future so long as government leaves the market alone and resists the urge to help people.

What free markets do well, of course, is to ensure that every kind of *good* will be available at the cheapest possible price, but not that every *person* will have the money to buy things, even cheap things. As Amartya Sen made so vivid in his studies of famine, whatever necessities people cannot produce themselves, they must acquire by other means. With luck, they can produce something they don't need, sell it, and use the cash to buy things they do need, or they can sell their labor and use their wages to buy what they need. But when markets for their goods or labor don't provide them with enough to live on, only government can make sure everyone has entitlements to basic necessities.

Economists have another law that seemingly transforms help into harm. It doesn't have an official name, so I'll call it the Law of Giving. According to the Law of Giving, it's impossible to give help without losing some of the resources you're trying to help with. Whenever government tries to transfer money from the rich to the poor (to take the favorite example), some of the money it takes from the rich never arrives in poor people's pockets. That's because some of the money meant for the needy must go toward running the transfer system—paying the people who administer it and providing them with offices, paper clips, computers, checks, envelopes, postage stamps, and vacations. No organized system of help runs by itself, after all. There's no way to avoid these costs. All possible means of transporting money from the better off to the worse off are "leaky buckets," to use economist Arthur Okun's memorable image.[75] In the transport of precious resources from one set of people to another, society's total assets diminish. That is why whenever government tries to redistribute, it unwittingly harms the entire society.

Now, a giant money-moving machine is bound to have some leaks and breakdowns. Most people accept the idea that nothing's perfect. In an imperfect world, most of us try to make things better rather than sit on our hands until we are sure our efforts will succeed perfectly. If we were at sea in a leaking lifeboat and all we had for a bailer was a leaky bucket, most of us would start bailing. Many economists, including Okun, conclude that leaks or not, if there's a huge disparity of well-being among citizens, it's worth transferring some resources from the best off to the worst off, even though some resources will dribble away in the process. It's worth helping the needy because it's morally right to help them, and because even if we can't cure all the world's troubles, it's better to have tried, and it's certainly better to cure some of them than none. If some folks among us have inside knowledge of where the leaks are, then let them get busy with their plugs instead of telling the rest of us not to bother.

Still, those who believe free markets are always superior to government think the problem with government help goes beyond leaky buckets. In their eyes, government redistribution programs are not inert objects, like rusty buckets. They're ripe opportunities for social parasites. To use Milton Friedman and Rose Friedman's metaphor, some of the money en route from rich to poor gets "siphoned off."[76] Some of it is purloined by bureaucrats who make their own jobs unnecessarily complicated so they can earn more money and amass more power. Some of the money goes to people who don't really need it, because bureaucrats don't have complete information about everybody's needs, and even if they did, they're only human so they're easily swayed by sympathy, sentimentality, their own biases, or sometimes bribes. Some of the money passing through our well-meaning aid program ends up in the hands of cheats, people who are good at playing the system but who wouldn't receive any help if the system operated perfectly. In the free-market cosmology, organized systems of help are immoral because they permit these kinds of illicit private gain at society's expense.

Troubling as these problems with government aid may be, however, there is no trouble-free alternative. It's not as though the private sector is free of embezzlement, swindles, fraud, accounting shenanigans, and other creative forms of corruption. The question isn't which kind of social regulation is more pure—politics or markets?—but rather how we as citizens can make all of our lives better and use all the tools at our disposal to minimize skullduggery. Imagine how you would have felt if the federal government had decided not to send water to New Orleans after Katrina so that none of the precious liquid would fall into the hands of looters and price gougers. Better to send the water, along with reinforcements for the local cops. A government that lets people suffer so as not to enable cheaters has declared its moral bankruptcy.

Democracy is not a superstore. The conservative cult of self-reliance and personal freedom denies our essential vulnerability and our dependence on each other. Free-market ideology fosters this delusion. It defines freedom as the right to choose from an array of goods in every aspect of our lives. We're not free, we are told, unless we can choose our children's school, our long-distance carrier, our Internet provider, our electricity supplier, and our health plan (never mind that most people would prefer the freedom to choose their doctor). Define freedom as consumer choice and anything so common as public schools, public utilities, public transportation, public pensions, or public health insurance encroaches on it. This is a shriveled concept of freedom, akin to a rat's freedom inside a Skinner box. The rat is perfectly free to choose between the lever that delivers food or the one that delivers a shock, but it is not free to roam outside the cage to search for possibilities beyond those its captor offers. Market freedom, too, is freedom within limits.

There's yet a bigger flaw in this vision of the good life as being set loose in a superstore. Most of us, as we begin to fashion our life plans, want some things that can't be had off the shelves. We want to roam in our imaginations and to create things that don't yet exist. We want connectedness as well as autonomy. We want to love and be loved. We want understanding, compassion, and loyalty. We want the pleasure and purpose of working with others on some larger project. No one, least of all the market or anyone in it, can produce and package any of these things for us. These aren't things we can choose. We have to make them, and we can't make them alone.

Individuals by themselves can't create these things, but neither can markets. Markets are designed to disconnect people at the first sign of trouble. When the savvy consumer is disappointed with a purchase, he may complain once, but he'll soon go looking elsewhere for another product or another store. Like a child with its toys, when our consumer selves get tired of something or it fails to please us, we up and leave. Albert Hirschman dubbed this consumer behavior "exit."[77] Freedom to choose is ultimately the freedom to walk away from any commitment, the freedom to extricate one's money and one's energies from common ventures, and the freedom not to have to care about anybody else.

There is a better response to disappointment, but it's one that markets don't foster. Hirschman called it "voice," a lovely shorthand for democracy. Instead of walking out, we can speak up. We can reason, persuade, cajole, and bargain. We can, in short, seek others' help in getting what we need and fulfilling our dreams. Cooperation, benevolence, and mutual aid have always been the way people got by, the way communities coped with adversity, and the way societies progressed. Commitment to a helpful government turns out to be a more capacious freedom.

3

Everyday Altruism

No man giveth, but with intention of good to himself.
—Thomas Hobbes, *Leviathan* (1651)

Thomas Hobbes launched modern political thought with this bleak assessment of human psychology: we are self-interested to our core. Everything we do is ultimately for our own benefit, and every seeming act of kindness is really a form of self-satisfaction. The Good Samaritan turns out to be a selfish soul, just like the rest of us.

One day, a story goes, Hobbes was strolling with a friend, when they came upon a beggar. Hobbes gave the fellow some money. The friend, thinking he'd caught Hobbes in an act of charity, gleefully pointed out the contradiction between Hobbes's behavior and his philosophy. Hobbes, however, had a ready explanation: it made him feel terrible to see the man so wretched and miserable. He had given money not to relieve the beggar's suffering, but his own.[1] Even in charity, Hobbes thought, every man is out for himself.

This way of thinking imagines self-interest and altruism as opposites: self-interest means acting to promote one's own welfare, altruism means acting to promote other people's welfare, and never the twain shall meet. We're motivated by one or the other, but it can't be both. Alexis de Tocqueville exploded this dichotomy a little shy of two centuries later. Instead of sitting in a study, imagining how people behave and what makes them tick, Tocqueville traveled around America and talked to people. He was awed by how much Americans joined together to help each other and promote the common good. Americans grasp "the principle of self-interest rightly understood," he wrote in his report, *Democracy in America.* They readily explained to him how "an enlightened regard for themselves constantly prompts them to assist one another and inclines them willingly to sacrifice a portion of their time and property to the welfare of the state."[2] In other words, these yeoman philosophers understood what the great academic minds of Europe did not: when we help others, we help ourselves, too. Self-interest and altruism are quite compatible, if not the same thing.

The philosophical separation of self-interest and altruism confuses motive and result, and makes altruism impossible. If we define altruism as acting in order to benefit someone other than ourselves, then when we discover, as Hobbes did, that we get pleasure from helping another, we think our motives must not have been pure. Altruism vanishes, and we are left with a one-dimensional view of human nature. Nothing but self-interest all the way down. In everyday life, when people help others, they feel richly rewarded. "You get more than you give," rejoice helpers of all kinds. That paradox makes no sense in our normal accounting schemes, but like Tocqueville's "self-interest rightly understood," it captures a spiritual wisdom that ordinary people grasp.

To find everyday altruism, we have to remove the cultural and scientific blinders that prevent us from seeing it. In this chapter, I travel through America if not exactly as a foreigner, then as an intellectual alien, someone who has never felt at home in the self-interest paradigm that dominates American political thought. I report on an astonishing breadth and depth of everyday altruism outside the voluntary associations that so fascinated Tocqueville.

How to Look at Altruism without Seeing It

In the standard way of thinking about altruism, Hobbes's way, "true altruism" is "acting with the goal of benefiting others."[3] The test of whether an act is truly altruistic rests in the helper's motivation, rather than the effect of her actions. You could try to rescue a group of endangered children, and even if you didn't succeed, we'd still consider you an altruist, for your purpose was noble. The trouble with this definition, though, is that to find altruists, we have to be able to peer into people's minds and see their intentions.

Lacking CAT scanners that can reveal the brain's intentions, most social scientists try to sneak up on altruism from behind. They ask whether the helper received any benefits in the process of helping others.[4] If they can find evidence that a helper benefited from his attempts to help others, he doesn't deserve to be called altruistic. On the other hand, when someone tries to help others and loses something or suffers harms in the process, they conclude that he is a genuine altruist.

By insisting that a true altruist can't get any satisfaction out of helping others, even though personal satisfaction is not her main motive, social science has written altruism out of the realm of human possibility. As one review put it in 1990, "For a long time it was intellectually unacceptable to raise the question of whether 'true' altruism could exist. Whether one spoke to a biologist, a psychologist, a psychiatrist, a sociologist, an economist, or a political scientist, the answer was the same: Anything that *appears* to be motivated by a concern for someone else's needs will, under closer scrutiny, prove to have ulterior selfish motives."[5] Just when you think you've found altruism, the scientists make it vanish into thin air.

How does this vanishing act work? Social scientists erase altruism by imagining opportunities for personal gain in every act of help. Say you look out the window and notice a child being attacked by a dog. You leap up and run outdoors to help the child. Surely, you're entitled to call yourself an altruist.

Not so fast, says modern science. Maybe you rescue the child to make yourself feel better, because you're distressed at the sight of a crying, frightened, injured child. By helping the child, you relieve your own distress. Bingo: self-interest. Or maybe you help the child to avoid feeling guilty, since you've been brought up to help people in distress. You're just helping the child to relieve your guilt or to get the satisfaction of knowing yourself to be a virtuous person. Bingo: self-interest. Or perhaps you anticipate some kudos from other folks when, looking out their windows, they see your heroism. A little admiration sure feels good. Bingo: self-interest. Or maybe you think that by acting heroically, you'll enhance your reputation, and, of course, you never know what opportunities a good reputation will bring you. Bingo. Or maybe you calculate that by acting altruistically now, you'll boost the chances that somebody will help you in the future. Bingo.

There's one last chance to rescue yourself from the dark truth of pure self-interest. Perhaps you are one of those rare people who, quite uncharacteristically, get pleasure from helping others. These are people most of us would call altruists, people whose goal is to benefit others. Some social scientists, though, say that if such people do what gives them pleasure, then they're just like everybody else. They have unusual tastes, to be sure, but they're still self-interested. Help all they might, people who get pleasure from helping others still do it to boost their own pleasure. Sorry, say most scientists, but helping others is just egoism all the way down. "Scratch an altruist and watch a hypocrite bleed" goes a famous aphorism of altruism skeptics.[6]

Against this dreary tide of pessimism, evolutionary biology comes running with good news: despite what you may have learned about Darwinism in school, life isn't all competition and struggle to the death. Everywhere in nature, from the tiniest creatures to man himself, we find altruism. Organisms often cooperate, share food, or help rear each other's offspring. They sometimes put themselves in jeopardy to protect their fellow creatures, even sacrifice their own lives to defend the group.[7]

Don't rejoice too quickly, however, for the new evolution doesn't make us look terribly nice, either. It turns out that altruism is just another strategy our genes use to perpetuate themselves. According to modern biology, the struggle for survival isn't a fight among animals or people or organisms of any kind;

it's a war among genes. A gene's only goal in life is to replicate—to perpetuate its kind. Now, if a gene somehow inclines its hosts (that's us) to be cooperative and helpful, and if cooperation increases the chances that the hosts flourish and make a lot of off-spring, that cooperative gene is going to be mighty prolific. But *any* characteristic that helps an organism survive and multiply will tend to last—brown eyes, bushy tails, barbarism, whatever. Genes associated with traits that help organisms multiply will themselves become fruitful, and so, therefore, will the traits they determine. What looks like helpfulness and self-sacrifice at first glance is only the side effect of natural selection. Helpful behavior among humans is nothing but some of our successful genes expressing themselves. Altruism isn't really altruism. It's merely behavior that kept genes going for a long, long time.

I suppose there's some comfort in knowing that nice genes and therefore nice people tend to win out, but the evolutionary explanation for altruism doesn't speak to the lives of individuals. It explains how populations thrive (or don't) over the long run, but it doesn't explain what thoughts and feelings course through someone as she's deciding what to do today or reflecting on what she did yesterday.

To find everyday altruism, I bypass all these existential ruminations about whether altruism is real. I start with a simple, straightforward concept of altruism that captures the phenomenon I want to explore: people helping other people. I go out looking for occasions when people think they're helping others, when people think someone else has helped them, and when observers think people have been helpful. Instead of seeking a pure, ideal kind of altruism, I look for ordinary acts of kindness and care that enable us to grow up, live, and achieve a modicum of human connection and happiness.

Are Americans Altruistic?

The largest social science effort to quantify altruism among Americans, the General Social Survey, listed fifteen activities and asked people whether they had ever done any of them.[8] The list mentions routine daily activities, rather than heroic rescues or major sacrifices. Not surprisingly, a high proportion of people say they do these kinds of things. The list includes some common courtesies: 89 percent have "given directions" to someone who asked, 47 percent have "given up a seat" to someone else, and about the same percentage have "carried someone's belongings." The list includes small favors: 59 percent have "helped someone who was away," perhaps bringing in the mail and watering the plants; 42 percent have "loaned an item"; and 42 percent have "returned extra change" when the cashier made a mistake. It includes big favors, too, such as "helping someone find a job" (61 percent did that) and "loaning money" (the survey doesn't ask how much money, but 52 percent loaned some). And it includes rather more substantial commitments: "giving to charity" (79 percent), "giving blood" (a mere 17 percent report having done that), and "volunteering for a charity," by far the least-frequent altruistic activity of Americans in this survey, with only 7 percent donating their time and labor.

As testimony to the altruism of Americans, the General Social Survey is tepid stuff, but that's not the fault of Americans. The survey asks mainly about common courtesies and trivial favors instead of more meaningful experiences of altruism. It also makes some odd presumptions about what counts as altruism. It includes "helping others with housework" (79 percent claimed credit for pitching in), as though housework is somebody else's responsibility. Sorry, but no altruism points for helping with the family dishes. Curiously, the survey counts "talking to a depressed person." Americans earn a near-perfect score on this item—93 percent—which perhaps says more about our mental health than our altruism.

For a slightly more meaningful concept of altruism, we might look at the "Giving and Volunteering" surveys performed every few years by the Independent Sector. These aim to measure the extent to which Americans make charitable donations and do volunteer work. According to the most recent survey (done in 2000), 44 percent of adults did some kind of volunteer work (far more than the 7 percent who told the General Social Survey that they volunteer), and they work an average 3.6 hours a week, be it licking envelopes for fund-raisers, visiting the sick, driving meals to shut-ins or shut-ins to medical appointments, staffing hotlines, working soup kitchens and food pantries, donating their professional skills, or serving on boards of non-profit organizations.[9]

Some smaller surveys find even higher rates of altruism. According to Princeton sociologist Robert Wuthnow, who surveyed some twenty-one hundred adults about their compassion and caring, levels of caring for others are extremely impressive. Three in four people had helped a relative or friend through a personal crisis, six in ten people had visited someone in the hospital, and the same portion had lent more than one hundred dollars to a friend or relative. More than half had tried to get someone to stop using alcohol or drugs. Compassion didn't extend only to friends. Six in ten people said they had stopped to help someone with car trouble, and half had given money to a beggar, nearly a quarter in the previous year.[10]

Perhaps the richest survey of everyday altruism is also the smallest. In the Boston Area Diary Study, Paul Schervish and John Havens asked forty-four people to keep track of all the money, goods, unpaid help, and emotional support they gave and received over the course of a year, without counting help to spouses or dependent children. Virtually everyone gave material assistance. All but one person gave money or goods to nonrelatives, usually a close friend or coworker; all but three gave money or goods to relatives; and almost half gave money to their adult children. But the level of unpaid help and emotional support was the real surprise. All told, participants averaged eighty-seven person days per year (counting eight hours of help time as one day)—forty-three days of unpaid help and forty-four days of emotional support. That's almost three months, a quarter of the year, that people spend helping others. The bulk of the unpaid help consisted of caring for children and elderly people, and giving people rides, but in addition, people helped with word processing, bookkeeping, pet and plant care, snow shoveling, house cleaning, shopping, cooking, tutoring, moving, medical care, religious instruction, and lawn care.[11] No doubt keeping track of these activities made the participants more conscious of them, and probably boosted their recollection. But think about it: a quarter of our lives giving the kinds of help we take for granted and don't count unless some nosy researchers pester us to keep track.

The very ordinariness of everyday altruism makes it so invisible. We couldn't live without everyday altruism, nor do we, and so we take it for granted, like breathing. Reporters and social scientists who interview altruists and do-gooders almost always encounter puzzled, uncomprehending reactions. Who, me? I don't do anything out of the ordinary. I'm not particularly caring or generous. I just do what I do, like everybody else. Anybody in my position would do what I did. On and on. One woman, pressed by Robert Wuthnow to describe the kinds of caring she does in her everyday life, told him, "Those are the kinds of things you don't talk about. It's almost embarrassing for me to tell you the kinds of things I've done, because I haven't done them to get recognition."[12] This is why I have no doubt that Schervish and Haven's diary method did not inflate everyday altruism; it simply rendered the invisible visible.

Trying to measure altruism is something of a shell game. It's all in what you count and how you count it. If, like the General Social Survey, you count talking to someone who is depressed and giving directions, you're likely to find that nearly everyone's an altruist. If you count donating blood, most of the altruists disappear. Even more challenging for accurate surveys, people's recollections about giving and volunteering are quite malleable. When survey takers prompt respondents with suggestive examples of kinds of giving or volunteering, the respondents tend to recall more of their own giving and volunteering, and, of course, they then report higher levels.[13]

But by far the worst problem with surveys is that they have a downward bias. Trying to quantify altruism—for that matter, trying to quantify anything—requires that we first narrow our sights, decide in advance what we'll look for, and then look for only those things: the finite list of activities in social surveys. The very questions in a survey signal people not to bother mentioning things that don't immediately seem to fit. That's why prompts with suggestive examples lead more people to say yes—the suggestions broaden their idea of what the survey taker is after.

What's noteworthy, though, is that even with all these problems and even by the minimal standards of social surveys, most people recognize themselves as sometime-altruists. If we don't try to quantify and if we expand the concept beyond the relatively trivial favors, volunteerism, and charity that surveys measure, we can get a much richer picture of altruism.

As I began to think about altruism, I worked from my own experience—the kinds of help and caring for others that I noticed in my everyday life and reading. Instead of aiming for a census of altruists, I sought to compile a photo album of altruism. Starting from my intuition that people do things to benefit others all the time, in big and small ways, I tried to look at the world expansively, and sure enough, I began to notice more and more altruism.

Once a few years ago when bears had just started frequenting our neighborhood, a friend came by to say she'd been out in the woods and seen a lot of claw marks on the trees. Excited to see evidence of bears, I asked her if the marks were hard to find. She answered, "No, once you see one, then you see another and another. The more you see, the more you see, if you know what I mean." I stopped my gardening and went into the woods in search of bear signs. She was exactly right. The more you see, the more you see. And that's how it is with altruism.

Caregiving

Mothers and fathers are the original altruists. Maybe they don't always act out of love for their kids, but most of the time they're raising kids, they're putting their children's interests above their own. They're waking when they'd rather be sleeping, putting food in a child's mouth when they're hungry themselves, sacrificing a thousand pleasures in hopes of giving their children a good life. Among low-income single mothers, according to two sociologists, "the norm of self-sacrifice is so strong that a woman risks social censure if she has nicer clothing than her children." One seventeen-year-old mother told them, "I can't see my son walking around with Payless sneakers on with me walking around with Nikes or Reeboks or something. My *son* is gonna have Nikes and Reeboks on. *I'll* wear the Payless shoes. My son will always come before me."[14]

According to one school of economics, when people decide to have kids, they're buying future labor for the family economy or investing in old-age insurance.[15] They may make short-term sacrifices, but they expect to receive long-term rewards. I'm not such a cynic. Besides, as economist Nancy Folbre points out, would-be parents would get a much higher rate of return if they refrained from having kids and invested in something else besides child rearing, and single moms would definitely prosper financially if they ditched their kids to their fathers or an orphanage.[16] But most people don't ditch their kids, and parents sometimes take on enormous risks and even social stigma to do right by their children.

Besides raising children, families devote extraordinary time and labor to taking care of the frail elderly and people with chronic illness, disability, retardation, and dementia. The federal government collects data on family caregiving through large interview surveys. Here's what we know: in 1997, approximately twenty-six million people were providing care to adults who need assistance—*adults*, people over eighteen, not children. At the time, this was almost four times as many people as the professional and paraprofessional caregivers employed in the paid home-care sector.[17] According to a 2003 survey, one that defined caregiving quite stringently, more than forty-four million people—more that one-fifth of adults— were caregivers to other adults.[18]

Time-wise, caregiving can be equivalent to a full-time job. Nearly a fifth of caregivers to adults spend forty hours a week or more. Half of informal caregivers devote more than eight hours a week to taking care of others, the equivalent of an extra workday or more. Most would say they find caregiving rewarding, but they also sacrifice a great deal. Half say they have less time for family and friends, and more than 40 percent say they give up vacations, hobbies, and social activities. Even more striking are the sacrifices working people make on their paid jobs to devote themselves to caregiving. More than 60 percent of informal caregivers who are also in the paid workforce have made some adjustments in their work, including going to work late or leaving early, taking time off, taking a leave of absence, working fewer hours, taking less demanding jobs, refusing promotions, taking early retirement, or leaving the paid workforce altogether. The average caregiver devotes 4.3 years to the job.[19]

Statistics don't begin to convey the heart of the matter. My favorite caregiving story is one that never happened, John Steinbeck's *Of Mice and Men*.[20] It's a tale of two itinerant ranch hands, an unlikely couple, but the kind of pair Steinbeck would have us know teems through human history. Lennie is very large, very retarded, very good-hearted, and very, very strong. When his mother dies, leaving him an orphan and unable to fend for himself, his first cousin George takes him on as his charge and working partner. George is as rough as they come, yet as gentle, too.

Lennie often gets into trouble, costing both men their jobs, usually because he doesn't understand his brute strength and inadvertently kills animals he means to pet. He does understand that he's a burden to George, though, and so he offers to "jus' as well go away an' live in a cave." George tells him he can "jus' as well go to hell," and gathers Lennie in tighter with fantasies about how they'll one day have a place of their own with pigs and chickens and soft furry rabbits for Lennie to tend. Meanwhile, he constantly tutors Lennie in how to survive. Don't drink dirty water out of a puddle. If you get lost, just stay where you are and wait for me to find you. Around other people, let me do the talking.

Together George and Lennie roam, looking for work and board. When at last they find a ranch with openings, the boss can't fathom their relationship, or why the big man doesn't talk. Whenever he asks Lennie what kind of work he can do, George answers, praising Lennie as "strong as a bull" and "a hell of a good worker."

"Then why don't you let him answer?" the boss asks. "What you trying to put over?"

"Oh! I ain't saying he's bright. He ain't. But I say he's a God damn good worker," George insists.

The boss finally thinks he understands: "Say—what you sellin'?" he asks George. "What stake you got in this guy? You takin' his pay away from him?"

What stake you got in this guy? The question sounds the clash of self-interest and altruism, two ways of understanding human relationships and two ways of being in relationships. George does have a stake in Lennie, but devotion is not the kind of stake the boss can grasp.

When doctors advise parents to put their profoundly disabled children in an institution, when friends suggest to full-time caregivers that they ought to pack their loved one in a nursing home and get a life, when supervisors refuse to accommodate an employee's caregiving schedule—these are all ways that altruism and self-interest collide in contemporary life, and people's stakes in each other are met with the ranch boss's dim bewilderment.

Neighborliness

Neighbors and friends are everyday altruists. All the simple care, the watching out for one another, and the little kindnesses that go into these relationships are things people do to benefit someone else: giving someone a ride when his car is in the shop or he can't drive, picking up someone else's kids from school, minding each other's kids, shopping and cooking for a friend who's under the weather, looking in on an ailing neighbor, letting the plumber or the meter reader into the neighbor's apartment when she can't be home, helping fix the storm door or move heavy furniture, shoveling a neighbor's walk, taking a family in when their heat or power fails, having a party to introduce a new neighbor around.

In her study of aging in the inner city, anthropologist Katherine Newman discovered informal safety services. Tenants of housing projects establish patrols, escort services for the elderly, and self-imposed curfews. Neighbors on a floor listen for unfamiliar footsteps and check on each other if they think something's amiss. Missy Darden, a woman in her seventies, told Newman that after being mugged a few times, she was motivated "to do something to help herself and others." She started a civilian patrol and a buddy system. "People who come home from work late at night get together and have a telephone chain of people who are coming in at the same hours so people come in together. A person wouldn't have to walk down the street by themselves." Darden used the buddy system as a vehicle to educate her neighbors about how to be streetwise. She also organized a yearly fair in her housing complex to bring the neighbors together, and she sometimes took groups of teenagers to African American festivals.[21]

Altruism skeptics think all these little favors are just so much self-interest in disguise. They dub it "reciprocal altruism," meaning "I'll do for you now, hoping you'll do for me later," and they think it's about as altruistic as the Godfather. No doubt, sometimes people do hope for payback somewhere in the recesses of their mind, but most of the time, people help their friends and neighbors because they care for them and because they want to live in a community where people help each other. Rather than disdain reciprocity as somehow venal, Newman's inner-city residents have a keen sense of self-interest rightly understood: "I think neighbors should look out for one another, for the elderly," a plumber told her. "My neighbors love me. Whenever they ask me for something, I will try to help them out. Some people will try to take advantage of me. But if you are nice people and I see you need help, well . . . what goes around comes around."[22]

Hidden Altruism

Everywhere in nooks and crannies of America, there are hidden kitchens, as two reporters for National Public Radio discovered. Around midnight, behind a taxicab depot in San Francisco, a woman named Janete prepares Brazilian food for the fleet's drivers, all of whom happen to be Brazilian. Her makeshift kitchen is the focal point for Brazilian music, Portuguese conversation, companionship, and a sense of home. In another San Francisco neighborhood, the reporters learned, such cooks are called "old stoves." They're "the people who have put in some serious time in the kitchen cooking for their community for decades on end." Lou Marcelli, the caretaker for a swimming and rowing club near Ghirardelli Square, presides over a galley kitchen in the boathouse, and once or twice a week, he whips up a meal for the lonely old-timers just so they have a place to go. Families who come to the club don't need him, he told the reporters. "It's the bachelors and people that live alone, they don't want to go home. They just want company, the camaraderie. When I cook, I always cook enough for a few more people, and there is always somebody around."[23]

The more you see, the more you see. In the part of rural, very small-town New Hampshire where I live, funerals are catered by the church folk, with nary an order form or a price list. Somehow, lavish spreads of finger sandwiches, Swedish meatballs, cheese and crackers, cakes and cookies materialize after the service. For years, the Country Kitchen restaurant in the neighboring big town (population 5,000) sponsored a free Thanksgiving dinner for people with no other place to go. The owners ran three seatings, served more than 200 people in the restaurant, and delivered more than 300 meals to homes. Co-owner Pat Tremblay organized the event, but the operation was staffed by innumerable volunteers—chefs, servers, and people who roasted turkeys and baked pies in their home ovens and brought them to the restaurant.[24]

We could spend a lot of time trying to find out what all these underground cooks get out of doing what they do, and whether they're self-interested at bottom, but if we did, we'd miss the point: they enjoy bringing people together and nourishing them, and because they enjoy such things, they are community spark plugs.

Then there are hidden rides. I became conscious of them when my neighbor Dave Diehl told me he spends a day a week driving people to the university hospital for medical treatments—chemo, dialysis, whatever they need. It's a one-hour trip each way, plus however many hours he has to wait for the person's treatment. Once I was aware of Dave's driving, I noticed the hidden network of drivers for people who need outpatient care but don't have relatives or friends who can drive them. I hadn't seen it before because no one in my close circles needs rides (yet).

The more you see, the more you see. The local Council on Aging has more than 130 volunteer drivers on call for people who can't drive, whether for medical appointments or just getting around to live their lives. The volunteers donate not only their time but use of their vehicles and gas costs, too. Sometimes the grateful riders offer to chip in for gas, but the drivers almost never accept. In 2005, volunteer drivers for this one agency made eight hundred trips and logged more than fifty-four thousand miles.[25]

Of course, transportation isn't the only service these drivers provide. Laurie Buckley, a forty-seven-year-old single mother, had a brain aneurysm and stroke that left her temporarily unable to walk and talk, much less drive. There was a time, she told a reporter, when the council's drivers were "the only adult interaction she had all day." And I know from my friend Dave that he became confidant and shoulder to the people he accompanied on their journeys through terminal illness.[26]

Besides driving, there are many other forms of keeping company that I count as everyday altruism. Volunteers log thousands of hours visiting patients in hospitals, nursing homes, rehab centers, and at home in companionship programs or hospice care. Murl Eastman, eighty-four years old and a World War II veteran, dons a suit and tie every day to visit with patients at the VA Medical Center in Ann Arbor, Michigan. "They just like to know somebody cares besides their family, and they like to talk about their experiences," Eastman said, explaining the value of what he does. One outpatient of the center drives all the way to Ann Arbor from Toledo, Ohio, because he cherishes the attention from the volunteers. "When the nurses are busy, they fill in. They'll come by with a tray of things, or to give company." Another volunteer, seventy-eight-year-old Jane Bowen, explained the importance of company from the volunteer's point of view: "You get a whole new extended family here. Everybody here is concerned for everybody else."[27]

Visiting and keeping company are so much a part of everyday life that it's hard to think of them as altruism, and especially hard because the benefits go both ways. But company is so crucial to human well-being that formal programs to provide it now abound, and thousands of people volunteer through them, offering their regular company to strangers.

Through Meals on Wheels, volunteers deliver not only food but also smiles and small talk. "Our food is our signature," said one program director in Tampa, Florida, "but it's the knock on the door and the 'How ya doing today?' that means the most to individuals." Marvin Burrows, a driver for the program in Hayward, California, echoed a common refrain among volunteer drivers: "Sometimes we're the only people they see all day." One of his clients, ninety-two-year-old Elviro Ferro, explained to a reporter what she loves about the program, besides that "it's fun to just look in the bag: Marvin says hello and we say a few silly words. It's nice to have a visitor." Like the drivers in most Meals on Wheels programs, Burrows uses his brief contacts with homebound clients to check up on them and report any undue problems. In the Hayward program, drivers use a checklist to monitor clients every six months, looking for signs of decline or need for further help with dressing, cleaning, or eating.[28] Although I've lumped Meals on Wheels volunteers in with other kinds of company keeping, it's worth noting that each program also fields large volunteer staffs who cook, wrap, and pack meals in church basements and wherever else programs find kitchen space, without coming into contact with clients—another kind of hidden kitchen.

Meals on Wheels drivers typically have relatively little time for company keeping, because their primary goal is to get hot meals to people within a small window of midday mealtime, but there are other programs whose missions are explicitly company keeping. Senior Companion programs link older volunteers with older adults who are homebound. Respite-care programs arrange for volunteers to step in for a family caregiver so she or he can have time off. Medicare requires its hospice programs to train volunteers and provide them as part of the package of services for the terminally ill. All of these programs, including Meals on Wheels, must meet government standards and they survive primarily with government money, but volunteers do the actual work. Were it not for armies of people willing and eager to help their neighbors, these programs wouldn't exist. And were it not for government funding, these opportunities for everyday altruism would vanish.

Even the briefest glance at some of these more formal programs highlights the altruism in informal visiting as well as in the formal programs that are becoming part of the landscape of late-life years. For the visited, visitors offer "someone to be talking and complaining to," in the words of an eighty-one-year-old. In these visits, people reminisce about their families and their pasts; share tips on how they cope with this and that; gripe, laugh, cry, and pass the time with somebody besides TV characters. And because two's always company, the visitors receive some benefits of company as well, even though it may meet different needs—perhaps a sense of connection to family or a window into experiences the visitor never had. The people who receive visits as well as their families appreciate this company keeping for the act of generosity it is. Carl Hubbard, who took care of his mother full-time before she died, said of his mother's senior companion, "When on the weekend a person like Cynthia visited, I was beneficiary of that good will. I appreciated her cheeriness as much as my mom."[29]

On-the-Job Altruism

I count as everyday altruism occupations and paying jobs whose purpose is to improve other people's well-being. Medical care, social work, elder care and home care, child care, teaching, firefighting and emergency work, police work, counseling, religious ministry—all of these seem to me to count as forms of altruistic behavior. Not every person in every one of these occupations is altruistic, and few people are altruistic 100 percent of their working hours. These occupations are replete with altruism, though, because the job description for every one of them reads the same: "Assess somebody else's needs and respond to them. Make the other person better off."

That these people get paid for their work doesn't make them any less altruistic. They could be doing all kinds of other things with their time, and they could be earning their incomes in all kinds of other ways. They choose to spend their working hours helping others when not everybody does. Science may say there's no such thing as genuine altruism, yet who of us believes a teacher, a nurse, or a day-care worker does it mainly for the money? Yes, I know that some of these people can be mean, cruel, and abusive some of the time. But most of the time, most of the people in these occupations define their jobs as promoting the well-being of others. And most of the time, they get paid a pittance in comparison to the value and arduousness of the work they do.

Then there are professionals who choose a public-service career instead of a more lucrative private-sector route: biomedical researchers who devote their talents to a state health department, trying to prevent epidemics, for far less money and glory than they might attain developing a new drug for a pharmaceutical company; lawyers who serve as public defendants or represent indigent clients in legal-aid services; doctors who do the best they can for patients in understaffed, underfinanced community health clinics; experienced soldiers who stay with the armed services instead of switching to a private security firm to do the same dangerous job for ten times the military pay.[30]

Utility, highway, and transportation workers are frequently called upon to work overtime and in dangerous conditions, helping communities to recover from storms, power outages, explosions, road washouts, and other calamities. True, they get paid for their work, but in crises they put themselves on the line and exert themselves far beyond any pay. We might not think of them as everyday altruists because their help doesn't go to people directly, but rather to objects—roads, utility poles and wires, underground pipes, bridges, and culverts. However, by maintaining the communal infrastructure, they serve the common good, and they rise to crises with a dedication to something beyond themselves. Largely invisible, they form a vast network of hidden repair-and-recovery squads.

I also count the often invisible work of cleaning and maintaining common spaces—offices, public restrooms, roadsides, parks, paths, and picnic areas, even parking lots. I count it as mild altruism when people pick up after themselves (raw self-interest would lead them to leave their mess for somebody else), even greater altruism when they pick up after others, and perhaps even greatest when workers take on the degrading tasks of cleaning homes and public restrooms for others. I once heard a nurse's aide, a union member, explain the value of her work in plain bedside talk: "We clean up your caca when you can't."[31] Anyone who's ever been sick and incontinent or had an incontinent relative knows what a gift it is to give someone her dignity while cleaning up her accidents.

I count cleaning jobs as altruism because even though they are paid jobs and even though the people who do them usually don't feel they have other options, cleaning workers often give far more than they receive. They give away their own dignity and social status, in return for a pittance, to elevate the dignity and comfort of the people they clean for. Swallowing your pride seems to me an act of generosity, even if it's what you have to do to eat.

I also count cleaning jobs as altruistic because, often, the people who do them develop loyalty to their employers far beyond the scope of the job. One employer told Judith Rollins why she kept employing a woman who routinely came late and didn't clean very well. "It's worth much more to me to have her loyalty and her trust. And know if I'm sick, she'll come and take care of me, know I can count on her being there." A domestic worker explained to Mary Romero why she continued working for an elderly woman in a financially nonsensical job with low wages and a long commute: "I guess you can say she needs companionship.

I feel sorry for her, you know. . . . I go once a month to her house. I like to go early so I can sit and talk to her."[32]

Beyond-the-Job Altruism

There's a kind of altruism that might be called going beyond the job description. Every occupation and every workplace has such people: people who do things not required by their jobs in order to make things more pleasant for their coworkers, customers, and clients; people who put in more time and go the extra five miles because they want the job to be done right; and people who give far more to their jobs than what they receive in pay.

An inner-city school bus driver in Boston's Roxbury neighborhood took it on herself to do more than transport the kids, because, as she said:

I want to see these kids make it in life. I want to see them survive. . . . When I'm driving the bus, I call some kids to be up there near me, sitting, and I've done my homework—I've checked into *their* homework!—and I'm ready for them. I'll quiz them. I'll try to give them hints about how to do better in school. I'll teach them about obeying and keeping quiet and speaking out at the right time. If they're doing good, I reach into my bag, and I give them a chocolate bar—and it's extra good, not just the five-and-dime-store kind. "Made in England" is what it says on the wrapper—and I get them to read it.[33]

Where I work, Dartmouth College, the department administrator's job includes organizing the course schedules, making sure every class has a room to meet in, collecting and filing the student grades, and a host of other administrative duties. Kathy Donald, however, does many other things that are nowhere in the college's official job postings but create a sense of community. She keeps tabs on birthdays, babies, illnesses, and family deaths and organizes the appropriate cards, gifts, and parties. She maintains the faculty lounge, keeps up newspaper subscriptions, makes sure the plants are thriving, and stocks the coffee machine. She not only nurses the department's printers and high-tech copier but also patiently coaches everyone in using them and bails us out of jams. She makes artful displays celebrating faculty publications and awards and student achievements. She makes sure there's food whenever people get together. Because of Kathy, we all know each other better and care about each other more.

In the village where I live, town government is definitely a beyond-the-job-description affair. At every election, eight or ten people staff the polls as registrars and ballot clerks. They, along with the town moderator and town clerk, remain in the polling place for eight hours or more depending on the type of election, then stay even later to count ballots and make sure everything is done right. Most of them volunteer. The moderator, who has a private law practice, gets paid fifty dollars per election, so he effectively donates his time. Poll workers sometimes bring refreshments for the voters; voters sometimes bring refreshments for them. Because all these people give of themselves, elections in our town are social events and draw unusually high turnouts. So it goes with every town organization. The planning board, whose members get paid two hundred dollars per year, officially meets once a month. During 2005, board members put in seventy-two long evenings (they all have day jobs) because there were so many requests from landowners and developers needing the board's approval. Much of the town's business wouldn't get done at all but for the extra efforts of these people, and none of it would get done as well as it does but for their dedication.

Pick anyplace where you live or work and run the same kind of analysis. If you don't live in a small town, pick a community within your city instead—a school, a soccer club, a condo association, the Rotary Club, the neighborhood association. Ask yourself who keeps things running and how. (Cynics might say that none of this beyond-the-job activity counts as altruism because the people I describe get their jollies from serving as they do. But then we're quibbling over words. In my book, anyone who gets her jollies from serving others or the common good is by definition an altruist.)

A few years ago, my hairdresser opened my eyes to everyday altruism in the beauty world when she told me she was learning to style wigs for a customer getting chemotherapy. Soon after, I noticed a news article about two hairdressers who had taken training with the American Cancer Society. Now they donate their time to fitting and styling wigs for patients at the regional cancer center, and if a patient is uncomfortable being fitted in public, they make time in their shops outside regular hours.[34]

The more you see, the more you see. I learned that these hairdressers were only three of some twelve thousand cosmetologists who volunteer more than one hundred thousand hours a year to the American Cancer Society's "Look Good, Feel Better" program. The program teaches cosmetologists beauty techniques for cancer patients, and they in turn run small groups or do individual consultations, passing on their knowledge of makeup, skin care, nail care, and dealing with hair loss. Like so many altruists, when they are singled out and honored, they emphasize that they are only doing what seems right. "It's not about us," said Vilma Colon Cobb when she won an award from the American Cancer Society. "It's that we're able to give something to the patients. God gave us a talent to do hair, and makeup, and nails, et cetera—and this is the time that we pay back. To somebody that's in need. That's what all of us volunteers are about."[35]

Everyday altruism shows up in the workplace when people help a coworker who is swamped, stay late to help the boss, or go the extra mile for a customer. While Barbara Ehrenreich spent a year working an assortment of low-wage jobs for her book *Nickel and Dimed,* she benefited from this kind of unspoken assistance in every job. At a restaurant where she waitressed, the cooks, busboys, and waitresses "form a reliable mutual support-group. If one of us is feeling sick or overwhelmed, another will 'bev' a table or even carry trays for her. If one of us is off sneaking a cigarette or a pee, the others will do their best to conceal her absence from the enforcers of corporate rationality." In her job as a dietary aide in a nursing home—which she thought would be primarily serving food to residents but mainly entailed carrying trays, scraping and washing dishes, collecting and washing table linens, sweeping and vacuuming floors—she got by "thanks to the nurse's aides, who pitch in with serving."[36]

Even some Holocaust rescuers, people we think of as part of the "race of saints," turn out to be beyond-the-job altruists. Miep Gies helped hide Anne Frank's family in the attic above Mr.

Frank's office. "During a time when everyone was on ration cards," writes political scientist Patricia Siplon, "everyone in the attic was fed. For over two years, Miep went back and forth on her bike to the public library every Saturday to exchange everyone's library books, and she made sure that everyone's birthday was celebrated with a cake and a present—items almost certainly acquired at great cost through the black market. One has to wonder how many meals, afternoons, and personal possessions Miep and the others had to forego to carry out their ordinary altruism. By focusing only on the bravery," Siplon notes, "we lose sight of the fact that these people were also motivated to simply improve the quality of life of the people in the attic."[37]

Employers and business owners are frequently beyond-the-job altruists, too. Aaron Feuerstein, owner of Malden Mills, famously kept his workers on the payroll after the factory burned down, and then struggled for years to protect them against creditors as his textile business had more and more trouble.[38] Feuerstein was hardly what you'd call an everyday phenomenon; he made national news precisely because financial sacrifice of that scale by a CEO for his employees is rare. But if the scale of what Feuerstein did was unorthodox, the spirit is common.

Andre Medina, a Cuban immigrant in Boston, built a chain of supermarkets. That in itself wouldn't be remarkable, but Medina opened his stores in low-income neighborhoods where no other chains would put a supermarket, and hired former convicts and addicts to give them another chance. "He opened doors for me that no one else would," said Felix Fresneda, a fellow immigrant who had spent fifteen years in jail and lived in a halfway house before Medina hired him. Under Medina's tutelage, he worked his way up from painter to store supervisor and was able to buy a home.[39]

A pawnshop might be the last type of business where one would expect to find altruism, but a *New York Times* portrait of "Mr. Pawnbroker" in the South Bronx tells otherwise. The owner, Radames Rosado, has tight relationships with a core of regular customers. He helps them by giving them loans against jewelry, and they, for their part, are grateful because most of them have no one else to turn to for help, certainly not banks or credit companies. He sometimes holds customers' jewelry for them long past the four-month contract and stops charging interest. One customer told the reporter that Mr. Rosado did her a favor by giving her eighty dollars for some gold hoop earrings. "I'm glad [the shop] was there, because I needed that money. I didn't have to ask anybody for money, even family." More than the cash, the pawnbroker gave independence, the ability to fend for herself without burdening others. She needed the money, it turns out, because she, a social worker earning nineteen dollars an hour, had given all she had to her father so he could take her three sons to Disney World. Thus, the pawnbroker also gave her the means to be generous with her own family. "Mr. Pawnbroker" enables a good deal of this everyday generosity. One man raised cash to send his son to Puerto Rico for his birthday. Another woman pawned jewelry to help her sister pay her mortgage and, sometimes, to be able to shop for Christmas presents. On occasion, a customer turns the tables and does a favor for Mr. Rosado. One customer pawned her engagement ring when Mr. Rosado first opened his store—not because she needed the money, she said, but "to welcome him to the neighborhood."[40]

Little Benefactors

Philanthropy is only a small part of what I consider everyday altruism, but it does have the virtue of being measurable, and its numbers are impressive. According to *Giving and Volunteering in the United States, 2001,* the most oft-cited survey of charitable giving, a whopping 89 percent of households made charitable contributions, and the average household gave $1,620, which was just over 3.1 percent of its income.[41] Yet impressive as these numbers are, they largely reflect responses to well-financed fundraising campaigns and donations to organized charities, and so they fail to capture the kind of grassroots philanthropy I see as part of everyday altruism.

"Anonymous Donor Pays Seniors' Bill" ran a headline in the *Bethel (Maine) Morning Sentinel.* A few days earlier, the paper had published a story about an elderly couple who lived on an $1,162 Social Security check and $66 worth of food stamps per month. The state's Department of Health and Social Services decided it had overpaid them almost $1,600 in food stamps and, following federal rules, told the couple it would deduct $10 a month from their food stamp allotment until the debt was fully recovered. (By my calculations, the deductions would have lasted thirteen years, perhaps longer than the couple.) After the first story, the paper received calls and e-mails from people wanting to help the couple. A stranger dropped off $40 at the couple's home. And within a few days, an anonymous benefactor had walked into the department and paid off the entire debt.[42]

News stories often call forth this kind of small-scale philanthropy, especially when the needy people seem deserving and their fates seem cruel or unjust. (News stories about general poverty rarely call forth individual donations, in large part because general stories don't offer people specific ways to help.) After reading about a struggling food pantry in his native New Hampshire, a North Carolina race car driver donated a building with a playground to the organization. After the *Boston Globe* ran a series on unscrupulous debt collectors and their penchant for impounding poor people's cars, a retired schoolteacher e-mailed the paper: "I felt compassion for the people who were so taken advantage of." He and his wife had a 1996 Saturn SL ("registered, runs well, and wears an inspection sticker"), he wrote, "and we would be willing to donate it to one of the people in the article."[43]

The principal of New York's P.S. 139 found himself on the receiving end of an unusual donation. A pupil's father, Ping-nan Fung, had been a violinist with the Hong Kong Philharmonic before emigrating to the United States. One day, with the help of a translator, he walked into the principal's office and offered to give free violin lessons as well as provide the instruments. Fung donated twenty child-sized violins, some brought from Hong Kong, the rest purchased with money from his savings. Soon, with the help of Mrs. Fung and supportive parents, the school had a music program and an orchestra. In words reminiscent of John Steinbeck's ranch boss, the principal admitted that he was initially skeptical: "Being a New Yorker, I kept wondering: What's the angle here?"[44]

Like big-money philanthropy, everyday philanthropy has its fund-raising side, too. Charity runs, walks, and rides mobilize thousands of people to gather pledges to fight hunger, cancer,

AIDS, and other scourges. The largest of these events are typically organized by for-profit firms who skim off up to half the proceeds to cover the organizing and marketing costs, as well as their profits. Nevertheless, the people who walk, ride, run and gather pledges from friends, family, and coworkers, as well as the many people who volunteer as event staff—their efforts meet my working definition of altruism, acting with the intent to benefit others. That they get high on endorphins or have a grand time wheeling through beautiful scenery doesn't take away from their altruistic purpose; after all, they could (and often do) enjoy running or riding without giving to something beyond themselves. Outside large cities where the professionally organized charity events occur, small local groups organize suppers, flea markets, car washes, runs, and motorcycle rides to raise money for uninsured families, medical research, or memorial scholarships. Among twenty- and thirtysomethings, the Internet has become a vehicle for small-scale fund-raising. Web sites, links, blogs, and social-networking sites enable amateurs to create personal fund-raising campaigns for causes that move them. One site, Network for Good, lets people create a "charity badge" for their cause of the moment. The badge is the electronic equivalent of the thermometer signs that used to dot church, library, and hospital lawns. It shows up-to-the-minute figures on how much money has been raised and how many donors have contributed. "I basically blasted everyone I knew," twenty-six-year-old Samantha Millman told the *Wall Street Journal* about her campaign to raise money for a legal-aid program with a charity badge. She raised more than $15,000 from 406 donors, and exalted that she was able effectively to donate so much more than her "meager paycheck" would have allowed.[45]

Maybe there's a lot of everyday philanthropy, you might be thinking, but not enough to call it a political phenomenon and certainly not enough to make a dent in public problems. Sure, people donate small sums when they read about particularly sympathetic characters, people like themselves and people with whom they can identify, but constant reports of ongoing dire poverty in the United States and around the world don't call forth much widespread generosity. News reports about uninsured children, say, don't stimulate a lot of checks (where would you send them, anyway?), nor do they rouse voters to press government to raise their taxes to pay for children's medical care.

Everyday philanthropy as I'm describing it isn't itself the answer to social problems, but it does provide a window into human motivation. It suggests that empathy for strangers can be strong enough to make people sacrifice for others' well-being, and that wise political leaders can tap this reservoir of willingness to contribute to the common good.

Receivers as Givers

From the "Metropolitan Diary" of the *New York Times:*

> Ned Helfand was walking past Madison Square Garden recently when a homeless man, holding a cup for contributions, approached him. Mr. Helfand reached into his pocket, retrieved some change and put it into the cup. The homeless man then passed a table with two large jars on it and a man exhorting

passers-by to donate. "Just one penny to feed the homeless," he intoned. "One penny can make a difference. Can you find it in your heart to give just one penny?"

The homeless man reached into his cup, selected a penny, deposited it in the jar and continued on his way.[46]

Most of us imagine help as going in one direction, from helper to helped. Look closely, though, and everyday altruism travels round-trip. Ruth, a once-wealthy divorced mother of three, was reduced to using a food pantry after her husband stopped making child-support payments. A food pantry runs on donated odds and ends, so some household essentials are scarce commodities. Yet even when scraping by at the food pantry, this frightened, ashamed, destitute woman retained her sense of generosity. "There's almost never any toilet paper or paper goods. So, if someone has donated four rolls of toilet paper, you want to grab the whole package, but you know it wouldn't be right so you open it up and just take one."[47]

Lars Eighner's *Travels with Lisbeth* is part memoir of homelessness, part survival manual. Like many homeless people, Eighner scavenged Dumpsters and retrieved a continuous bounty of fresh food, new clothes, unexpired medicines, appliances, and electronics. Unlike most scavengers, though, Eighner proofed his finds with the meticulous scrutiny of a public health inspector. He also saw himself as a distribution agency. "I found more canned goods than I could use or store and I formed the habit of taking the food that was perfectly safe to the drop point for the AIDS food bank at Sleazy Sue's [café]. I often wished I had a little dog cart, for Lisbeth seemed to very much enjoy towing the loaded bicycle as we carried things to Sue's. Perhaps it is not too much to suppose a dog knows when it is doing something useful. And perhaps it was not much different for me."[48]

A homeless woman who lived under a bridge in Portland, Oregon, came into Sisters of the Road Café one day. There she heard other people talking about a baby girl in need of just about everything. The next day, one of the café owners saw the homeless woman arrive carrying a pair of booties. "She had nothing, but she found some way to get those booties. I would never romanticize poverty—it is a harsh and dreadful way of life—but even here there is joy in very small things; there is sharing even when there is almost nothing to share."[49]

A mile north of the World Trade Center, Ronald Williams runs a crisis center for the Bowery Residents' Committee. The clientele are homeless, most of them plagued by mental illness and addictions. On September 11, frightened, bruised, exhausted crowds streamed past the center. "My clients, people who were homeless, people at the lower end of society, were making suggestions to the staff," Williams marveled. "We put chairs outside, we had a hose attached to a faucet, a nurse came out with what first aid we could muster. When people started coming by covered in stuff, we hosed them off. . . . My clients were the ones doing this. They were out offering water, offering help. The clients just pitched in as if they were staff. They were sad because of what was going on, but they were glad to be part of something, to be doing something. They were there."[50]

Beggars as helpers. They seem rare, and so they sometimes make it to the news. But such stories are not really rare, or news. They are rare only because our stereotypes screen them out.

Sixty-five-year-old Natalie Hefflefinger sleeps in the parks of Harvard Square, frequents Dunkin Donuts, and works as a self-appointed park cleaner-upper. She drives a shopping cart loaded with broom, mop, Windex, and plastic trash bags she purchases from CVS. According to the *Boston Globe,* "The soft-spoken woman is one of the few homeless people allowed to linger in local cafés. She always pays for her coffee, and, after parking herself in a chair for a few hours, she pulls a bottle of Windex from her cart to wash off the table. She also tips." Of her park clean-up work Hefflefinger says, "It's a way to give something back. People think of the homeless as always taking from society. This is how I can thank society for letting me sleep in the parks."[51]

Beggars *can* be choosers. They can choose to help, and that makes all the difference. The need *to* help is as human as the need *for* help. When the chips are down, when we dare face our essential vulnerability, help, not self-reliance, is the only path to autonomy. When we help others, we can forget for the moment that we, too, need help.

Here, I think, is the most important clue to why we are so blind to everyday altruism: No one wants to need help. The American worship of self-reliance reinforces the natural human tendency to deny dependence. When Katherine Newman asked inner-city residents about how they helped their friends and neighbors, she heard plenty of stories. When she asked them whether they could turn to others for help, she got an earful of independence talk: "I am a loner, I depend on me. I do the things I do because don't want to depend on nobody." "I don't like to bother people. I prefer to do things myself." "I don't need nobody. I don't need support from other people to keep me happy. I do what I got to do." Even Missy Darden, the community spark plug who had formed a civilian patrol, created a residents' buddy system, and organized neighborhood fairs—even she staked her identity to the American delusion: "Most of the time, I'm on my own. I've had to do it alone and you form habits of not involving other people with what you consider your own problems. I mean, I talk to people, but I don't depend on anyone but myself. I'm independent to a fault."[52]

Accidents and Crime Scenes

In the biblical parable of the Good Samaritan, the setup for the quintessential altruist is an accident—an injured man, lying by the side of the road, in need of care. Comb the news, review your own personal week, and you'll see that accidental good Samaritans are common. "Men Pull Lady from Burning Car" sounds rare enough to warrant a headline, but such seemingly extraordinary things happen in every community, if not every day, then often enough.[53] And when they do, the Good Samaritans almost always refuse praise, because they see themselves as no different from the rest of humanity: "Anybody would do what I did." They also think that helping strangers in need is part of their character, not a question of sacrifice but of who they are.

In Syracuse, a bus driver and janitor named Kendall Eggleston stopped to help stranded motorists on an overpass over Interstate 81. A passing van hit him and knocked him off the bridge, leaving him partly paralyzed and uncertain about whether he might be able to work again. A reporter asked him whether he'd do it again—stop to help people. "I have to think twice about it in that situation, because of the condition of the highway, but I would still help people, absolutely," he answered. His working life had changed, he said, "but as far as my character is concerned, that is never going to change."[54]

Beyond the more dramatic car wrecks, fires, explosions, and disasters, help arises in everyday slips and trips. It's a familiar scene, so familiar that people rarely record it, but who doesn't recognize a moment like this?

> I was walking up Third Avenue, happily absorbed in my cup of mocha chip gelato, on my way to a physical therapy appointment. I suddenly found myself sprawled on the sidewalk, having lost my balance. Within seconds, a young man was kneeling beside me, helping me up; an elderly man cleaning the street had thrust a clean towel in my hand (I was covered with ice cream, not blood); and a police car stopped at the curb with two solicitous cops asking if I needed help. In less than 60 seconds I was upright, again on my way to the physical therapist, and the four knights had faded into the crowd.[55]

And then there are crimes, muggings, rapes, beatings, stabbings, shootings, the real stuff of the Good Samaritan tale. In 1964 in Kew Gardens, New York, thirty-eight people witnessed Kitty Genovese being attacked and murdered and did nothing. The incident mushroomed into an urban legend whose moral was that altruism is dead. But research provoked by that incident showed that such obliviousness is rare. It tends to occur when there a lot of bystanders who are aware of each other's presence. Each person assumes someone else will do something; no individual feels responsible.[56] When people believe they are supposed to help or when they think they are the only person available to help someone else, they are very likely to respond.[57]

Real life is even more heartening than the research. Researchers who want to study altruism usually contrive artificial situations to test how people respond, and they can't ethically put their subjects in danger. Real-life crimes, accidents, and disasters do pose dangers, yet Samaritans respond nonetheless. Crispin McCay had just finished a twelve-hour shift as an emergency medical technician and was heading home when he heard a radio call about a shooting only a block away. The woman had been shot through the carotid artery. McCay stemmed the bleeding and saved her life. Later he told a reporter that he had debated about responding to the call. "You don't know what's going on. A scene like that, it can become very, very difficult to control," he said, and he worried that the assailant might still be around. But after hesitating initially, McCay said, he went because "it's something I would want someone to do for my mother, my father, or my brother."[58]

On a single January day in Boston, two crimes tested ordinary people's willingness to plunge into danger in order to help a stranger. At Santana's Towing shop, two workers saw a woman running toward them, bloody and shrieking for help, pursued by an attacker. They tackled the man, knocked him to the ground, and held him until the police came. At a Walgreen's store in another part of Boston, a security guard and clerk wrestled a gun from a would-be robber and held him until the police arrived.[59]

At first glance, these rescue acts seem morally uncomplicated, like the Good Samaritan parable itself. But people's reflections on these two incidents were nuanced and ambivalent, and they teach us something about the strength of altruism in the human psyche. The police cautioned citizens against getting involved in such situations; better to mind your own personal safety, call 911, and let the police handle things, they said. By contrast, a spokesman for the mayor said, "Certainly there is no higher civic duty than personal responsibility, and we commend any Bostonian who would engage not just in an act of personal responsibility but an act of bravery." The tow-shop workers thought more like the mayor than the police, though the notion of bravery didn't enter their minds. They didn't think about their own safety, they told a reporter; they thought about stopping something bad. "People . . . they get tired, you know, of street muggings, the stabbings, the shootings. It's time to do something about it," said Angel Seary, one of the rescuers. City councilman John Tobin shared Seary's sense that citizen rescues, foolhardy though they may be, are political statements: "These types of things you are going to see more and more of, because people in the city are starting to rise up and say enough is enough." For her part, the attack victim expressed a simple faith in everyday altruism. She said she had deliberately run toward the tow shop after freeing herself from the attacker's grip. "I knew that they would help, because they're nice people. They always wave and say hi." And the owner of the tow shop illuminated the powerful bonds that form between strangers suddenly thrust into a helping relationship. "You think about [the victim] like it was your mom."

Certainly, the police caution was reasonable—beyond reasonable, eminently sensible. (Once, after I had lectured about everyday altruism, a man in the audience chided me, "I think what you are saying is very good and very inspiring, but I think you lack common sense." I bit my tongue and asked what he meant. "I wouldn't want my daughter to stop to help strangers in every situation.") Most people, hearing these crime-intervention scenarios, would probably advise caution and leaving things to the pros. Even the pro, the emergency medical technician, thought twice about wading into a shooting scene to help someone. Yet in all these stories, what actually happened violated common sense, and that's an urban legend worth believing.

You Had to Be There

There is a quality about altruism I call "thereness," and it overrides rational thought. Altruists, if they saw a child attacked by a dog or, in Nazi Europe, a Jew hiding in their garden, wouldn't stop to calculate anything. They would not even think. They would just help, because the person is there, the need is there, and they are there. One rescuer of Jews recalled how he had saved a drowning boy when he was twelve. "I don't know why I did this. It was just spontaneous. You don't think. You just do it." Reflecting on his later Jewish rescue activity, he said, "You do things because you are human, and because there is need."[60]

Sometimes good Samaritans *do* think, though cogitation doesn't seem to slow them down. Kathleen Moore was driving with her seven-year-old daughter when she saw a car on fire on the side of the road. "I heard a man crying, 'Help me. Help me. Help me,'" she told reporters later, as she recounted her thought process, step by step. "I was scared to death. I could see the flames light up in the dark. I was thinking, 'Oh, my God, I'm going to go down there and help him and that car is going to blow up and my daughter was going to be left on the side of the road motherless.' I just said to myself, 'I can't leave somebody to burn to death. I'm going to help him.'"[61] Even though Moore envisioned the consequences of her action, helping was something of an automatic reflex, something she would do no matter what she was thinking. She knowingly put her daughter at risk because right in front of her there was someone who would die if she did not help, right then.

Still, it's hard to understand what makes anyone sacrifice his or her own family to help a stranger. Migdalia Ramos kept asking herself that question after September 11. Her husband, Harry Ramos, was the only employee of his firm to die in the World Trade Center attack. All the others had rushed down from the eighty-seventh floor. Mr. Ramos stayed behind to help a stranger. The Ramoses had two sons, a five-year-old and an infant, plus a hefty mortgage. Mrs. Ramos's mother had died only ten days earlier. How? she asked herself. How could her husband have put a stranger ahead of his family? Then one day she found herself in a similar position. She acted. She did what her husband had done. And she understood.

On September 30, Mrs. Ramos went with "a retinue of brothers, in-laws and small children" to clear out her mother's apartment. While they were hauling out her mother's possessions, the fire alarm went off. They all ran downstairs. Mrs. Ramos handed her baby to her sister-in-law. As the *New York Times* tells the story, "Learning from the superintendent that the firefighters had not yet arrived, she did not even stop to think. She turned and ran back up. Her in-laws were gaping, but she knew that her mother's neighbor across the hall was nearly blind and could not get out by herself." Mrs. Ramos gave the *Times* reporter another thought script from the front lines: "When I was running up the steps, I was thinking, 'Harry, what am I doing?' The feeling I was having, it crossed my mind that he had had those same feelings." No one answered when she banged on the neighbor's door, so Mrs. Ramos made her way to another apartment, from whence smoke was billowing. Inside, she found a toaster oven on fire and a frightened woman her mother's age struggling to breathe. She put out the fire and opened the windows. With some sense that the woman was now safe, Mrs. Ramos suddenly remembered her five-year-old and ran back downstairs. "I did the same thing Harry did," Mrs. Ramos told the *Times*. "It took me to how he would be feeling. I realized that Harry did what he did because that was Harry's nature."[62]

Harry Ramos's nature, as Migdalia Ramos learned, is *our* nature. Altruism is a powerful human instinct, powerful enough to overcome, at least sometimes, the supposedly most powerful instinct of self-preservation, and the supposedly second-most-powerful instinct of family protection. Confronted with human need, right there, right now, people often respond to need.

The people I have called professional altruists—health care workers, child care workers, teachers, social workers, police, EMTs, firefighters, utility and infrastructure workers, and community activists—are, in a sense, THERE, more THERE than most of us. They are on the front lines, where there is almost always someone in need RIGHT THERE. The "thereness" of their jobs stimulates their compassion and their altruism and induces them to forget self-interest.

This is not to say that every person in one of these roles is altruistic, nor that anyone who regularly does any of these kinds of work acts with altruistic motives every hour of every day and night. Nor is it to say there aren't powerful constraints on individual altruism. It is to say that there is a lot of kindness and generosity going on right under our noses, and that we might have a different view of ourselves and our moral obligations as a society if we weren't quite so oblivious to everyday altruism.

We are used to hearing about altruism in accidents, emergencies, and wars because that kind of altruism is loaded with easy footage, drama, and heroes. It has all the makings of news. The altruism of everyday life rarely makes the news. It takes a special breed of documentary journalist to see the altruism in a nursing home, on a school bus, or at a street corner, and to eke out some footage from it. The kind of stories in the *New York Times*'s September 11 obituaries probably never would have made it into print had the lives not ended in a national calamity. Indeed, most of the victims would never have had an obituary of any kind in the *Times*. These stories illuminate the underground of altruism.

Everyday altruists see everyday life as composed of everyday emergencies. They deliberately hover at the scene of the great human accident. Their altruism comes in little doses, more like an IV drip than a shot of adrenaline. But we will never notice this kind of altruism or understand it unless we acknowledge what is impossible in our dominant intellectual paradigm: people are motivated to give as well as to get.

Here is precisely why I invented the concept of everyday altruism—to bring it to social notice. Everyday altruism recognizes that people sacrifice their self-interest to help others all the time, in big and little ways. These sacrifices are real, even when they don't entail risking one's life, and all help, even the less-than-death-defying gesture, is a form of rescue. Moreover, everyday altruism is irrational. It can't be explained by the ordinary logic of self-interest, yet everyday altruism is the fabric of our lives. We should treasure and honor it, because it's a testament to the human spirit, and because everyday altruists make excellent citizens.

4

The Samaritan Rebellion

While I was doing research on home health care, I met an aide whose careful phrasing and reluctance to talk tipped me off to the kind of underground resistance many home care workers were staging. I had asked Nina (as I'll call her), "Do clients ever ask you to do things that maybe aren't on the care plan, or that you don't have time to do, or you feel you shouldn't do?" I was looking for ways aides go beyond the job on behalf of clients.

Nina told me about a "gentleman" who lives alone. His daughter lives some distance away. Sometimes he asks Nina to pick up a quart of milk for him, so as not to make his daughter go out of her way. Nina had an air of kindness as she talked. She clearly didn't mind these requests.

"Any other special favors you do for people?" I probed.

"Well, probably too many to mention. Things that you don't want to mention."

"I think I'll turn this thing off," I said, ostentatiously reaching for my tape recorder.

With the recorder off, Nina still seemed nervous, but she grew a bit more expansive with the details. "The man lives three miles from the store. His daughter lives all the way down in [another town]. It's very inconvenient for her to bring him milk. So how's he going to get milk? How's he going to get a loaf of bread? I'm going right by. It's on my way home." She told me of other favors she does for people. Then she came out with a confession: "How can you say no? You can't. You're a human being. I go out of my way to do things for people. I guess I'm guilty."

Nina used the word *guilty* two more times while talking about her kindnesses. "It's curious to me that you use the word *guilty*," I said. "You're doing something *nice* for these people. Why should you feel guilty?"

"They tell you you're not supposed to have contact with patients outside work."

I had heard from several other people about doing "little extras" for clients during off-hours. No one had been quite so secretive about it as Nina, so I said to her, "Others have told me they do all kinds of things off-hours for clients. Do you talk about this with other aides?"

"No," Nina answered, "we don't talk. But we all know we do it. Everybody does it. You cannot shut your feelings off, or your concerns."

I had stumbled into a puzzling clash of moralities. These women who are hardworking and generous to the core feel like lawbreakers. They're altruistic, yet they feel guilty. They think they have to be clandestine about giving in to their humanity. "You don't broadcast it," Nina said, telling me again about "being human," and adding, "I don't think it's wrong."

Suddenly, I understood that Nina wasn't arguing with me. She was arguing with the agency's policies that prohibit aides and nurses to give any kind of help to their clients outside the prescribed care plan or their shifts. She was arguing with the policies of her government, because she's had it drilled into her that the agency must abide by Medicare rules. She was arguing with a public morality that conflicted with her personal morality, and which she believes is a higher morality.

Both Nina and a nurse in the same agency had told me about a client with multiple sclerosis. He'd been getting home care for about ten years, but because of a recent Medicare budget cut (in 1997), he was probably going to be terminated, even though he was so debilitated by this point that he couldn't walk and had the use of only one arm.

Now, with the tape recorder still off and Nina warming to the topic of illicit caregiving, she blurted, "I told the guy with MS, 'Hey, if they cut you off, you won't go without a bath.'" To me, she said, "If he gets cut off, I don't know what he'd do," as if *his* problem were *her* problem, too. The man gets less than eight hundred dollars a month, Nina told me, and he can't afford to hire aides privately. "It's not right, it stinks," she declared, talking about the Medicare rule-tightening and budget cutbacks. Then she circled back to the man with MS. "I told him I'd stop by after work and do it. They can't stop you on your own time. After 3:30, you're a private citizen."

Nina's phrase, *private citizen*, put me in mind of *Antigone*, Sophocles' play about civil disobedience. The motive force of the play is precisely the state's refusal to recognize ancient human obligations of care. When the play opens, Antigone's brother Polynices has been killed in battle—actually, he was leading a band of rebels in a civil war for the throne of Thebes. With the rebels now defeated, King Creon, the king of Thebes, decrees that Polynices' body may not be buried: "None shall give him funeral honours or lament him, but leave him there unburied, to be devoured by dogs and birds, mangled most hideously." Funeral rites were as important in Greece as they are in most cultures. The ancient Greeks believed that the dead would not accept the soul of a newly deceased person unless the body was first buried. So Antigone defies the law, buries her brother, and when confronted by King Creon declares, "I deny nothing. I avow my guilt."[1]

Here was Nina, defying Medicare policy, caring for her patients, and avowing her guilt. I had discovered something I never expected to find and wasn't even looking for—rampant resistance among home health care workers. This resistance is subtle, nuanced, and varied, but it's pervasive. It's not the usual kind of labor unrest. These care workers weren't struggling to better their own working conditions and pay. They were fighting to be able to give better care to the clients and families who depend on them.

Civil Disobedience on the Home Front

Everyday altruism creates bonds of loyalty and fierce attachment. When people care for others, the simple act of helping intensifies their desire to help. Desire and need become one. It doesn't matter whether they're helping their own children, somebody else's mother or father, a patient, or strangers. They want to do more, as much as possible. They go beyond the job description, beyond norms and expectations. If necessary, they cheat, disobey rules, and sometimes break the law to carry out the kind of help they feel they owe. Their loyalty to the people they help overrides their loyalty to people outside that bond, notably employers and law-makers, people who hold great power over them. Help doesn't work this way all the time, or for everyone, but rule breaking and civil disobedience in the name of altruism are powerful under-ground currents. If we hope for citizens who have a strong attach-ment to their communities and their government, we need to understand this wellspring of human loyalty.

You might question whether Nina's defiance was really civil disobedience or just good old-fashioned altruism. But by visit-ing and helping an agency client after hours, Nina was taking a huge risk—if not Antigone's risk of capital punishment, then certainly occupational death and financial ruin. Most agencies, including the one that employed Nina, forbid caregivers from having any contact with clients outside their regular working hours. Nina, like every caregiver who works under such rules, knew she risked losing her job. Home care agencies maintain this rule in part to protect the workers against liability. Should anything untoward happen while caregivers attend clients after hours, or should someone even accuse them of anything unto-ward, they risk personal liability because they wouldn't be cov-ered by the agency.

You might also think that what I'm describing isn't civil dis-obedience because the rules in question are private agency rules, not laws of the state. But nurses and aides perceive little distinc-tion between the state and the agency they work for, because Medicare pays for the lion's share of home health services and keeps most agencies in business. To Nina, and to Medicare's beneficiaries, Medicare *is* the state. The man with multiple sclerosis was a Medicare client, and Nina directed her intense anger about the situation to Medicare. Nina knew the agency didn't want to terminate him from its rolls, so it was against the state that she protested.

The form and purpose of civil disobedience in *Antigone* is quite different from that in two other great texts on the subject, Thoreau's essay "Civil Disobedience" and Martin Luther King's "Letter from the Birmingham Jail." Both Thoreau and King are concerned with breaking the law in order to right systemic injustices. They argue that each person has an obligation to remedy injustice for anonymous other citizens who may live in other cities or regions. *Antigone* is about civil disobedience in the service of obligations to kin. The king, Antigone says, "has no right to keep me from my own."[2]

Antigone represents a different kind of civil disobedience—the elevation of private, personal relationships above public roles and responsibilities, or as one critic put it, "the absolute valuation of the bonds of blood and affection."[3] The caregivers in my research engage in this same defiance of man-made law to serve what they regard as a higher law. Like Antigone, they sometimes break the law to fulfill their ancient obligations of care. They put loyalty to persons above loyalty to the state.

Antigone can be read as a grand cultural story about what happens when rules and laws interfere with the moral duty to help others. People rebel. The current American political scene can be read as a reincarnation of King Creon's Thebes. King Creon's dictates are widespread: they govern workplaces, hospitals, nursing homes, welfare offices, and other public assistance programs.

Rearing Up at Work to Rear at Home

A mother on welfare who left her children alone for several hours a day would likely be dragged through the child protection system, charged with neglect, and threatened with loss of custody. Yet when an employer coerces parents to neglect their children through job requirements and threats of firing, the law looks the other way.

My neighbor Judy worked for a large mail-order computer company until she was fired for making Antigone's choice. She is a divorced mom with two kids. Her employer had a policy of "three absences and you're out." Judy used up one day when her daughter was sick. She used the second to attend her uncle's funeral. Then one day her seven-year-old son was sick and couldn't go to school. She stayed home with him, knowing what she was risking. The next day she was escorted to her cubby and told to gather her things and leave the building without talking to her coworkers.

Then there's the case of Joanna Upton, a Massachusetts woman who was fired for refusing to work mandatory overtime. When she was hired as a professional management consultant, she was told her hours would be 8:15 AM to 5:30 PM. That was hard enough for a single mother with an eight-year-old son. But her management position often kept her at work until six or seven in the evening. Then the company demanded she work overtime, until nine or ten at night. Upton refused to abandon her motherhood responsibilities, or her son. The company let her go. Upton sued her former employer under the quaint theory that firing her violated the state's policy favoring "care and protection of children." The state's Supreme Judicial Court reluctantly rebuffed her. She was an employee-at-will (meaning she had no contract), the court said, and no state public policy "mandates that an employer must adjust its expectation . . . [for] an at-will employee's domestic circumstances."[4]

The Family and Medical Leave Act (FMLA) is supposed to soften the conflict between family caregiving and workplace rules, but it's a minimal cushion. The law requires large employers to grant their employees twelve weeks of unpaid leave to care for new babies, sick children, or sick relatives.[5] The law often fails, and when it does, people often make Antigone's choice.

Dana Wilson worked for a local insurance company in Milwaukee. When her seventy-seven-year-old father began having a cascade of medical problems, she sought an unpaid leave to be able to accompany him to his medical appointments. "He's always been there for me, so whenever he needs me I'm there," she explained. But because she had not yet worked a full year for her employer, she was denied the leave and warned not to miss any more work. "They basically told me it was your father or your job." When her father fell in the hospital and became disoriented, she stayed to take care of him and lost her job.[6] Antigone's choice.

Chris Schultz had been a building maintenance worker at Advocate Christ Hospital in Chicago for twenty-six years, and was the first nonphysician or nonnurse to win the hospital's employee-of-the-year award. He requested a leave under the FMLA to take care of his ailing mother. His father had Alzheimer's, so when his mother died, Schultz had to continue to take intermittent short leaves to care for his father. Meanwhile, his employer established new productivity standards that Schultz couldn't possibly meet on his reduced schedule. The employer held him to the new standards, then terminated him for poor performance. Schultz went to court to enforce his rights to care for his parents under the FMLA. In

2002, a jury expressed its moral outrage by awarding him nearly twelve million dollars, most of it in punitive damages.[7] This is still the largest award in a new type of lawsuit known as "family responsibilities discrimination."[8]

At first glance, Schultz's story seems to show how well the Family and Medical Leave Act works, for he received a big sum of cash. But the jury award is just the happy public face of this story. To enforce his right to care for his parents, Schultz had to get fired first, suffer a legal injury, then bring a suit, then wait two years for a verdict. He had to endure all this on top of losing both parents, but still have the emotional stamina and financial wherewithal to bring a suit. It didn't matter that the nice law was in place to protect him. While his parents were sick and dying, he had to make a choice between fulfilling his employer's requirements and fulfilling his moral duties.

The Family and Medical Leave Act, then, isn't all that effective in stopping employers from acting like King Creon. Deep down, the FMLA doesn't respect people's human obligations to care for their kin. In the eyes of the law, devotion to one's family isn't normal for a worker. The normal worker has minimal caring duties—or desires—that can fit into whatever work schedule the employer requires. Under the Family and Medical Leave Act, caring is a special need that arises only under special circumstances—childbirth or adoption, accident or illness (one's own or a relative's, but illness nonetheless). Outside these special circumstances, in what is supposed to be normal everyday life, a worker's family relationships are merely "domestic circumstances" (as the Massachusetts court characterized Joanna Upton's predicament)—as irrelevant to an employer as where its employees live or what color wallpaper they have in their parlors.

The Family and Medical Leave Act, like the workplaces it is meant to modify, assumes that an employee's desire to care for someone else is unusual, infrequent, and short-lived. The law addresses births and major illnesses, typically the ones that require hospitalization, but children and others who need care don't typically concentrate their needs into tidy time blocks.

The problem with the way work is organized, law professor Joan Williams argues, is that the normal or ideal worker is someone with no care responsibilities toward anyone else.[9] The Family and Medical Leave Act alters the ideal worker a smidgen, adding on temporary and sporadic care responsibilities—rather like unbuttoning the waistband of a garment that's too tight. The law doesn't refashion the ideal-worker template into one that fits people who care for others as part of the fabric of their lives.

These workplace stories illustrate how little scope our employment model gives to altruism. The organization of paid work in the United States, and in all market economies, imagines people as self-interested, self-sufficient islands. They are supposed to meet their needs by earning income, and if they have any "dependents," as tax lingo dubs our deepest human connections, they will meet their moral commitments with cash. Too often, people have to defy their employers and lose their livelihoods to carry out their moral desires to care.

In the low-wage sector, working parents often find themselves fighting for the right to care for their families against jobs that, as one woman put it, "don't give a rat's butt about family."[10] Women are the main fighters in this underground because mothers overwhelmingly take responsibility for children. As we saw with the FMLA cases, middle-class and professional parents occasionally must fight for the right to care. For workers at the bottom of the wage scale, they already live so close to the bone that they must constantly choose between work and care, every day, almost hour by hour. To manage this squeeze, they rely first on their own ingenuity and second on help from family and friends. When things get desperate, they turn to government for help.

Through painstaking collaborative research, sociologist Lisa Dodson has assembled a portrait of how low-wage parents manage the work-family squeeze.[11] Mothers, and sometimes fathers, find secret ways to bring their children to work "under the radar." Janitors sneak their children into the buildings they clean at night, set them up on blankets, and move them from floor to floor as they work. Home health care workers, house cleaners, and even retail workers bring their children to the job, and refuse jobs that don't permit them that liberty. One home aide told Dodson she worked only for clients who were bedridden, so that she could park her child in another room, never to be discovered. Often, supervisors collude with mothers, looking the other way, but if push comes to shove, mothers will quit a job and look for another that allows them to watch over their children.

Low-income mothers get very adept at managing their supervisors. Only 11 percent of working poor mothers have paid sick leave that they can use to care for sick children, so, as Dodson puts it, they make their own flextime.[12] One mother who had battled her office supervisor over time off told Dodson, "I call into work and let them know that I can't be in; I have a sick child. They cannot go to day care because what if the stuff that she has is infectious? Look, I don't care about 'do I have sick time, do I have vacation time?' I'm not coming because I've got a sick child.

If you can't understand that, fire me. My child comes first."
Mothers ignore their supervisors' demands that they work overtime and their bosses' stingy allotments of vacation time. Sometimes they beg, sometimes they try to shame their supervisors,
but when they feel themselves up against a wall, they just "yes"
their supervisors, put their children first, and deal with the consequences. "Whatever their rules, whatever. I say 'yeah, OK' but I
am going to do what I need to and get ready to move on."[13]

These mothers, Dodson finds, know perfectly well how their
supervisors regard their efforts to take care of their children: as
tardiness and early departures, absenteeism, noncompliance, unre-
liability, irresponsibility. But these women don't accept the reigning political definition of personal responsibility as holding a
paying job and earning one's keep, period. Most of them think the
essence of personal responsibility is caring for their families. They
hold to a generous definition of caring, besides—not only providing food and shelter but also making sure their children are safe,
healthy, and loved. They define responsibility as having a certain
kind of relationship with their children, not merely providing the
material necessities. They want to be available whenever their
children get sick, have problems at school, have fights with their
friends, have upsets, or just need to talk.

In that calculus of responsibility, many mothers think it is more
responsible to sacrifice a high-paying job or a promotion for a lesser
job that allows them to be better mothers. "I have had better-
paying jobs than I have now, but none of them understood that my
kids come first," one woman explained to Kathryn Edin and Laura
Lein why she quit a $6.00-an-hour job for one that paid $5.50.
"At least this job understands that if my kids are sick, I just won't be

in that day." Another woman left a job as a bookkeeper in a health clinic for a job with a dry cleaner because the health clinic (of all places) didn't provide health insurance. "I don't think I could accept a promotion," another mother said. "I mean they have talked to me before about being a manager, but I need the availability."[14]

Financial planners and job counselors might see these woman as irrational, lacking any basic economic sense. Some conservative moralists might see them as insufficiently motivated to get ahead. In the moral economy of everyday altruism, however, these mother-workers are as wise and steady as they come.

And on this score, low-income mothers are no different from family caregivers in general. In a recent survey of family caregivers to elderly and disabled adults—about 40 percent of whom are men—57 percent said they had gone in to work late, left early, or taken time off because of their caregiving. And like mothers, caregivers to adults often make economically irrational choices. They reduce their paid work and sacrifice their income, even sometimes their careers, to accommodate their caregiving responsibilities. In another survey of family caregivers to adults, of the two-thirds who were in the paid workforce, more than half had changed their daily schedules, taken leaves of absence, worked fewer hours, taken less demanding jobs, turned down promotions, taken early retirement, or left paid work altogether, all in order to devote more of themselves to caregiving.[15]

These portraits of devoted mothering and caregiving may seem overly rosy, perhaps even romantic. Families certainly have their dark sides. Few people treasure each and every relative. Most people are not willing to help everyone who asks or needs. Relationships have their rifts and reconciliations. Caregivers can come to resent how much they are asked to do and pull back. Care sometimes turns into neglect or abuse. When not all members of a family thrive, the more stable and upwardly mobile members may want nothing to do with their downwardly mobile kin. They may throw their dysfunctional relatives out on the street or do their best to disassociate.[16]

More often than not, though, family bonds are so potent that they override fatigue, resentment, disappointment, and even good sense, as social workers sometimes discover to their chagrin. Despite stern advice and firm resolve not to succor criminal, drug-addicted, or alcoholic relatives, people relent because these problem-ridden no-goods are "blood." As Jason DeParle put it in his *New York Times* series on welfare reform, "Addicted sisters, imprisoned brothers, needy cousins and aunts—the great national drive from welfare to work winds through a forest of familial distractions." Lashanda Washington was one of Wisconsin's hard-core welfare cases. She couldn't seem to live by the textbook work ethic because she put safeguarding her alcoholic, disturbed, sometimes abusive mother above almost everything else. On the day she was supposed to start training as a nursing assistant and launch herself on the path to self-sufficiency, she spent the morning caring for her mother instead, getting her sober and tending her bruises. DeParle encountered ten-year-old Tremayne Franks, who had been abandoned by his father (in prison) and his mother (gone south to work as a stripper, not heard from since). His grandmother worked the night shift as a hospital housekeeper and during the days had no energy and little patience for Tremayne. Yet, at age ten, Tremayne already knew he wanted to be a lawyer so that he could "make a lot of money so I can take care of my dad, and if she comes back, my mom."[17]

Blood transports oxygen, but "blood" carries forgiveness. If I have painted a somewhat one-dimensional picture of families, I did so to emphasize the ferocity of family ties. We can and should acknowledge the complexity and ambivalence of family relationships, but we should never forget the intense family bonds at the core of human experience. Rules and policies that ignore this yearning for connection drive citizens underground.

Creon's Welfare

In the stereotypes of welfare debates, poor people choose between work and welfare. They resort to welfare because they lose a job, are unwilling to look for one, or are too lazy to keep one. In reality, poor mothers choose between work and family care, and they resort to welfare because their work-and-care system has collapsed.[18]

The precursor of today's welfare payment was called a Mother's Pension. When forty states debated and eventually adopted these pensions between 1910 and 1920, the public rhetoric elevated motherhood to high heroism. Pensions were "salaries" for women who "serve[d] the state by giving all their time to rearing good citizens." "The pension," proclaimed the Illinois Congress of Mothers, "removes the mother and her children from the disgrace of charity relief and places her in the class of public servants similar to army officers and school teachers."[19] Mother's Pensions were issued mostly to widows, but also to some women whose husbands had deserted them. If these destitute women could be *paid* for raising children, the thinking went, they wouldn't have to choose between caring for their children and earning a living, or between keeping their children in extreme poverty and placing them in an institution.

This same vision—public support for family care—inspired what later came to be reviled as "welfare" but was more formally known first as Aid to Dependent Children and then as Aid to Families of Dependent Children, or AFDC. But if the original purpose of public assistance was to enable single mothers to care for their children, the sole purpose of it now is to get mothers and fathers into the workforce. Indeed, the main aim of welfare since the reform of 1996 is to force poor people, especially single mothers, to choose paid work over caring for their families.

Here's how welfare reform worked for Regla Belette and Angel Martinez, a New York couple with three children living in New York.[20] As their five-year lifetime limit on public assistance was coming to an end in 2001, they received a letter from the Department of Human Services suggesting they come in for an appointment "so you can discuss how you plan to manage your household expenses." They both worked, he as a warehouse man in the Brooklyn Navy Yard, she as a child-care worker. Despite these jobs, and despite Martinez's working all the overtime he could get, they struggled to keep hunger at bay and pay the rent.

In order to qualify for assistance, Belette had to be working for money, so instead of taking care of her own children, New York City paid her to take care of her sister's three children, while her sister worked in her own workfare assignment. Shades of King Creon: we forbid you to take care of your kids, on pain of hunger and deprivation. And the story gets worse. At some point during her time on public assistance, Belette went to Florida to take care of her sick father. While she was away, she missed some appointments with the welfare office, a transgression for which the family was punished with loss of its food stamps and rent subsidies.

Since the 1996 Personal Responsibility and Work Opportunity Reconciliation Act, public policy requires almost all mothers to work outside the home for pay and to put their kids in child care. If a mother refuses to do this, she doesn't get benefits. In a strange and perverse twist, if a woman takes care of *other people's* children *for money*—as a babysitter or a family day care provider—then welfare policy considers her to be doing something valuable and earning her keep as a citizen. We, her fellow citizens who are in a position to help her, will give her vouchers to purchase care for her children on the market, but we will no longer help her, or seem to reward her, to take care of her own kids. Likewise, we will help her if she takes care of someone else's parents as a paid home health aide or nursing-home assistant, but not if she takes care of her own parents out of honor, loyalty, and love. As long as she exchanges her care for cash, we will help her if she still earns too little to support her family. Welfare policy pays people to put their families out on the market.

In today's public policy, taking care of family is no longer honorable, something to be encouraged, at least not for poor families. A century ago, government offered poor mothers aid so they could care for their children. Today, government tells them to find child care so they can go to work. A century ago, poor women could fulfill their citizenship obligations by rearing children, our future citizens. Today, they must fulfill their citizenship obligations by becoming self-supporting. A century ago, a woman's proper sphere was in the home. Society expected her to sacrifice any yearning for a career or a profession to care for her family. Today, a woman's proper sphere is the workplace. Society expects her to sacrifice any yearning to care for her family that conflicts with her ability to earn a living—in that bitter irony, she has achieved equality with men. A century ago, caring for her own children was a moral duty and a calling. Today, caring for her own children is a luxury merited only by those lucky enough to have a high-yielding spouse or portfolio.

By one of those uncanny coincidences of politics, two pieces of legislation about family caregiving arrived in Congress at the same time, one for the poor, one for the rich. The Family Support Act, passed in 1988, was a run-up to the 1996 welfare reform. It tightened the work requirements for poor mothers on welfare by requiring them to work even if they had very young children. Meanwhile, Congress was discussing the Family and Medical Leave Act, passed in 1989. It loosened the work requirements for those middle- and upper-class parents who could afford to take leave without pay to indulge in family caregiving. In debates over the Family Support Act, stay-at-home moms were reviled as poor role models for their children, transmitters of a parasitic culture. In debates over the Family and Medical Leave Act, a stay-at-home mom could be a perfectly good role model for children, as long as she had a high-earning husband by her side.[21]

Even more than people covered by the FMLA, people who must rely on low-wage work or public assistance or some combination find themselves in tension between two ethics: the work ethic and the care ethic. Most poor people want desperately to work so they can hold their heads up in a society that prizes work and self-sufficiency. Most poor people also love their families and want desperately to take care of them, especially their children. The harshness of life at the bottom forces brutal choices on people who have family they love. They have to choose between paying for food and paying for heat, or between food and medicine.

Between getting to work on time and making sure their children are in safekeeping. Between showing up for work and tending a sick baby or an ailing parent. Between being a responsible employee and a responsible human being. In today's workplace, everyday altruism sometimes requires Antigone-like defiance.

And this is what we know about poor women: they usually choose care. When they choose welfare over paid work, they usually do it because it is the least-bad way for them to care, not because it is the most lucrative way to live. Kathryn Edin and Laura Lein interviewed several hundred low-income mothers, some on welfare, some working. Most of them, even the ones who weren't currently working, could tick off the added expenses of working—child care, transportation, work clothes, and medical care (because they often lose Medicaid when they leave welfare for work). Some pulled out envelopes or scraps of paper with the calculations they'd already done for themselves. Working is "not worth it," one woman told Edin and Lein. "It's not worth it 'cause you have kids and then they gonna be sick and you gonna have to go to the doctor and you gonna have to pay hundreds of dollars and that's why." It's not worth working, even for extra money, if you can't afford to take your kids to the doctor. On welfare, you get a Medicaid card. On welfare, you can often take better care of your kids. The truth, as the women know, is that they get a better net return from welfare than from working in the kinds of low-wage, no-benefit jobs available to them.[22]

Contrary to popular belief, most women on welfare hate to need it and are loath to make their first claim.[23] Their sense of responsibility for their children overcomes their sense of shame. "Almost without exception," political scientist Joe Soss finds, "the women I interviewed argued that a good mother must do whatever is necessary to provide and care for her children, including swallowing her pride and accepting the indignity of welfare." As one woman explained, "To have to go down to the welfare agency was really scary, but I did it because I had to do it. I knew those kids had to eat." An unemployed former military surgical technician explained her decision to apply for welfare as a simple calculus: "All I knew was that I was going to be able to feed my son." After Karen Roberts and her husband separated, she worked two part-time jobs, waitressing and cleaning, but still needed assistance to support her children. "When you've got two kids, you do what you have to do. That's really the main reason I went on it, too, because of the kids. I had no choice."[24]

A twenty-year-old mother told sociologist Lisa Dodson how she sacrificed her pride and her self-image to get help from welfare officials. To receive welfare, mothers are required to identify their children's father(s) and cooperate with the state to establish paternity and pursue child support. Luscious (as Dodson calls her) received much support and kindness from her child's father, though not formal child support. His parents gave her their succor and a lot of child care as well. So Luscious kept the father's identity from the welfare officials. She hated the lie, but explained to Dodson, "If I'd of told on Lennie, it would have ruined everything." Protecting her extended family relationships meant saying that "I didn't know who the father was . . . like I was so loose I didn't know who I'd had sex with." Dodson observed: "This deceit was antithetical to everything Luscious had been raised to believe and value. It meant accepting the most disrespectful label a woman can have."[25]

Claiming welfare can be an act of resistance. It means resisting the social stigma, the contemptuous looks as you hand the cashier your food stamps, the humiliation as you submit to the caseworker's condescension and oversight.

For many, many women, claiming welfare is also an act of altruism, a way of helping others. They use their welfare benefits to enable them to take care of grandchildren, parents, and sometimes partners, though they must conceal such uses, since by and large welfare rules don't recognize a person's caregiving obligations to anyone other than children. Josephine, a mother with a very low income, was getting along without assistance, but when her mother got sick, she felt obligated to take advantage of the program for which she knew she was eligible, in order to help her mother. "I needed to help her medical expenses, so I went on AFDC. I was upset about it, and I wouldn't have planned on doing all this. It wasn't much of a choice or much to think about. Who is going to pay for the medical bills?" A homeless woman in Los Angeles told researchers the state had denied her homeless assistance because she had once given some of her AFDC money to her son, who had just gotten out of prison. "I don't care, the money is there for me, too," she told them. "I can do what I want [with it] and I'd rather help my son." An epileptic woman whose public assistance paid her extensive medical bills imagined her life without it. She would have been consigned to a nursing home, where, she knew from experience, having worked in one, she would have been strapped into a "geri-chair" with a helmet and left to sit all day long. "I much prefer the situation I'm in now. I think I can give more to the community besides." To many if not most welfare recipients, welfare represents not something they receive but something they give.[26]

Defying Creon

For poor people, if government help means welfare, it also means "the law," and to low-income parents, "the law" looks much like King Creon's dictates. Low-income women feel forced to leave their children in risky child-care arrangements (which often means home alone or home with a slightly older sibling) because they must earn money by working outside the home and can't afford better care. On their meager wages, they often cannot feed, clothe, and shelter their children adequately. They fear poverty, but they fear "the law" even more. "The law" to them does not mean what the welfare program's name suggests, Temporary Assistance for Needy Families (TANF). "The law" means state child-protection agencies that would take away their children if their child-care arrangements were discovered. "The law" means caseworkers who have the power to declare their standard of living neglectful and call in the state protective service. "The law" means siccing the state on your children's father so it can garnish his wages—"puttin' the law on him," as the expression goes.[27]

In fact, these mothers' perceptions of the law are deadly accurate. The TANF legislation encourages states to wield tough child-care standards and to sanction "bad" mothers by reducing or ending their benefits, making it even harder for them to provide decent care. It requires mothers to cooperate with paternity-establishment and child-support enforcement, and pressures them to grant custody and visitation rights to fathers, even if the mothers don't want the fathers involved. And always over this downward spiral looms the threat of child removal.[28]

So, as Dodson says, low-income mothers hew to their own higher law. They lie about their child-care arrangements, even to researchers who hope to help them by documenting the need for better child-care policy. They don't dare tell caseworkers the full extent of their need, even when they are desperate for help. They teach their children to cover up, too.

Virtually every person on welfare cheats. They have to in order to survive because it is simply impossible to live on the income from welfare. Most work off the books, doing things legal and illegal. Some pay professional shoplifters to get clothes for their kids. Some use false ID cards to get food, jobs, and, more often, health care. Doctors and clinics sometimes abet these families by looking the other way or even suggesting that Mom bring in Tommy under cousin Johnny's Medicaid card.[29]

Like Luscious, many women receive goods, services, and money from their children's fathers or grandparents. They don't report these gifts, as they are required to do. They lie to caseworkers about the identity and whereabouts of their children's fathers. In effect, they build their own child-support systems, because the official one would confiscate all but a smattering of any child support fathers paid, instead of using it to support the children.[30]

Mothers collaborate with their children's fathers to maximize benefits from the earned income tax credit. To get this rebate at tax time, a parent has to have worked (and earned income) *and* has to have had children living with him or her for at least half the year. If the mother has custody of the children but doesn't work, and the father works but doesn't have custody, the family loses out on the benefit. If they report that the children live with him, however, everyone benefits. When asked a hypothetical question by a reporter, Deborah Morton, a cashier at a discount store, saw nothing wrong with letting her daughter's father claim, falsely, that the child lived with him. She explained what was to her a simple moral calculus: "She is his child and he helps me with her."[31]

Juan, a young man in Harlem, regularly used part of his paycheck to help his mother, in addition to helping support his son and his son's mother. Juan's mother had been on AFDC seemingly forever, Juan still had younger siblings at home, and he felt responsible for helping to pay for the necessities. But when welfare authorities got wind of his help, they threatened to reduce his mother's grant. To protect his mother, Juan moved out, even though that meant couch surfing with friends, so that the welfare department could no longer count his income as part of her household income. Of course, he continued to help her, off the books.[32]

Nemesis, another of Dodson's informants, recalls the time when she was eleven and the police raided her mother's apartment. Her father had been an alcoholic and a batterer, and her mother had thrown him out. Her mother, unable and unwilling to live "on the dole," ran a gambling parlor, and kept the proceeds in a box of tissues. As the children were being taken off to relatives, her mother handed Nemesis the tissue box and told her to take care of the other children and wipe their faces. Later, Nemesis's mother talked to her children about the law and breaking rules. "My mother said it was wrong to tell lies and to cheat and to break the law. But she said there were bigger wrongs. Having hungry children, being dependent on people who abuse you, are bigger wrongs. She said that you feed your children first. You belong to nobody. The other comes later."[33]

When honest work, lying, and cheating have failed to provide for the family, stealing suggests itself. "Ruth" descended into poverty after her physician husband left her and their three sons. As is so common in divorce, he routinely flouted the child-support order. Ruth did everything she could to keep the family going, including volunteering at her synagogue so she could feel right about continuing the boys' Hebrew lessons even though she couldn't pay tuition. As part of her volunteer work, she was asked to run the synagogue's food pantry program. "I began to take, I mean to borrow, some of the scrip that belonged to the synagogue," she confessed. "I'm a mother. These are my children, my babies we're talking about. Am I really going to make them eat peanut butter for weeks on end when I have access to all this food scrip?"[34]

Twenty-three-year-old Carmelina Smith, with two kids to support, thought she'd supplement her meager wages with a cashier's job at a university bookstore. She pilfered eleven thousand dollars from the cash register and wound up in jail. "I couldn't buy my kids milk and Pampers—that's why I did what I did," she told Jason DeParle. "I wasn't able to put clothes on their back the way I should have." Did she feel like a criminal? Not at all, DeParle reported: "Ms. Smith recalls the moment as a rare time of inner peace. 'It felt good. I felt like now I can take care of my kids the way I want to.'"[35]

Women on welfare consistently define personal responsibility on their own terms, terms that put family care above all else. "They [welfare officials] act like because you're on welfare, you're not working a job, and so you must not have anything better to do," one woman told Joe Soss. "Well, just because I'm not working a job doesn't mean I don't have other important things to do. I do have a family, you know." Lisa Dodson got some of her informants together for a discussion of rule breaking. Luscious, the woman who pretended she didn't know who had fathered her child, opened the discussion by announcing, "We all be creative with our accounts." Nemesis, the woman whose mother had schooled her in putting family above the law, had another name for creative accounting—civil disobedience. Luscious agreed: "I say this to the law," she said, snapping her fingers. "You're breaking the law by making sure you and your kids don't starve on the street—well, that's not *my* law."[36]

Antigone, too, lectured King Creon on the status of his law:

> It was *not Zeus* who published this decree,
> Nor have the Powers who rule among the dead
> Imposed such laws as this upon mankind;
> Nor could I think that decree of yours—
> A man—could override the laws of Heaven
> Unwritten and unchanging. Not of today
> Or yesterday is their authority;
> They are eternal.[37]

Creon's Medicine

In a classic study of Holocaust rescuers, Samuel Oliner and Pearl Oliner tried to understand why some people helped Jews and others didn't. They interviewed rescuers and nonrescuers, and concluded that rescuers had certain predispositions to begin with. When rescuers were confronted with an "external event," they sprang into action. What kinds of events caused rescuers to stop to help? Sometimes a Jewish person asked them for help, sometimes someone else personally asked them to help Jews, and sometimes they responded to a new anti-Semitic regulation or a rumor of a roundup. But not every person with altruistic predispositions sprang into action when confronted by one of these events.

Oliner and Oliner were especially puzzled by a doctor who said her parents had taught her to be loving, kind, helpful, and considerate of others. Yet when a Jewish man arrived in the hospital where she worked, a hospital that was forbidden to treat Jews at the time, the doctor didn't treat him, even though she knew he would die without emergency care and even though the ethics of her profession ought to have reinforced her parents' teaching. "I could do nothing," she told Oliner and Oliner matter-of-factly. Other people with a similar upbringing, faced with just such a human emergency and the same draconian laws against helping Jews, decided to help. Oliner and Oliner concluded that objective external events by themselves didn't cause caring people to help. Rather, they thought, people confer their own subjective meanings on events. Rescuers interpreted events differently than nonrescuers, and their interpretations caused them to act, not the events themselves.[38]

Interpretations are where politics and altruism come together. Except for life-threatening events, people aren't hardwired to respond automatically. With our higher brains, we give meanings to events. These meanings are subjective in the sense that they're personal, but they are not completely of our own making, immune to outside influence. The meanings we give to events come from experience, from our upbringing, our education, and our own encounters with helping and being helped. They come from messages we get from others. And nothing shapes these messages and our own interpretations more powerfully than public discourse—how a community talks about help.

Consider how the contemporary health care community talks about doctors' ethical obligations to their patients. In the national quest for cost control, the new professional ethics tell doctors to treat populations rather than patients. Every time doctors decide whether to test or treat a patient, they should consider whether the procedure has been found to be cost-effective when done for large groups of patients. They should give less consideration to their judgment of whether the test or treatment would help the individual patient. "Practitioners need to develop an allegiance to the entire membership of their health plan," admonishes a leading health policy adviser (himself a physician) in the *Journal of the American Medical Association*. "This will be difficult for those who see themselves as serving as their patients' advocate in a struggle with administrators and insurers." Doctors who see themselves as advocates of their patients need moral correction. They need to understand that putting their patients' interests above those of "the membership" is "hoarding" resources for their own patients and "taking from other patients."[39]

Suppose we could transplant the doctor who puzzled Oliner and Oliner so much—the one who "could do nothing" for a dying patient—into contemporary American medical practice. Suppose that now, as then, she has been brought up with values of altruism. Suppose that now, as then, she trained under a code of medical ethics that obliged her to put her patients' interests first. But now suppose she is practicing medicine and imbibing moral lessons from the house organ of the American Medical Association, the organization that promulgates her profession's formal code of ethics. How will she be likely to respond when faced with a conflict between a patient she believes will suffer without her care, and rules—even rules of thumb—that discourage her from treating that patient?

Along with its moral lessons, her medical association includes some advice on exactly how to withhold the care she thinks might benefit the patient. It even scripts the conversations for her: "It will not do to have a practitioner say, 'I'd like to give you this [treatment] because it has lower risks, but I can't because the administrators are forcing me to save money at the expense of your life.'" Instead, her professional association advises her, she should either keep silent ("in most cases there will be no need to say anything at all"), or simply tell her patient what she is going to do, without discussing possible alternatives ("Well, for patients like you, the appropriate approach is . . . ").[40] After enough lessons like these, it would hardly be surprising if she did nothing for the patient. And at the end of the day, she would turn off the lights and say to herself, "I could do nothing."

No doctor makes medical judgments in a social vacuum. Doctors are subject to constant moral tutelage through their training, supervision and peer review, and through articles in medical journals, lectures at professional conferences, and the health policy debates they watch and read along with other citizens. This moral tutelage in turn shapes the way they relate to their patients—how they interpret their roles and responsibilities and whether they respond with compassion. And since the 1970s, economic thinking has played a bigger and bigger role in shaping medical morality.

Economic thinking encourages doctors to think about social efficiency rather than individual compassion. Unlike the Good Samaritan of the parable, the socially efficient doctor would pause before reflexively trying to help, read up on the literature, canvass the streets for other sick and injured people, and only then decide where his help might do the most good. This kind of thinking denigrates medical Samaritans as inefficient and backward, as followers of personal feelings instead of scientific evidence, as hoarders of resources and traitors to the common good.

Moral tutelage is only one way that society molds doctors' sense of themselves. The other way is more direct and coercive: financial incentives. The moral mind-set of economists contradicts the moral mind-set of healers, so economists have run into a great deal of resistance to their prescriptions for reforming medical care. Resistance is exactly what the American Medical Association anticipated when it exhorted doctors to shift their loyalties from the individual patient to the "health plan membership," and then lamented, "This will be difficult for those who see themselves as serving as their patients' advocates."

To overcome this resistance, economists recommended changing the way healers get paid so that their excess compassion costs them personally. Starting in the 1970s, first hospitals and then nursing homes, home health agencies, rehabilitation centers, and many outpatient providers now receive a fixed pot of money from government health insurance programs. Just as parents give children allowances to teach them that they can't have everything they want, government's new way of paying healers is designed to teach them that they can't help everyone they would like to help. It's up to each provider to make the pot last by deciding whom to help among the many needy people in its beds or at its doors. This payment method was the core of the managed-care revolution in private health insurance, too.

The new payment method deliberately pits healers' financial interests against their compassionate mission. They can stay in the black only if they harden themselves to the plights of the sickest and neediest people. People who need a lot of chronic care and those who need expensive care stand out as budget busters, consuming an outsized share of the common pot. And that is exactly the purpose of this payment method—to spotlight very sick people as financial drains. In crass economic terms, as *Barron's* magazine once put it, patients have become "cost centers" instead of "revenue centers."[41]

Never mind the bland bureaucratic name for this new health care payment method, "prospective payment system." The new pay scheme performs the kind of brainwashing that moral tutelage alone could not accomplish. It reinterprets sick people in doctors' minds, transforming them from human brethren who deserve help to losses on the business ledger. And if doctors, nurses, therapists, aides, and other healers don't get it, their front offices do. At the same time, it transforms medical altruism from help (for the patient) to harm (for the healer). Dark magic indeed.

Medicine, better than any field I can think of, illustrates how politics mediates altruism. Healing, after all, is the central metaphor of the Good Samaritan parable. It's easy to think that doctors, nurses, and other healers are genetically altruistic, that people who go into helping professions are caring "by nature." In fact, whether healers respond altruistically depends as much on the moral politics that surround them as on their personal predispositions. I say moral *politics* rather than moral *climate*, because moral tutelage and reward systems are not weather visited upon medicine by mysterious meteorological forces. They are intentional, purpose-driven human policies.

Medical Resisters

Health care is governed by the desire to help. "First, Do No Harm" goes the Hippocratic Oath, but most health care providers aren't satisfied by such a minimal standard. They didn't train for eight or more years only to refrain from injuring people. They hope to do good. They hope to help. In their medical education and their on-the-job training, they learn to defy illness, injury, infection—anything that can go wrong with the human body or mind. When things go wrong with the social system, they learn to defy that, too. Rules that interfere with healing are meant to be broken.

Doctors and nurses fudge the charts to provide the care they deem right. "Doctors Say They'd Lie to Get Insurers to Pay" ran one headline in *USA Today*. In a survey of 169 doctors in eight cities, 58 percent supported the principle of lying so a hypothetical severely ill woman could get bypass surgery, even though she didn't meet the insurer's criteria. Forty-eight percent of doctors admitted actually lying to insurers, the story reported. "Doctors think they're being ethical in getting the patient what he needs, so you've got a huge outbreak of civil disobedience," commented bioethicist Arthur Caplan.[42]

At dinner one night with a friend who is a practicing gerontologist, I mentioned my interest in rule breaking in the name of medical altruism. "I do it all the time," he said, as though he were talking about grocery shopping. His college-student daughter was with us, and her ears perked up. "What do you mean? Like what?" she pressed him. My friend explained: "Insurance companies will pay for a drug only for certain diagnoses, so you embroider the diagnosis to get the patient's drug paid for. And I steal things from the hospital to give to patients." Now my ears perked up. "What kinds of things? Drug samples?" I asked. "No, samples are free; that's not stealing. Things they can use—stuff for testing their blood sugar, or Foley catheters."

In the cubicles of the federal agency that oversees Medicare, civil disobedience, if there is any, is well hidden, but one such act made the front page of the *Wall Street Journal*. Sixty-six-year-old Edward Petraiuolo Jr. desperately needed a liver transplant. He had hepatitis B; Medicare didn't cover transplants for patients with hepatitis B. Petraiuolo's doctors were confident he could do well with the aid of some new medicines, and apparently were willing to donate their surgical services. However, without coverage of the post-transplant drugs—costing some $400,000 over five years—a transplant was futile. Through Mrs. Petraiuolo's pleas to their congresswoman and senator, the case reached the desk of Jeffrey Kang, the person then in charge of setting Medicare's coverage policies for specific diseases like Edward Petraiuolo's. In violation of Medicare's rules, Kang authorized Medicare to cover a liver transplant for Petraiuolo, then called Mrs. Petraiuolo with the news: "I wanted you to be able to sleep tonight." Kang was reprimanded for "exceeding his legal authority." He was accused of responding to congressional political pressure. "Dr. Kang says he wasn't responding to congressional pressure," the *Wall Street Journal* reported. "Rather, he says, he made the medically correct decision to help move a dying patient onto a transplant waiting list."[43]

In hospital emergency rooms and clinics, doctors and admitting clerks are sometimes caught between anti-immigrant eligibility rules and sick immigrants. Medical care for immigrants has become a hot-button issue, leading to tightened restrictions in many states. Many medical personnel, socialized into an ethic of helping sick people, skirt the rules to fulfill their moral sense. In 1996, California's governor issued regulations to prohibit doctors from treating pregnant undocumented immigrants. Twenty thousand doctors signed pledges to disobey the law. Doctors in Boston pledged to ignore a welfare regulation denying service to undocumented immigrants.[44] Resistance sometimes takes the form of foot-dragging rather than outright disobedience. Clinic staff often try not to know about the immigration status of their clientele. "Should I wonder whether this is the guy from Third Avenue who doesn't have the money or the guy from the third world who doesn't have any? That's not my job. I'm a doctor," the emergency services director at Bellevue Hospital told the *New York Times*. Parkland Memorial Hospital in Dallas doesn't ask about patients' immigration status, even though Texas is home to a large illegal immigrant population and prevailing public opinion thinks citizens and legal immigrants should come first. "I don't want my doctors and nurses to be immigration agents," the hospital president explained. "We decided that these are folks living in our community and we needed to render the care."[45]

In nursing homes, aides sneak in their patients' favorite foods, release them from restraints to give them much-needed freedom, and take time away from their routine duties to sit and chat with a resident. "A major blowup occurred in the middle of my fieldwork when Ana was caught violating bureaucratic procedures in an effort to help one of her patients," writes sociologist Nancy Foner in her study of a nursing home. Ana, it seems, ordered some kind of protective gloves for a patient after her many requests to the nurse in charge were ignored. Only a week earlier,

Ana had incurred the wrath of her supervisor for taking a wheelchair-bound resident downstairs to the dining room. The resident had beseeched Ana to take her, Ana had obliged during one of her breaks, but wheeling residents downstairs was supposed to be someone else's job, not the aides'. "The sheer onslaught of rules has a numbing and demoralizing effect on the caregivers," Foner comments.[46]

In private homes, health aides bring gifts for their patients, visit on their days off, and frequently purchase groceries for them using wages earned at seven to nine dollars an hour. Tiny things, to be sure, but each of them is a violation of rules that could (and sometimes does) get the aide reprimanded or fired. Sometimes aides take patients outdoors for a stroll, flouting Medicare's requirement that patients be "homebound." Medicare won't pay for home health care if patients are capable of leaving their homes, or if they do leave for anything other than attending church or medical appointments. Nurses are supposed to enforce this rule by asking each time they visit, "Have you been out at all?" The homebound requirement is particularly irksome to home care nurses and aides. Like the clinic staff who don't ask about immigrant status, many home care nurses don't ask about homebound status, don't write down the answers they hear, or tell their clients, "I don't want to know about it." When I asked a group of aides in New York City about rule breaking to help their patients, a few of them told me they sometimes "cheated" by wheeling their patients outdoors. "Everyone has a right to fresh air," protested one.

In my home care research, I also heard about record fudging to keep patients eligible for services—exaggerating symptoms or substituting diagnoses acceptable to Medicare for ones that aren't. A physical therapist told me about one of her patients with multiple sclerosis. Having already heard the story of the "guy with MS" who was being "cut off" from Medicare, I asked this therapist how a person with MS could be eligible for services. She worked in a different state, and for a moment I thought perhaps Medicare regulations might be interpreted differently in her state. "Oh, I don't put down MS," she answered matter-of-factly. "I write down 'gait disorder' as the primary diagnosis." Caregivers have a keen sense of justice, and they frequently do a little "creative coding" to ensure that the agency gets reimbursed for their services or that clients remain eligible. During one case conference I attended, people talked about a patient who needed "cardiac rehab." Someone said, "Medicare won't pay for that. They'll go deconditioning, but no cardiac rehab." Someone else added, "So you just have to not word it as cardiac rehab."[47]

Another common form of cheating I encountered was recording that the worker was helping the official patient when she was in fact helping the patient's spouse. Home care personnel aren't allowed to help someone unless there's a care plan prescribed by a doctor. But often, they go into an elderly patient's home and find a spouse who's just as needy. One aide scoffed at the idea that aides should refuse care for a needy spouse. "What am I going to do—cook for him, and not feed her?" she huffed, treating the issue as a matter of common decency. At a team conference, the group discussed a family in which the elderly husband was getting services for leg ulcers and other problems, but his wife, who was not a patient, had Alzheimer's, among many other problems. The social worker on the team was reporting on her latest visits and the wife's problems. The case manager started to write down which team members had been in the home during the prior two weeks. "I was in there under Phil," the social worker cautioned her. "So put me in under Phil. Although I was really there for Mary, but don't put me there for Mary." Wink, wink, nod, nod.

In one home health agency, a few nurses were so troubled by a continuing tension with the homebound rule that they brought the case to the agency's ethics committee, where I was a fly on the wall. The client was an elderly farmer who had been paralyzed in a tractor rollover accident some years before. He needed home nursing mainly to tend his recalcitrant skin wounds. The couple's children lived nearby, the family owned a handicapped van, and often they trundled the man out to family gatherings, church social activities, and the local Wal-Mart—a favorite spot for the mobility-impaired because it provides electric carts. Knowing the homebound requirement, the nurses on this case told the farmer's wife that her husband was not allowed to go out and still receive care. They told her repeatedly, and she repeatedly gave them a piece of her mind: "If you make me take a choice between losing services and taking him out, I will take him out." They tried to up the ante by telling her they were very sorry, but the government has these rules. She countered: "If Mr. Clinton wants to come in here and tell me I can't have services, let him come." In frustration, the nurses gave the woman to understand that if she took her husband out, they didn't want to know about it.

As the ethics committee deliberated, the consensus became clear: it's good for the man to get out of the house and socialize, and we wish every disabled person had loving, nearby relatives who could afford a handicapped van. So the nurses looked the other way, but they knew they were breaking the law, and they were worried. The members of the ethics committee subtly backed the family and the nurses by assenting to the consensus.

Still, the nurse who spoke before the ethics board seemed acutely uncomfortable, as if she were on trial. The Law of the Land had caused these nurses to doubt their own compassion and clinical judgment and had made them feel like petty criminals. At the time of this case, the ethics board was a new innovation within the agency. As I observed its deliberations in the context of the legal climate for home health care, a time when the federal government was vigorously prosecuting home care agencies for fraud, it seemed to me that the agency had created an ethics forum primarily to help the staff cope with Antigone-like choices.

Many on the Right would read these tales as stories of lawbreakers who should be punished. I read them as skirmishes in a political struggle over the right to care for others. I read them as stories about the ways business and government prevent us from caring, about government's failure to protect citizens from employers and businesses who behave like Creon, and about citizens gone private, abiding by a higher law. Finally, I read them as parables about what happens to democracy when a community doesn't allow its members to honor their deepest convictions about what it means to be a good person. When citizens can no longer respect the public sphere, they retreat into more humane private worlds. Honoring altruism is the key to democratic revival.

5

Engines of Democracy

Leaders must constantly ask themselves what kind of citizens they would like to cultivate. Who makes a better citizen for democracy, the self-interested person whose ambition spills over to benefit others, or the altruistic one whose intentional generosity surely helps others but is just as surely limited? Which kind of citizen should government encourage? American public philosophy has long bet on self-interest.

In 1922, traumatized by the Russian Revolution, Herbert Hoover pedalled furiously to define a uniquely "American individualism" that could satisfy the human yearning for compassion without upending capitalism. In an essay written years before he would become president, he acknowledged that American ideals were molded "from the instincts of kindness, pity, fealty to family and race; the love of liberty; the mystical yearnings for spiritual things . . . [and] the impulses of service to community and nation." Yet for all these noble sentiments, Hoover rued, "the day has not arrived when any economic or social system will function and last if founded upon altruism alone."[1]

Hoover then made a prophecy at once soothing and frightening: "With the growth of ideals through education, with the higher realization of freedom, of justice, of humanity, of service, the selfish impulses become less and less dominant, and if we ever reach the millennium, they will disappear in the aspirations and satisfactions of pure altruism. But for the next several generations *we dare not abandon self-interest as a motive force to leadership and to production, lest we die.*"[2]

Today's American individualists are less sanguine about a millennial dawn of altruism. Yet even years after the fall of the Soviet empire, they still share Hoover's terror of socialism, because they understand the strength of the human yearning for kindness and compassion. In 1998, law professor Richard Epstein painted the collapse of the Soviet Union as "a clear warning about the limits of universal altruism in the organization of our political life."[3]

This is not to say that altruism was hounded out of American politics by Lenin's ghost. Human nature was a topic of intense interest for the founding fathers. To design a proper constitution, they had to know what sort of men they were dealing with. If government is the art of coordinating citizens' behavior for the common weal, governing well depends on understanding why people behave as they do. James Madison famously assumed that people are intensely self-interested and would get into fractious fights in the pursuit of their self-interest, so he recommended a constitutional design to neutralize human nature. The key to his design was a large republic. By placing citizens in a large arena where everyone would hash it out with everyone else, Madison reasoned, people who opposed each other on one issue would find common cause on other issues. Add Alexander Hamilton's checks and balances and the political system would grind up vicious self-interests into a sort of social sausage with bits of something for everybody's tastes.[4] The American Constitution was designed to produce altruistic results from self-interested motives.

Just as the founding fathers chose a view of human nature to write into the Constitution, leaders of every generation choose which motives they write into laws and policies. Yet the motives assumed in law influence how citizens behave. Our motives and morals are never fixed. They come into being continuously as we choose how to act. Politics shapes motives as much as motives shape politics. Since the late 1970s, economics has become the premier science of government. No discipline or profession has been more important in shaping how American leaders understand human motivation. And in the economic worldview, self-interest is the engine of social progress.

There is another logic of human motivation—the logic of love, help, kindness, and care. Altruism moves us in every facet of daily life and sometimes moves us to accept great losses and punishments in order to help others. Yet as strong and pervasive as altruism is, our political culture virtually ignores it. Political leaders and thinkers are so deeply imbued with the self-interest model that they wittingly and unwittingly promote it.

The Logic of Self-Interest

Charles Schultze, the chair of President Carter's Council of Economic Advisors from 1977 to 1981, laid out the case for self-interest with elegant simplicity. Societies have only three ways of coordinating citizens' behavior: coercion, self-interest incentives, and the "emotional forces" of "compassion, patriotism, brotherly love and cultural solidarity." Each society combines these mechanisms in its own proportions, but in the United States, coercion and the emotional forces are less available. With our love of freedom, Schultze said, Americans won't countenance too much coercion. With our ethnic and racial diversity, we can't rely on cultural solidarity, and "*compassion, brotherly love and patriotism are in too short supply* to serve as substitutes [for cultural solidarity]." That leaves self-interest. Fortunately, though, "harnessing the 'base' motive of material self-interest to promote the common good is perhaps *the* most important social invention mankind has yet achieved."[5]

Self-interest is a motive we can count on. Everybody's got it, and no one's self-interest will ever run out. Two decades after Schultze inventoried human motives, biologist Edward O. Wilson reached the same conclusion: "True compassion is a commodity in chronically short supply." Milton Friedman listed another advantage of self-interest as a social engine, in addition to its abundance. Self-interest is a "much stronger and more dependable spur than human kindness."[6]

If we want citizens to put their energies toward the public good, economists reason, government should tax or punish bad behavior and reward good behavior. By wisely arranging carrots and sticks, government can get people to behave in ways that benefit them in the short run but help society in the long run. In other words, smart leaders can trick people into acting altruistically by appealing to their self-interest. Government's job is not so much to help citizens but to manipulate them through incentives into serving the public good inadvertently.

Self-interest is supposed to be an engine of social progress, too, because people are—or at least most social scientists think they are—driven by their own want. When they have unsatisfied desires, they strive to fulfill them. Want stokes ambition. If deprivation, need, and desire spur constructive behavior, then help blunts effort and stifles ambition. Because social progress is nothing but the sum of individual actions, the best way to ensure social progress is to withhold help, so as not to interfere with individual ambition.

This view of human nature casts people as fundamentally lazy, unlikely to make much effort unless they have a strong need that can't be satisfied by lounging around. But, as everyday altruism shows, people habitually put themselves out to help others, for reasons that have little, if anything, to do with their own material needs. If we shift our focus from how helping supposedly affects the people who receive help to *how helping affects the helpers*, we begin to see the powerful motives and rewards that move people to act altruistically.

The Paradox of Altruism

A few years ago on public radio, I heard a Vermont woman who volunteers two days a week delivering meals to elderly shut-ins. She described how much she enjoyed her visits and how rewarding she found the work. Then, as if confessing, she told the interviewer, "I get so much more than I give when I visit these people. I'm really very selfish."

The Meals on Wheels driver is not alone. The more I talked and read about altruism, the more I heard her refrain: "I get more than I give." Generous people steadfastly refuse to see themselves as giving, or only giving. They often parry praise with comments like, "I'm really doing it for myself" or "I'm doing it for a very selfish reason: It makes me happy."[7]

When sociologist Robert Wuthnow surveyed some two thousand people about help, 91 percent agreed that "when you help people in need, you get as much from it as they do." A man celebrated by a local paper for teaching English to immigrants tossed off the "giving is getting" idea as cliché: "It's the proverbial 'I'm getting more than I'm giving,'" he said, explaining that the immigrants nourished his long-standing interest in foreign cultures. Congressman John Kasich asked some teenagers why they were giving up their Saturdays to make sandwiches for homeless people. One of them answered as if he were stating a simple equation: "It helps people—it makes me feel good."[8]

"I get more than I give" is the mantra of helpers and the paradox of altruism. When philosophers and social scientists refer to the paradox of altruism, they mean something quite different. They mean that it's incomprehensible why a self-interested creature would ever sacrifice for others. Self-sacrifice doesn't jibe with self-preservation. In a Darwinian world of each for oneself, altruism should die out. This is the puzzle most recent scholarship on altruism aims to explain: how can the motive of self-interest lead someone to behave altruistically?

From the voices of altruists, a more remarkable paradox emerges: Most people don't experience altruism as self-sacrifice. They experience it as a two-way street, as giving and receiving at the same time. When they help others, they gain a sense of connection with other people. Giving and helping make them feel a part of something larger than themselves. Helping others makes them feel needed and valuable and that their time on earth is well spent. Helping others gives them a sense of purpose, and when they invest in others, they simultaneously invest their own lives with meaning. Judging from how people talk about their altruism, self-interest and altruism merge into one.

Like the Vermont Meals on Wheels driver, ordinary people often use the language of economics to talk about their altruism. They talk about exchange, about giving and receiving. They often describe their feelings with metaphors of money, bank accounts, wealth, rewards, income and outflows, debts and paybacks, and they invariably paint themselves in the black. But despite the economic language, theirs is not textbook economics, as the following four vignettes show.

One: After Dr. Jack MacConnell retired to posh Hilton Head, South Carolina, he started a health center for people who couldn't afford medical care and staffed it with other retirees and neighbors, all volunteers. "I have the best retirement anyone in the world could have: giving yourself away in service to others," he says. "When I come off the golf course, I'm always diminished a bit, and when I come out of the clinic, I'm elevated and feel good about myself and my life." A reporter asked another volunteer doctor how he liked "working for nothing." He rebuffed the question: "I make a million dollars every day. What I get from this clinic you can't buy with money."[9]

Two: When Irene Gut Opdyke was sixteen years old in German-occupied Poland, she was drafted as housekeeper to a German major. She used her position to sneak food to Jews in the nearby ghetto and, eventually, to hide twelve people in the major's basement, feed them, and keep them alive. Reminiscing about her rescue activity fifty years later, she explained, "I didn't do it for the money or glory or anything. But the older I get, the more I feel I am very rich. I would not change anything. It's a wonderful feeling to know that today many people are alive and some of them married and have their children, and that their children will have children because I did have the courage and the strength."[10]

Three: In a book of daily meditations for nurses' aides, Bethany Knight notes, "One hour of the muffler installer's services costs you four hours of your pay." But then she adds, "How many people hear 'I love you' from the people they work with? Once you realize your heart is your bank, you'll never feel poor again."[11]

Four: Novelist Isabelle Allende says she learned her most important life lesson while caring for her daughter Paula, who was comatose for a year before she died. "When she died, I thought I had lost everything. But then I realized that I still had the love I had given her. You only have what you give. I don't even know if she was able to receive that love. She could not respond in any way, her eyes were somber pools that reflected no light. But I was full of love and that love keeps growing and multiplying and giving fruit." Paula's lesson became Allende's teaching: "It's by spending yourself that you become rich."[12]

No investment adviser would counsel people to spend their money or give it away in order to get rich. Getting fulfillment by making others happy is not the core of standard social science, but it is the stuff of life, and so we need a new way of understanding altruism. The puzzle is not how or whether altruism can exist, but why people so consistently describe helping others as enriching and fulfilling. How to explain that when people devote themselves to others, whether for an instant or a lifetime, they usually feel rewarded and renewed instead of depleted and diminished?

Altruism blurs the distinctions between many categories we ordinarily consider separate. In moments of helping, altruists don't experience sharp differences between self and other, motive and reward, giving and receiving, benefit and burden, pleasure and suffering, choice and necessity. If this all sounds too abstract, try a thought experiment: close your eyes and think about taking care of your very sick child, spouse, partner, parent, or close friend. You probably didn't experience your caregiving as all burden, giving and suffering with no pleasure from making the other person happier or more comfortable. And you probably didn't experience your caregiving as something you were forced to do, with no trace of desire to do it in your heart.

In addition to metaphors of wealth and abundance, helpers often use metaphors of energy. They describe getting a rush, a high, a thrill, an uplift; they feel pumped up, energized, rejuvenated, euphoric, and even addicted. A nursing-home volunteer explained her sensations as similar to an athlete's high: "I go home tired, but with a new spurt of energy such as one feels after a really good game of tennis." A kindergarten teacher who "sort of adopted" children from low-income families described her feelings as "like I had been zapped by an energy bolt." A woman who gave up a nursing career to help a friend set up group homes for mentally disabled children reported, "I've never been happier. I have endless energy."[13]

Helping others, people say, takes them outside their own problems and recharges their batteries. No matter that they expend energy on helping others; focusing on others gives them respite from their own worries. A former provost of the University of Texas–Austin drove a regular route for Meals on Wheels, not a typical daytime activity for university provosts. "I consider volunteering a way to *refresh* and get away from the normal demands of the regular routine," he explained. "It's a *time out*—a totally different thing to do and, in addition to being very gratifying, it helps you keep things in perspective."[14]

Helpers sometimes speak of pride as a source of energy that keeps them moving on altruistic paths. When they see that their help made a difference, that the people they helped succeeded or simply suffered less, they feel successful. Geoffrey Canada runs programs for inner-city youth in Harlem, programs that emphasize curbing violence, giving kids solid education, and inculcating a strong work ethic. In LaGuardia Airport, as Canada tells the story, "this young man in greasy dungarees came up to me. 'You don't remember me,' he said. And it was true, I couldn't place him. 'I was the one who was always getting in trouble. But I work here now, on a ground crew.' He was so proud of his job and what he'd done with his life. I thought, 'That's what keeps me at this job, remembering how proud that young man was.'"[15]

For my research on home health care, I interviewed many home care aides. Almost all of their patients were frail, homebound elderly people in their declining years, often widowed, and terribly lonely because their physical and mental problems kept them socially isolated. These were not patients who were likely to improve much or recover many of their lost abilities; the best they and their families could hope for was that their decline would be gradual and that they would come to terms with their diminished worlds. One of my standard questions to the aides was, "Would you tell me about a time you felt very successful or like you'd done a really good job?" The first time I asked this question, the aide, who had been very reserved until then, suddenly smiled and answered, "I got her to smile." She didn't say whom she'd gotten to smile. She didn't bother with the back story, apparently, because my question had transported her to a moment when she'd made someone happy and the memory was still making her happy now.

The majority of aides answered my success question in a similar way: "I had this woman who was very depressed. After a few weeks of my going, she wasn't so depressed." Or, "I had this one woman, and her family told me that she was sad all the time, but when *you* come, she is happy." What's so striking about aides' rendition of "success" is that making people smile isn't part of their formal job description. They are supposed to follow nurses' orders, doing things like help people stand, walk, and go to the bathroom; fix meals; give showers or baths and get people dressed; and change bed linens and do laundry. But they are everyday altruists, and they know that the most important thing they do is befriend people and make them feel loved. They make their own definition of a job well done, and they find fulfillment in meeting it.

On his fiftieth birthday, rock drummer Eddie Tuduri broke his neck body surfing. Lying in his bed in the rehab hospital, barely able to hold one drumstick in his right hand—the only one that still worked—he asked an aide to rap the side of the bed with the other stick. Before long, he had the room full of patients, nurses, and doctors clapping, rapping, and tapping however they could, and soon after that, he brought the improvised percussion band to the hospital's occupational therapy class, whose staff saw how much it improved patients' coordination, memory, and self-confidence. Tuduri now runs his own rehabilitation program, the Rhythmic Arts Project (TRAP), using percussion instruments to help people with disabilities learn to speak, spell, count, and coordinate their movements. Nine years after his accident, Tuduri told an interviewer that he continues to have shooting nerve pains and spasms. "But during TRAP sessions, when faces light up as the students find their own rhythm, the pain is worth it."[16]

One might be tempted to dismiss all these professions of good feelings from altruism as just so much happy talk, the heart-warming, fuzzy stuff of magazines and missionaries. But there is by now a well-established neurophysiological basis for the good feelings that people get from connecting with and helping others. When people (and some animals, too) befriend others, certain hormones are released that have a calming, soothing effect.[17] When we merely observe emotion in another person—say a wince, a smile, or a look of fear—neural pathways in our own brain are activated, pathways that make us feel the same emotion. These pathways not only make our own emotions mirror those of the people we are with but also activate other pathways that lead us to take action to respond to the others' emotions. As Daniel Goleman puts it in *Social Intelligence,* "The neural networks for perception and action share a common code in the language of the brain. This shared code allows whatever we perceive to lead almost instantly to the appropriate reaction. Seeing an emotional expression, hearing a tone of voice, or having our attention directed to a given topic instantly fires the neurons that the message indicates. . . . To feel *with* stirs us to act *for.*"[18]

This neural circuitry explains why many scientists now believe that the human brain is wired for kindness and that we are biologically constructed to help each other. It also explains, or at least makes plausible, why altruists experience the drive to keep helping more and more. If helping makes other people feel better, they will show their happiness in their facial expressions and words. Seeing and hearing that happiness, the helper will experience the same emotion. Perhaps that's why altruists commonly say, "I get so much from the people I help" and "It makes me feel good to help people." Neuroscience isn't far enough along to prove that altruism is self-reinforcing. Nevertheless, scientists have uncovered an uncanny resemblance between brain physiology and how people say they feel when they help others.

Help, care, giving, service, kindness, altruism—by whatever name, the phenomenon defies ordinary logic. In the material world, when you give something away (or sell it, for that matter), you have less of it for yourself. Altruism obeys the laws of passion rather than the laws of economics. Instead of "The more you spend, the less you have," the altruist's law reads, "The more you give, the more you receive, and the more you want to give." Instead of metaphors of scarcity, zero-sum, and pies with only so many slices, people talk about altruism in metaphors of fertility, continuity, circular flows, and widening ripples. "In the cycle of grace," Kathleen Brehony writes in her book about altruism, "determining who has been giving and who has been receiving is not so easy."[19] The world of altruism, far from being an economy of scarce resources and mine-or-thine, operates as an economy of abundance and mine-*and*-thine. Fortunately, all signs point to a hopeful assessment of the world supply of altruism, because it is often self-fulfilling, self-reinforcing, and self-generating.

If you are tempted to think that all these stories of rich rewards and endless energy prove that altruism is nothing but self-interest in disguise, think again. These stories prove that helping others brings people spiritual sustenance and transcendence that they don't get from pursuing their own self-interests. A politics that offers people incentives to get more for themselves can't compete with everyday altruism for personal satisfaction.

Why Altruism Withers

Altruism depends on empathy. People are much more likely to want to help someone whose plight they can feel themselves.[20] In a candid essay in *Newsweek*, Joe Troise described his experience delivering meals to terminally ill patients.[21] Unlike the Vermont Meals on Wheel driver who "got more than she gave," Troise became disgusted and was perpetually on the verge of quitting. He felt little sympathy for his clients, much less empathy. He was angered by a man who hallucinated food thieves and sometimes demanded that Troise "double back to the kitchen and deliver a second meal." He was put off by a dying alcoholic man who lived in his car and sometimes chastised Troise for not arriving sooner. He was especially annoyed to find a well-to-do woman on the client roster: "It's hard to accept that the well-to-do need food. Can't they just hire a gourmet chef?" One of the women on the program staff tried to explain that for some terminally people, "It's not the money. Some of them don't like to be seen . . . ah . . . in their condition." I knew immediately what the woman meant, because I have had close relatives who refused to allow family and friends to visit in their dying weeks, saying, "I don't want people to see me like this." Troise was unmoved, I suspect, because he lacked the experience of close friends with mental illness, alcoholism, or terminal illness.

Empathy is the lifeblood of altruism. Lack of empathy prevents the altruistic cycle from getting started. People are much less likely to feel empathy toward those they believe are responsible for their own predicament. In fact, people who have problems that others consider within their control tend to elicit anger and neglect rather than empathy and help.[22] One senses that this factor played a role in Troise's reactions, too. He seemed to think his clients could have made different choices and wouldn't have needed help with meals if they had. If so, Troise shared a common belief that mental illness and alcoholism are problems within one's personal control.

The same connection between blame and the willingness to help others shows up when opinion surveys ask about whether *government* should help people in trouble. Citizens consistently give strong support to programs that help people they believe are innocent and deserving. In one survey, people were asked to rank the groups they thought should receive various kinds of government help. Poor and disabled elderly headed the lists, poor and disabled children ranked in the middle, and poor adults—described in the survey as "single moms" and "unemployed men"—came in last.[23]

Thus, when Ronald Reagan spotlighted a supposed Cadillac-driving, booze-guzzling welfare queen, he launched a devastating campaign to undermine empathy for poor people. From that moment on, the conservative establishment turned out reams of stories all designed to make disadvantaged people seem responsible for their own troubles in everyone else's eyes. Charles Murray's *Losing Ground*, published in 1984, led the charge. The conservative idea machine began framing all social problems as matters of personal responsibility—poverty, unemployment, hunger, homelessness, slums, and even illness (lifestyle, don't you know?). Conservatives found the perfect weapon to persuade Americans to walk past our neighbors without stopping to help. By interfering with empathy, they cut off public altruism at its source.

There's another brake on altruism—the fear that the people we help will exploit our sympathy and empty our pockets. James Buchanan dubbed this fear "the Samaritan's dilemma."[24] He pictured a world with two kinds of people, soft-hearts and parasites. If the soft-hearts believe that too many of the people on the side of the road are parasites, lying in wait for unsuspecting Samaritans to stroll by, they will be loath to offer help. And here's the dilemma: If we don't help, we feel badly for the other person— that parasite *is* a human being, after all—and guilty about violating our moral values. If we do help, we feel exploited. (Think about your encounters with panhandlers.)

Many people who escaped from poverty know this dilemma painfully well. Often, when one or two people in a struggling family make good or come into good fortune, they find themselves besieged with requests for help.[25] As Katherine Newman puts it, "To be the one stable earner in a sea of relatives who need help is to be caught in a dilemma without easy solution," and "a recipe for intergenerational heartache."[26]

People evolve their own ways out of the dilemma. Some cut ties completely. One man told Newman how he handled his drug-dealing nephew: "I kicked him out. I don't want him here.

Period. What he does, that's his problem. He's done here. I got rid of the rotten apple and the barrel was saved." Severing ties works (and may be the only way to protect oneself from an addict), but for most people, divorcing a family member or friend is a heartache they don't want. Many of these trapped Samaritans develop other ways of coping.

Darlene Cawley's alcoholic son was the parasite from central casting: "He felt that because he was my only child, I was supposed to just keep giving him and giving him and giving him. Every time he fell behind or owed somebody some money, I was supposed to go to the bank and just take it out and give it to him." Although Darlene had modest savings, she worried about her future security, what with her weakness for her son and for friends who asked for loans they didn't pay back. To protect herself, she put her money in a trust that she didn't control. "I figure if I get it into my hands, I'm a sucker for a sad story," she explained. Darlene could be the spirit of Ulysses, tying her hands so she can't respond to Siren calls for help.

Newman's inner-city residents face the dilemma we all face as citizens—to help or not to help—and like them, we can resolve the dilemma in two ways. We can close our hearts, steel ourselves, and shut the door. Or we can acknowledge our deeply human need to keep our ties intact and work out ways to protect ourselves while keeping our humanity. In Chapter 8, we'll see how these mechanisms can translate into social policy.

Conservatives shut the door by ending or starving social assistance programs. They gather support for their meanness by trying to persuade the secure ones among us that the needy are all parasites, and better to hold on to our money. They portray welfare recipients as loafers and swindlers who make babies for fun, and disabled people as malingerers who would rather live on a six hundred–dollar monthly handout than work. They foment generational warfare between young hardworking taxpayers and greedy geezers, hoping the young will withdraw their commitment to keeping the elderly out of poverty. (An example: "The history of federal Medicare and Medicaid spending on the elderly can best be described as reckless child endangerment.")[27] They don't mention that the elderly give away more money and assets through private transfers than they receive through government help.[28] They whip up resentment against immigrants by harping on how much they cost "us" in social services and ignoring what they contribute in hard work, self-sacrifice, and generosity toward their communities. All of these parasite narratives are so devastating because they undercut the natural human empathy so essential for vibrant communities.

Sometimes altruism doesn't get started because people feel paralyzed by the overwhelming magnitude of need. People don't stop to offer any help because they feel powerless to make a dent in the problem, not because they judge the needy as irresponsible or worse. "There are practical limits to the Samaritan impulse in a major city," Stanley Milgram observed way back in 1970, when cities were healthier than they are now. "If a citizen attended to every needy person, if he were sensitive to and acted on every altruistic impulse that was evoked in the city, he could scarcely keep his own affairs in order."[29]

Milgram used the idea of "overload" to explain why people in large cities can become oblivious to each other. Faced with overwhelming neediness, people develop coping strategies. They stop noticing homeless people by averting their eyes, crossing the street, or "assuming an unfriendly countenance" to discourage anyone from trying to approach. (Sound familiar?) They develop mental filters to distinguish people they can trust from those they can't. They pull inside themselves and ration their help. By failing to address social needs with public resources, conservatives overtax individuals and set in motion this kind of retreat from altruism.

When social problems become too overwhelming for individuals to alleviate through random acts of kindness, public life becomes a kind of demoralizing boot camp. Living amid so much hardship hardens citizens to the plights of others and teaches them to forgo the ordinary "luxuries" of kindness and generosity. Overload is a school for despair and selfishness.

When government permits such devastating conditions to persist, when it doesn't use every means at its disposal to help, when it models callousness and counsels its citizens not to feel badly about the suffering of others, it destroys the two most important qualities of a democratic citizenry: the desire to make life better for everyone and the will to take action.

Cultivating Altruism

In *The Kindness of Children,* educator Vivian Paley tells how she witnessed a simple act of children's kindness, turned it into a story, and watched it boomerang around the world. Paley was visiting a London preschool to demonstrate her method of having children make up stories and act them out as plays. On this particular day, a group of disabled children was visiting the class.

One of them, Teddy, spent most of his time strapped in a wheelchair wearing a padded helmet, but he also had a toy car in which he could, with great effort, inch himself around on the floor. A few children included Teddy in their plays, oblivious to his differences and his inability to speak. Late in the day when Teddy's car had already been packed in the school van, a boy noticed Teddy squirming and approached Teddy's teacher: "Your little boy needs his car. He wants to be in my story." The teacher demurred, explaining that the car was already packed in the van. The children took matters into their own hands and cast Teddy in their play without his car. They surrounded his wheelchair and one little girl prompted him, "Pretend you're the puppy and you didn't learn to walk yet."[30]

Paley returned to the United States and told the story to her mother, who lived in a hotel for seniors and hadn't yet managed to make any mealtime friends. Paley's mother used the story to strike up a conversation with another resident, and suddenly the two became mealtime buddies, linked by a story of kindness. When Paley told the story to other preschool children, they were moved to tell their own stories of times they or children they knew needed help and did or didn't receive it. Their reminiscences, now given shape by the Teddy story, tuned their antennae for hurt children on the sidelines of the classroom. Again and again, as Paley repeated the Teddy story in other classes, children far removed from Teddy and his classmates entered the story and performed little acts of kindness.

Just as altruism can be self-reinforcing, stories about altruism have their own generative power. The right kinds of stories can elicit empathy and altruism in the listeners. Thomas Jefferson appreciated this motive power of stories. He once recommended to a friend that he include fiction in his personal library, along with history, philosophy, and natural science, because fiction can cultivate good character: "When any . . . act of charity or of gratitude, for instance, is presented either to our sight or imagination, we are deeply impressed with its beauty and feel a strong desire in ourselves of doing charitable and grateful acts also."[31]

I learned the Jefferson story from Jonathan Haidt, a social psychologist who has put Jefferson's idea to the test. Haidt and colleagues showed a video clip of Mother Teresa to one group of subjects and a comedy sequence from *America's Funniest Home Videos* to another group. Afterward, people who had seen the Mother Teresa film more frequently reported "wanting to help others, to become better people themselves, and to affiliate with others." Haidt has since collected interviews and done more experiments that bear out Jefferson's wisdom: stories of kindness and charity move us to want to be kind and charitable people.[32]

Thus, leaders shape citizens' moral character by the kinds of stories they tell. When leaders tell the people that the altruism cupboard is bare, the people aren't likely to open the cupboard looking for any. Self-interest becomes a national myth that exercises its own power over how citizens think and behave. If they feel the urge to help, they assume they're in the minority and that most "normal" people are motivated by self-interest. Indeed, to judge from the studies of Dale Miller and Rebecca Ratner, young people woefully underestimate their peers' altruistic predispositions.[33] For that matter, adults underestimate their own altruistic motives, too. Like the Vermont Meals on Wheels driver, so many everyday altruists explain their service to others as helping themselves, and therefore selfish. The American story of self-interest has made the idea of altruism very nearly culturally extinct.

When leaders celebrate entrepreneurs as the noblest heroes and profit making as the highest social virtue, citizens will begin to doubt the social worth of their altruistic selves. Stories shape citizens' image of the kind of leaders they need and the kinds of political contributions they can make. American stories about politics are rarely tales of kindness, generosity, and help. They're mostly tales of unbridled ambition and wrongdoing. To follow the political news is to descend into a malodorous world of ne'er-do-wells and failed policies. No wonder, then, that citizens think a leader's primary job is to empty the world of evil rather than to fill it with goodness.

In American politics, Mona Harrington writes, "a political leader must pass the warrior test. Can he [and now she] rid us of our enemies, stamp out trouble, clean out corruption and waste, lick the Depression, the Nazis, the Communists, shield us from enemy missiles, get the government off our backs, wipe out deficits, welfare, and crime?"[34] When political campaigns define leadership as superheroism and success as vanquishing enemies, citizens get the idea that their meager abilities aren't worth putting into service.

The right kind of stories can give us faith that what we do matters. I once took a workshop on ecology and nature writing. The participants were all nature lovers, and each in our own way environmental activists. On the last evening, we sat around trying to sum up the week's lessons, but somehow we veered into eco-horror stories about drilling, logging, polluting, depleting, and killing. Finally, someone pleaded, "Doesn't anyone have any hopeful stories?"

A high school teacher named Mike volunteered a version of Loren Eiseley's essay "The Star Thrower." Eiseley, walking on a beach after a storm, finds the shore littered with thousands upon thousands of washed-up starfish. Then he comes upon a man who is picking up starfish one by one, hurling them back into the ocean. Eiseley thinks the man is conducting an exercise in futility. Eyeing the man's hand, cocked and starfish-loaded, Eiseley asks him, "Why are you doing this? You can't possibly make a difference." Eiseley sweeps his own empty hand around the shoreline, taking in the unfathomable multitude of dying creatures. The man stops in midthrow, looks at the starfish cupped in his hand, and says, "To *this one* I make a difference."[35]

Leaders can elicit altruism by asking for it. Famously, John F. Kennedy asked bluntly, "Ask not what your country can do for you. Ask what you can do for your country." Franklin Roosevelt, taking office in the midst of the Great Depression, asked rather more indirectly. He credited citizens with knowing why altruism is necessary and then told them he was confident they would act on their beliefs:

> If I read the temper of our people correctly, we now realize as we have never realized before our interdependence on each other; that we cannot merely take but we must give as well; that if we are to go forward, we must move as a trained and loyal army willing to sacrifice for the good of common discipline, because without such discipline no progress is made, no leadership becomes effective. We are, I know, ready and willing to submit our

lives and property to such discipline, because it makes possible a leadership which aims at a larger good.[36]

Roosevelt led with the power of suggestion. He put the idea of altruism in people's heads and then called on them to act on it. He also asked them to help him personally. He told them that without their help, he couldn't be a good leader. Roosevelt was a good psychologist—he anticipated by decades something research psychologists eventually learned about altruistic motivation. When children have done something helpful or generous, telling them that they are *helpful people* disposes them to be helpful in the future. Praising or rewarding them doesn't evoke nearly so much altruism as leading them to believe they are altruistic. Adults respond the same way. When told they have "an altruistic personality," lo and behold, they rise to fit the label.[37] Roosevelt brought forth altruism by telling citizens they had it in them.

Politicians cultivate altruism (or don't) by the way they appeal to voters. During election campaigns, they not only put forth their beliefs and positions but, subtly, also instruct citizens how to choose between candidates and how to think about politics and elections. Late in the 1980 presidential campaign, Ronald Reagan told citizens, "As you go to the polls next Tuesday and make your choice for President, ask yourself these questions: Are you better off today than you were four years ago? Is it easier for you to go buy things in the store than it was four years ago?"[38] The civics lesson: choose your leaders on the basis of your material self-interest.

In 2006, Deval Patrick ran for governor of Massachusetts, filling his speeches with Good Samaritan allusions. He repeatedly "challenged" voters—his word—to "see your stake in your neighbor's dream." Like a preacher, he called people to their higher selves. He self-consciously joined politics to the religious values of generosity and tolerance. When he won the race, he told his supporters that *they* were the "real heroes" of the campaign. They were the ones who "confronted your despair about the direction our Commonwealth has been heading in, and decided to take responsibility for her future."

Swirling in the euphoria of his election-night victory celebration, Patrick wouldn't allow his supporters to rest on their past good deeds. "What I expect from you is that you keep this renewed sense of community alive; that you see your stake in each other every day; that you ask what you can do to make Massachusetts stronger and just do it." And Patrick didn't stop with exhortation. He instructed the good citizens on how to engage in politics now that the election was over: "Just as you have built bridges across differences to create this grassroots movement, go build bridges with supporters of the competing campaigns. They are our neighbors, too."[39]

6

Bonds and Bridges

In the 1950s and early 1960s, the world was still preoccupied with fascism and political scientists were focused on understanding why some nations developed strong democracies but others didn't. Unlike dictatorships and totalitarian forms of government, democracy requires citizens to participate in making laws and policies—to govern themselves. But before citizens would be ready to exercise this power, political scientists thought, they would have to hold certain beliefs about government and politics and certain ways of relating to their fellow citizens. Gabriel Almond and Sidney Verba coined the term *civic culture* as shorthand for these attitudes conducive to democracy.[1]

Almond and Verba proposed three essential elements of civic culture. First, citizens must believe that government will help them solve problems that are beyond their individual capacity to fix. If they don't see government as a path to betterment, they have no reason to participate in it. Second, they have to trust one another and believe that cooperating is the best way to solve social problems. This element is what Robert Putnam later named

social capital. And third, citizens must feel some duty to participate in political life and have confidence in their ability to influence what government does.

Everyday altruism, in addition to providing the energy and
motive for citizen participation, can instill two of these crucial
qualities: trust in fellow citizens and confidence in one's own
power. In this chapter, I explore how everyday altruism builds
trust and cooperation, or bonds and bridges. In Chapter 7, I
trace how it can promote the desire and confidence to participate in politics. I don't pretend for a minute that calling upon
altruism can address the first element of civic culture, faith in
government—not when civic and intellectual leaders disparage
government and wish it away. Their widespread cultural disdain
for government has sent many a citizen fleeing to community
service as an alternative to politics.[2] To counter this threat to
democracy, government has to reclaim its mission of helping
citizens. In Chapter 8, I sketch some principles and ideas for
doing that.

Making Friends of Strangers

People won't cooperate to solve their common problems unless
they feel something in common with strangers and those who
are outside their tribe or close circles. Social scientists have tried
to explain what creates this mysterious social glue, or inhibits it.
In one school of thought, social contact among diverse people
breaks down the sense of strangeness and fear, and fosters social
harmony. When diverse people live and work together and have

occasions to get to know each other, they become more tolerant of differences and grow to trust each other. In another darker view, diversity undermines social harmony and breeds conflict. When diverse people live and work together, they tend to feel themselves in competition for scarce resources, and so they band together with their own kind against the people they perceive as threats.

Hopes for an integrated, tolerant, and fair society depend—crucially—on the first theory being right. Yet try as they might, social scientists haven't managed to convince each other that life really works this way, despite hundreds of studies that seem to show that contact between diverse groups typically reduces prejudice. In 2007, Putnam unnerved everyone who hopes for tolerance with results from his survey of social capital in forty-one American communities. The greater the diversity in a community, Putnam found, the lower the levels of all things civically good: trust in one's neighbors; belief that neighbors will cooperate for the common good; confidence in local government, leaders, and the media; and confidence in one's ability to influence government. Diversity even lowered volunteering, giving to charity, and working on community projects. Diversity, it would seem, is bad for social capital.[3]

Before we get too discouraged, though, here's something to consider: Putnam measured diversity by looking at the proportions of different racial, national, and ethnic groups in census tracts. The makeup of a census tract tells us little about social contact. People might inhabit the same census tract (do you even know which one you live in?), but how do they encounter people from other groups? Do they meet as next-door neighbors or do they collide as obstacles in a crowded supermarket? Do they talk as parents of kids in their children's playgroup or do they sidle silently past each other as white collars and dark overalls in office buildings? Do they come into contact *at all* with people outside their social class or racial, ethnic, or national group? Census tracts don't tell us.

If we want to find out why and how people come to trust strangers, we should go to places where people encounter strangers more than superficially: soup kitchens, food pantries, nursing homes, homeless shelters, Habitat for Humanity, prisons, community health clinics and home health care, organ donation clinics, Big Brother/Big Sister programs, and community organizations. These are all places where people not only come in contact with strangers but contact of a special kind: help.

Karen Olson founded the National Interfaith Hospitality Network to involve churches in sheltering and feeding the homeless. By now, the network is a large organization with many member churches and thousands of individuals who volunteer within their churches to provide food and shelter. It's hard to fathom that there was ever a time when Olson didn't imagine homeless people as people she could relate to. She recalls two pivotal events that shaped her view of homeless people. As a child, while walking with her grandmother in New York City, she noticed a bedraggled man carrying his belongings in plastic bags. "Let's help him," she asked her grandmother. "No, leave him alone—people like that want to be that way," her grandmother replied. That event hardened her heart, she says. "It was easier to pass people by after that."

Years later, as an adult working in a corporate job, Olson saw a homeless woman sitting on a crate. On an impulse, she went across the street to a deli, bought the woman a sandwich, and sat down to talk with her. Olson sensed that the woman, Millie, was probably mentally ill, but as Millie talked about her children, Olson also sensed that "Millie was much like everyone else": she needed human contact even more than she needed a sandwich.[4]

In interview after interview, altruists often say they help others out of a sense of "common humanity." The person in need of help "could be my brother" or "is no different from me." When a ten-year-old boy got lost during a family vacation in New Hampshire, volunteer searchers poured into the state. Asked to explain why they joined the search for a stranger in the cold New Hampshire woods, many said that they empathized with the parents. "I have a daughter," said one woman. "I hope somebody would help me if my daughter were lost." Another volunteer said, "I'm a father. I was looking at the little boy on television. He looked like a great little boy and seeing his dad and mother, I couldn't sleep last night." A well-to-do man who volunteers with Habitat for Humanity building affordable houses identifies with the parents he helps: "Our world is so different but we both want exactly the same things. We want to provide a good life for our children, keep them safe, give them everything we can. When you spend time with people who at first appear different, you understand that the truth is that we're exactly the same." A man who cares for patients in a chronic-care hospital says, "You have to be human and understand that these people are like your father and mother. They are the same. And you have to treat them exactly the same. You have to think at every moment that this is your mother, this is your father." Or, as one rescuer of Jews during the Holocaust said decades later, "You should always be aware that every other person is basically you."[5]

Altruism often forges sudden human connections. "It's like a thunderstorm, quick and intense," explained a woman who volunteers with Habitat for Humanity. "The chances are that you'll never see most of these people again. But you have this immediate sense of relationship with them." Kidney donors can develop a powerful sense of kinship with their recipients. "It's like marrying someone you don't really know," said one donor. "I never had a brother. Now I do," said another.[6]

When students at a military college in Vermont began work on a documentary about soldiers who had died in Iraq, they were afraid to call the families for interviews. They expected to be "cursed at, yelled at, and hung up on," they told a reporter. They had no idea how to connect. "I was terrified," acknowledged one twenty-two year old. "I didn't know what to say. I asked my professor and he didn't know what to say either." By the time they'd finished, the students had bonded with twenty-five families. They came to know the servicemen and their friends, and they cried with the families. For their part, the parents of the fallen soldiers came to consider the students as friends and helpers. "They've been so respectful and loyal and protective of the families," said one soldier's stepmother. "They have helped assure all these families that our soldiers will not be forgotten, and no one else has been able to do that."[7]

In my interviews with home health nurses and aides, almost all of them told me they were trained "not to get too close" to patients. They would not be able to do their jobs if they felt emotionally involved, or so they were taught. Their supervisors constantly reminded them to "keep their distance," not to "get personal," not to share personal stories or give out their home telephone numbers, and most of all, not to become friends with their clients. And to a person, everyone who mentioned this professional dictum of paid caregiving retorted with something like, "But you just do. If you're human, you do." Or, as one woman put it, "You can't help it."

Home health care workers, in fact, do worse than become friends with clients. They come to feel like kin, and patients and their families often come to treat them like kin. Along with stories of getting close, home care workers frequently say of their clients, "I feel like she is my own mother" or grandmother or grandfather, father, brother, child. Home health clients frequently express the same warm sense of closeness, calling their caregivers "my best friend" or declaring, "I love her like my own daughter."

One spring, when I told the chair of my political science department about my plans for research on home health care, I expected him to question me about what home health care has to do with political science. Instead, he launched into a story. He said his mother had a home health aide for a long time before she died. At his mother's funeral, he insisted that the aide ride in the limousine with the family. "She was my mother's best friend, the most important person to her, and I wanted her to have a place of honor." We never got to the issue of how caregiving and politics might be connected.[8]

What goes on in the minds of helpers to bring about this intense connection and loyalty? The most lucid thought script I have found comes from Julie Salamon's book on generosity, *Rambam's Ladder*, in a letter she received from her cousin Jimmy. Once while Jimmy was waiting for the subway, a drunken man fell off the platform and landed between the tracks.

> Without thinking of the dangers involved, I threw away my newspaper, jumped down onto the tracks, pulled the man off the floor, and half threw him up to where others could grab him and hold on to him until I got to safety, too. . . . My behavior immediately after the heroics seemed to be very inconsistent and strange. I felt I needed to put my arm around the drunk and keep him from harming himself anew. I felt very strongly that I had to continue to protect this drunken man and shield him from others until I could sober him up and take him home. *It was as if I'd become responsible for him because I had saved him; giving him another chance bonded me to him in unlikely ways.* I thought I had acquired a new cousin or brother, and I clearly remember calculating how to include him as if he were a new member of my extended family.[9]

In some of the classic studies of altruism, a key determinant of whether people will spontaneously help others in trouble is whether they think their role assigns them responsibility. If an experimenter tells small children that they're "in charge" when she leaves the room, they are more likely than children who haven't been assigned responsibility to take action when they detect signs of distress—say, the sound of a child crying in another room.[10] Helping others, whether through rescues, volunteer work, caregiving, or teaching, can generate the sense of role responsibility without any formal assignment or exhortation. Once a person helps someone, they *become a helper in their own mind*; they adopt the role and continue it for the person they helped and, sometimes, for people like the person they helped. As with so much in altruism, the effects are circular. A sense of personal responsibility moves people to help others, but helping others enlarges the sense of personal responsibility for those one helps.

Of Shoes and Bridges

Helping others can easily generate bonds between people who see themselves as similar. But even the smallest communities are not homogeneous, so to function well, they also need bridges between people who see themselves as different.

Research on altruism and helping is clear: People are more helpful to their own kind, to others whom they perceive as members of their "in-group." They are more likely to offer help to a stranger who is demographically similar to them. Even superficial differences matter. People more readily respond to a request for money from someone who is well dressed than from someone shabbily dressed, and they are more generous toward people whom they believe share their opinions on the most trivial of issues.[11] The same holds true for donating money and volunteering time to charities, and even for informal giving and caring. People tend to give their money and their time to their family and friends first, then to organizations that serve their family and friends and people like their family and friends. Only a tiny portion of everyday help and charity goes to people remote from our experience.[12]

If a sense of shared humanity stimulates empathy and a willingness to help others, creating that sense is one of the most important things we can do to promote neighborliness. It becomes important to know what kinds of experiences move people from thinking like Karen Olson's grandmother ("They want to be like that") to thinking like the grown-up Olson ("Millie was much like everyone else").

Strikingly, the very act of helping someone dissolves the sense of "they" and generates a powerful sense of "we." Although people are more likely to offer help to others whom they regard as similar to themselves, once help gets started, it creates a special kind of relationship that often connects people, even across great class and cultural distances. Helping others, altruists say, breaks down their own stereotypes and gives them direct personal experiences from which they can draw their own conclusions.

In a Washington, D.C. high school, students had the chance to work in a local soup kitchen and reflect on their experiences in class.[13] In their writings and class discussions, the students explained how their contact with homeless people changed the way they regarded and acted with them. "Before I used to just think that they were on drugs or, you know, alcohol; lost their job or something. Now they're homeless," said one. Another student reported, "I've changed. My outlook has changed as far as taking a moral stand." She and her friends used to make fun of a homeless woman in their neighborhood, she said, but "if they did that, I would say something now." Several students recounted that they had become more tolerant of rude behavior or insults. "When I was sweeping the floor, some guy picked up my broom and spit on it because he claims I ran over his foot. I just let it go." An alumnus of the program wrote, "Before going [to the soup kitchen], I always thought of homeless people as being dumb, uneducated, dirty individuals. After meeting with some of them, I realized that most of them did not want to be homeless or come to a soup kitchen. Most of them I talked with were college graduates, young mothers, and everyday people just like everybody else."

The students wondered why diners at the soup kitchen were sometimes mean, rude, or hostile, and in their class discussions, they tried to understand by identifying with homeless people. "Because they don't know any better," suggested one student. "Because everybody talks about them and puts them down," suggested another. "I guess I feel like I'd lose a little bit of pride having to be served at a soup kitchen," offered another. And another guessed, "I think they're frustrated because some of them feel that nobody's there to help them." Listening in on these student conversations, one imagines them trying on other people's lives as they'd try on different outfits at the Gap, assessing how each one feels and looks. Just as they might see themselves differently in different clothes, they saw homeless people differently as they dressed them in different explanations. Helping in a soup kitchen got the students to put themselves in homeless people's shoes.

Psychologists have learned something fascinating about how taking another person's perspective builds bridges. When we consciously try to understand how another person feels, we begin to attribute some of our own thoughts and feelings to the other person. Curiously, it doesn't matter whether we tell ourselves to imagine how *the other person* feels or to imagine how *we* would feel in the other person's situation. Either way, we end up ascribing our own traits to the other. We see ourselves in them, or them in us, and—here is the magic—we like them better and we judge them more favorably. This is how taking the perspective of others reduces stereotyping and biases.[14]

Helping others puts people in a very good position to take others' perspective. Community service, volunteer work, and even informal everyday altruism bring people from different social groups into close proximity. More than proximity, though, these situations tend to dissolve barriers because both helper and helped feel vulnerable. People who need help feel helpless and frightened because they need help; they're not sure whether they can trust these strangers who purport to help them. People who are trying to help—like the high school students in the soup kitchen—feel helpless and frightened for different reasons. They might feel ignorant about the strangers and uncomfortable around them, they're not sure how to help, and whatever knowledge and skills serve them in their own worlds aren't much good to them in this strange new world. Both helper and helped use their imaginations, as the high school students did, to get inside the other's skin. Perspective-taking is an exercise in imagination, and helping gives people a lot of practice.

Some kinds of strangers live among us, in plain view. After she had a stroke, May Sarton rued, "The trouble is, old age is not interesting until one gets there. It's a foreign country with an unknown language to the young and even to the middle aged." Julie Salamon, not yet having arrived in that country herself, had the same inkling: "The elderly poor represent a different kind of stranger. They are not 'us,' but rather who we might become, or who we might have been."[15] In a sense, every kind of vulnerability is a foreign land to people who have not experienced it. Caregiving and helping can be like a journey into one of those lands. Caring for others teaches us something of what it might be like to be different from who we are now—somebody old, young, sick, poor, illiterate, vulnerable, or trapped in a body one can't control. Through tending such people, caregivers learn to anticipate needs and they gain up-close knowledge of how it feels to be needy and dependent.

During one of my stints in Germany, I had a colleague who, like many men of his generation, had done community service in lieu of military service. Many of the community service jobs entailed caring for people with disabilities; his job had been caring for a boy with Down syndrome. My colleague told me that before that job, he could not have imagined having a severely disabled child, and that he and his wife would have chosen abortion if they learned she carried a severely disabled child. After his alternative service, he said, he was no longer afraid, and although he didn't hope for a child with Down syndrome, he was confident that raising one would be rewarding, that he and his wife would be up to the task, and that the child could have a worthwhile life.

Like caregiving, one-to-one volunteer work can build bridges between people who at first seem profoundly different. While helping people who are stigmatized, despised, foreign, feared, needy, lonely, or in any way trapped in a society they can't influence, volunteers learn something of what it might be like to be "that kind of person" instead of who they are, and what it feels like to be powerless in just that way.

A nine-year-old girl from a privileged, white suburban family explained to psychiatrist Robert Coles how everyday altruism had changed her mother's perceptions of people from Roxbury, a mostly low-income black neighborhood in Boston. The girl's sister had been treated for leukemia, and in the hospital, their mother met the mother of a black girl who was also getting chemotherapy. When the white mother learned how the black woman and her daughter struggled to reach the hospital on public transportation, she began driving them. Here is how the nine-year-old told Coles about the stereotype-busting she was picking up: "[My mother] goes all the way to Roxbury to help that family; they've become her friends. . . . She loves going to those people; she drives them to the hospital and she waits, and then she drives them back. She says she talks with them better than [with] anyone. Daddy is scared because of the neighborhood, but Mom says the people are very nice to her." Later, sharing more of her mother's newfound wisdom, the little girl added, "The lady has helped us a lot, too, Mom says—she has a lot of faith in God and she teaches you a lesson, that you can be poor and have a good soul."[16]

Like all bridges, this one went two ways, as Coles found out when he interviewed the black mother. "There are white folks who *care*, there really are," she repeated again and again, as if, Coles put it, she were "confronting an incredulity earned through the grim lessons of a lifetime." Surely, the empathy of their shared trauma brought them together in conversation. But it was the concrete acts of help—the driving back and forth, the conversations in the car, the trips through Roxbury alone and to-gether—that enabled the two women to see from each other's vantage point and, ultimately, build a bridge.

If even the casual altruism of giving rides can lead people to confront their incredulities, what of more concerted altruism? In

Coles's interviews with college students who tutor inner-city children through Big Brother/Big Sister programs, a common theme emerges. They see themselves as trying to make a connection between their middle-class worlds and the children's less privileged worlds. They hope to build a bridge, then entice the children to cross over it into a world where kids aspire to college, good jobs, and fulfilling lives.

As one young woman told Coles:

> When I first started teaching, I thought that if I could just go back a little to my own childhood and draw on it, then I'd make the connections I needed to make, and things would go well. But once I'd started going to the homes, it sunk in that these kids had to cross lots of bridges to get to me and my childhood, never mind me now. You can read a lot of books about "the culturally deprived child," but when you're sitting on a couch in a ghetto apartment building, looking and listening and wondering and worrying, then it's another story.[17]

Another tutor, a college student named Gary, also saw his work as bridge building. "A lot of what I'll tell him [his Little Brother, Juan] and his buddies—it's what my dad told me, and my mom, and her dad. Basically I'm trying to connect those kids with the middle-class world I come from. . . . I don't know how you persuade someone who is a stranger, except for an hour or two a week, to dream about a different life and then go to work to try to get there. But underneath it all, that's what should be happening between Juan and me." Gary was well aware of the long odds that Juan would make it over the bridge. He used his growing understanding of Juan's world to modify his strategies for helping Juan. "I've got to be as sensitive as can be—as *clever.* I don't mean to sound like a con artist, but you have to figure out how to do an end run around all of the enemies—everything that is pulling down, down, down on that kid's life."[18]

Those Who Need Help Erect Bridges

If there were ever a place where strangers shouldn't become friends, prisoner-of-war camps are it. POW camps spring into existence at times when enemies feel severely threatened by each other. As we know all too well from Abu Ghraib and Guantánamo, captors can easily lose their grip on the humanity of their captives.

Historian Allen Koop saw something quite different in Camp Stark, a World War II camp for German POWs in northern New Hampshire. Both captors and captives had been thrown together in a remote, harsh place. "None had chosen to come to Camp Stark or to have Camp Stark in their village. Someone else decided all this for them. They were little people, *kleine Leute,* caught in forces beyond their control. The apparent capriciousness of a war that so easily tossed about individual lives, regardless of which side they were on, could nourish empathy between victor and victim."[19]

At Camp Stark, the prisoners were forced to cut lumber for a nearby paper company. As the sun was setting one frigid afternoon, an American guard sat on a log while his young German prisoner worked a two-man saw to finish his daily quota of lumber. The work was going slowly, because a second prisoner who was supposed to man the other end of the saw had been called to another job. The guard was from Vermont, knew the climate and the work of logging, and knew how long he and his prisoner would be there if the work continued at its slow pace. "He looked at the struggling German and his wobbling saw, and suddenly could stand the sight no longer. He put down his rifle, walked over, and grabbed the other end of the saw."[20] Everything about these two men should have made them enemies. Their common predicament made them allies.

The German prisoners helped their American guards as well. Mechanics who had worked on tanks in the German army repaired the camp's trucks and tractors, even as that meant they and their comrades would have to resume their hard labor at logging. Cigarettes were rationed for American civilians; the German prisoners, with plentiful supplies through the prisoners' canteen, frequently gave cigarettes, packs, and even cartons to their civilian foremen. Once, when an American dozed off while he was supposed to be guarding the prisoners, the prisoners halted their talking to let him sleep. By helping each other through their joint misery, the German and American enemies acted like friends and became friends.

Vulnerability is the other side of help, and it makes people shed judgments and standards that they can no longer afford to hold. Tony, a rescuer of Jews during the Holocaust, was from a well-to-do upper-middle-class Dutch family. During the war, he formed a small raggle-taggle resistance unit, and in 1941 he was condemned to death by the Germans. A friend told him that if he ever needed sudden refuge, he should get to the red-light district because the prostitutes would always hide resisters. "And they would," Tony told political scientist Kristen Renwick Monroe.

"They were risking a death penalty for that. But these women would always hide you. They were the people whom I had looked down on socially before that. And I ended up working with a variety of much lower-class people than I would ever have associated with in my previous existence. That was a great eye-opener, to find that these people were in no way different."[21]

More recently, in a Massachusetts gay-rights controversy, help built some unlikely bridges. As the state senate was considering a ballot question on banning gay marriage, Senator Gale Candaras received several letters from constituents who said that they had changed their minds over the years and hoped she would, too. Candaras had voted for a ban earlier, but became one of nine senators who switched positions in 2007, sending the proposal down to defeat. One elderly woman began her letter acknowledging that she had previously asked Candaras to vote for the ban. "But since then," the woman wrote, "this lovely couple, these two men, moved in next door to me, and they have a couple of children and they're married, and they help me with my lawn. And if they can't be married in Massachusetts, they're going to leave—and then who would help me with my lawn?"[22]

Vulnerability shows us our common humanity, and help makes it real. When we need help and others offer it, nothing about their beliefs, lifestyles, or personal traits matters a whit. What matters to us is not "Who are they?" but "Who will help me?" Everyday need and everyday help are the great equalizers and connectors.

7

The Moment of Power

At first glance, everyday altruism, volunteerism, and community service seem to be outside the sphere of politics, and that is indeed how most people think. But at the core of every personal act of help there's a political moment—the moment when someone changes the world for somebody else and feels empowered. Stimulating everyday altruism may be the most important thing government can do to foster civic engagement.

In a fatalistic culture where people think nothing they do can possibly change their circumstances, they have little reason to put effort into politics. Even if their political system offers them opportunities, even if they believe governance is a worthwhile endeavor, and even if they trust their neighbors to cooperate for common ends, before they will participate in government, they have to believe they could have some influence. Without this faith in their capacity to make a difference, democratic politics doesn't leave the station.

We can get some idea of how people come to feel empowered by observing children, for they are the least-powerful citizens. Not having the vote pales in comparison to not being a grown-up. It turns out that helping others is the one experience guaranteed to empower kids. When Esmé Codell started her first teaching job in a New York City elementary school, she discovered that most of her fifth graders couldn't read because they hadn't yet mastered the alphabet. In order to teach them without humiliating them, she told them they were going to help the first-grade teacher teach first graders. She made each fifth grader responsible for teaching one letter; together, the fifth-grade class created an "alphabet zoo" and brought it to the first-grade classroom. Told they were the big, all-knowing teachers, the fifth graders rose to the occasion. They taught their letters and, while teaching, learned to read.[1]

Everyday altruism, volunteering, and community service put people in a position to help others. And no matter how people find their way into the role of helper, being in the role empowers them. The experience can transform even people who are already powerful by any conventional standard. Jeffrey Swartz heads the Timberland Company, a one billion-dollar footwear and apparel manufacturer. City Year is a youth service corps for seventeen to twenty-four-year-olds in Boston. When the head of City Year asked Swartz to donate fifty pairs of work boots, instead of just delivering the boots, Swartz stayed to help paint a drug rehab facility. Then, he says, "I went back to my office and sat at my desk thinking I had glimpsed power that I had never conceived of in business school or any corporate setting. The power I felt was that of a concerned citizen who could do something to help."[2] From that epiphany, Swartz got the idea of using his corporate leadership to stimulate altruism, and Timberland now runs a variety of volunteer service programs for its employees.

How Helping Empowers Citizens

When a thirty-year-old assembly-line worker first thought about volunteering in a nursing home, he couldn't imagine how he could possibly help the residents. But he had a friend whose father had lived in the nursing home, and who had told him that "the only good thing" about the place was the volunteer visitors. After the father died, the friend decided to continue visiting other patients as a memorial to his father. "So that was how we got started," the worker explained to Robert Coles. "He talked to me and I said yes, and he and I went to this nursing home, and we told them we aren't anyone special, but we like to have fun, and we could try to give the folks in there a good time." As is so often true with beginning volunteers, this man didn't think he had much to offer, but he learned by sheer dint of doing what he could offer and why it mattered. "We could bring them some cookies and we can sing . . . and we could always read from the papers, if someone was blind or had the shakes and couldn't hold the paper steady. They were glad we came, too."[3]

This story contains all the elements of how altruism empowers people. Because volunteer visitors were part of the nursing home's landscape, patients' relatives saw volunteers in action. Seeing how volunteers perked up the patients' lives, a son drew a lesson: even though he was powerless to keep his father alive, he might be able to enliven other people's days. He grabbed a friend for support. The two buddies didn't think of themselves as "anyone special," but out of a strong desire to do some good, they drew on what subjectively paltry resources they had—being able to sing and read, and asking their wives to bake cookies. And almost as soon as they started, they felt their own impact.

Dottie Barnes, a diminutive seventy-two-year-old, was out walking around her Florida condo when she heard screams and then saw an alligator dragging one of her neighbors toward a retention pond. Barnes grabbed the woman by the ankles and pulled her from the water, but not before the alligator had swallowed the woman's forearm. Insisting she hadn't done anything special, she told a reporter, "I think you're given strength when you need it."[4] Barnes's faith is more than a charming story. It's also a metaphor for the mysterious way people find mental and physical strength when they help others.

Adrenaline may explain the physical surge people feel in rescue situations, but how do we explain the emotional strength, the sudden ability to deal with new situations under extraordinary stress? Donna Frylinger, a social worker who has worked with addicts, abused children and battered women, sees helping as a kind of role-playing: "When you're in a position of helping someone else out, you tend to take the stronger-type role. When you are dealing with someone who is trying to get away from their husband, and they can't think, you sort of have to do the thinking for them."[5]

Seen in this light, the two nursing-home volunteers didn't believe they had any ability to help residents, but having thrust themselves into the role of helper, they suspended disbelief and played the part. Urgency, compassion, or both push people to improvise, to depart from the scripts they know. The urge to help leads people to take initiative. Hmm . . . sound familiar?

Isn't this exactly what self-interest is supposed to do—move people to action and stimulate them to innovate? But we're talking altruism here. I'll say it again: self-interest is not the only source of creative energy.

All helpers are figuratively rescuers. When they see someone desperate, about to go under, they don't think about what they *can't* do. They do what they can and hope it works. Gary, a college student and volunteer Big Brother, tried to save his Little Brother, Juan, from a bleak future by sermonizing about his own values and life philosophy. Gary's lectures came out so strong that he wasn't sure he believed them himself, he confessed to his faculty adviser, Robert Coles. "I'll tell him that he's fighting for his life and that if he doesn't watch out, he'll end up drowning. You may think I'm stepping outside my bounds," Gary went on a little sheepishly, aware that Coles was a seasoned psychiatrist. "I'm only nineteen years old, and I'm a history major and I've never even taken a psychology course. But when someone is floundering, and you're afraid he's going to go under, then you sure try your damnedest to throw out every lifesaver you can think of." Feeling that he was the only bystander, Gary empowered himself by making mental lifesavers to toss to Juan.[6]

There's a certain irony here. Current social policy aims to strengthen the weakest and poorest citizens by exhorting them to help themselves. Be responsible for yourself. Take care of yourself. Acquire the skills and work habits necessary to support yourself and your family. In a world where self-interest is the main human motive, self-help might be a straight route to empowerment. But in a world where altruism is a strong human motive, helping others may empower people far more effectively.

Making a Difference

Large organizations and big policies move slowly, in baby steps. For democracy to succeed, citizens need realistic expectations and a healthy dose of patience. If they expect to achieve big changes quickly, they will inevitably feel disappointed and disillusioned when they fail. And if failure confirms their sense of futility and powerlessness, they will withdraw from politics.

Helping others shows people the power of incrementalism. When altruists talk about the satisfactions they get from helping others, one of the most common phrases they use, up there with "I get more than I give," is "making a difference." They seem to mean it in a mathematical sense—a measurable, if tiny, difference between two states of affairs. For the home health aides I interviewed, the difference between a sad face and smile counted as a big accomplishment, a measure of their efficacy.

While spending her spring break in New Orleans cleaning up after Katrina, Molly Hercules, then a high school sophomore, told a reporter, "I am so tired. And we haven't even done much! But I know how much this kind of help really changes the people's lives."[7] I did not make up her name, but I wish I had. What could be more poetic than a fifteen-year-old girl discovering that to the people she helped, her puny strength equaled the power of her mythical namesake?

Molly Hercules experienced another paradox of altruism: "We haven't even done much," but "What I did changes people's lives." The mind of an altruist is a mind of comparison. Poised among people and places where need seems infinite, altruists can't help but compare the immensity of the problems to the smallness of the fixes they and their organizations can offer. Altruists stand within sight of overwhelming disaster, but they also stand face-to-face with individuals who bear their own particular particles of trouble. From their dual vantage points, would-be altruists might see success or they might see failure—a big difference or a drop in the bucket.

As president of the American Red Cross, Elizabeth Dole saw the big difference. In her resignation speech, she told her staff what the work had meant to her. "I've stood by your side in Florida as we braced for Hurricane Andrew. I've cradled a gaunt Rwandan baby in my arms. And I've sat with our men and women in uniform, far from home and loved ones, as they kept the peace in Bosnia. I have seen things that will haunt me the rest of my life. But I've been able to make a difference for people with dire human needs. This has been more than a job to me."[8]

By contrast, a college junior who tutored inner-city children in Boston saw the drop in the bucket. He taught fifth-grade math, took his students on field trips, brought them to his college campus to eat, and showed them a world beyond theirs. Sometimes when he took the big view, he mused that he might be more effective if instead of tutoring and mentoring, he became "a political organizer, something like that—try to change whole system. . . . What they do seems exciting for a while: fighting against lead poisoning, or dangerous stairways, or rats all over the place, or not enough heat in the winter. But you know, it's like a drop in the bucket: this is a neighborhood of thousands of people and they're locked in." Yet this student persisted with his small steps—he continued tutoring and mentoring his kids two days a week, and apparently gleaned huge satisfactions from his students' school successes and their heightened aspirations.[9]

Altruistic work is like the optical illusion in which you see either a vase or two faces, but you cannot see them both at the same time. No doubt most volunteers sometimes see the big difference, sometimes the insignificant droplet, yet, for the most part, they are able to keep a dual perspective. Especially when they work one-to-one, they see from the perspective of a single suffering person what a big change a little gesture achieves. One-to-one volunteerism can be so vital to engaging citizens in politics because it builds a bridge from despair to hope.

One-to-one altruism can empower people at the bottom of a bureaucratic hierarchy. In any service organization, white-collar administrators set policy, dictate the terms of everyone else's work, and preside over big decisions, yet the people in scrubs, overalls, and work uniforms actually deliver the services to clients. To the client, the staff person at the bottom of an organization is all-powerful. The caseworker, the intake clerk, the cop on the beat, the kitchen worker with the soup ladle in her hand—these are the people who determine what the client gets, or doesn't. Viewed from the penthouse office, their day-to-day discretionary decisions seem trivial. On the ground, the scope of their power looms large.[10]

"Have you ever considered the power you have?" Bethany Knight asks in her inspirational daybook for nurses' aides. In the formal hierarchy of nursing homes, aides are at the bottom. Their pay is abysmal, their workloads are impossible, and they are bound to follow somebody else's orders in most everything they do for patients. Yet Knight, herself an aide, understands how the helping relationship between aides and patients reverses the bureaucratic chain of command and makes the person at the bottom the most powerful rather than the least. "Do you realize that most of the people you work with would not and could not exist without you? Lying in their beds, or slumped in their chairs, they await your arrival. Just going to the bathroom is something they cannot do without you. . . . In their little still lives, you are the scenery that goes by. You are the beautiful view. You are the proof that life goes on."[11]

One could read this passage as a bit of power tripping, but judging from my own interviews with nurses' aides, I read it differently. In medical institutions, aides are considered the least-knowledgeable, least-skilled people in the system and, therefore, the least qualified to exercise discretion, let alone any significant decision-making power. Helping people who can't do simple things for themselves teaches aides that they do have both resources and power to do something significant for others. Those "others" become their barometer of significance, and this is the most important lesson in efficacy. Efficacy doesn't—can't—mean that aides restore people to the full strength and abilities of their younger or pre-disabled selves. It does—and must—mean that they improve the quality of their patients' lives, bit by small bit.

To feel oneself as politically effective requires exactly this kind of dual perspective on social needs and personal power. If citizens define personal influence as ridding the world of whatever problem they want to fix, they will miss their mark and likely despair. If, however, they define it as improving the quality of other people's lives—not everybody's but some people's—they open themselves to knowing their power. Helping others, no matter how unpolitical the work may be on the surface, instills this rudimentary appreciation for incrementalism, for what one person can do, sometimes alone, sometimes in concert, but always for someone else.

This same appreciation for the incremental makes political activists tick. Robert Coles was once asked to testify about the mental health of a young civil rights worker who had been arrested for trying to eat in a whites-only restaurant. Coles kept pressing Dion Diamond to explain what sort of satisfactions he derived from his political organizing. "You know what?" Diamond launched into one of his many riffs. "You look at those cops now—they've begun to respect us. They don't give us that big belly laugh anymore, they don't spit at us or sneer at us. They look real serious when they follow us around. And the other day, I couldn't believe it, one of them, he nodded at me and two of my buddies when we came out of the store. It was as if—well, hey, we sure do know each other! I thought I saw just the beginning of a smile on his face—just the start of one. You want to know why I do this work? To see that look on that cop's face."[12]

A nod. A smile. A look. Altruism and political activism come together in this simple human capacity to detect small differences in people's faces and to connect those differences to one's own efforts. Diamond suggested another way of seeing something large in something small:

I'm hearing [people] stop and think about what they're willing to do to change this world here in Louisiana. Isn't that enough—Isn't that a good reason to feel satisfied? If you can spend some of your life doing work like this, then you're lucky! There may be a sheriff out there waiting for me with a gun, but if he gets me, I'll die thinking: Dion, you actually *did* something—you were part of something much bigger than yourself, and you saw people beginning to change, right before your eyes, and that was a real achievement, and that's what I mean by "satisfaction."[13]

"Being part of something bigger" is another of those phrases, almost clichés, that pepper the language of altruism. On the personal level, altruists use this phrase to express their quest for meaning beyond the blip of a lifetime. On the political level, feeling part of something bigger is exactly what democracy asks of its citizens. Democracy asks you to vote not because your one vote might swing the election, but because if you plan to vote, you're likely to inform yourself about the candidates and their positions, and if you do that, you're going to put some thought into what kind of community you have and would like to have, and you're probably going to talk with your friends and neighbors about it, too. The popular vote empowers citizens not by the weight of one vote but by getting citizens to feel their significance as part of something bigger.

How Does Personal Empowerment Become Political?

Social scientists overwhelmingly agree: people who volunteer participate more in politics.[14] But how exactly does volunteering in a nonpolitical setting nudge people into politics? The scholars agree on that question, too. Associations provide people with the skills and knowledge to engage in politics. In these group settings, people learn how to speak in public, write letters and reports, conduct themselves in meetings, negotiate and compromise, manage and administer, and participate in group decision making. They pick up information about how organizations work and about public affairs. Most of all they learn how to cooperate with other people to get things done. Associations in effect hand people a toolbox for citizenship and give them practice using the tools.[15]

Everyday altruism suggests that toolboxes are not the primary reason volunteering leads to political engagement. Helping others engages the heart. The poignancy of helping relationships excites emotions, passions, and moral ideals. A toolbox surely *enables* people to participate in politics and feel confident that they know how to use a hammer, but personal altruism makes them *want* to bang the hammers.

Early in my research on home health care, an agency director suggested I sit in on some case conferences to get a feel for the whole business. During my first conference, the nurses, physical therapists, and aides began discussing a fifty-one-year-old patient who had recently been in a car accident that left her quadriplegic. Her husband was now caring for her full-time, and the couple was overwhelmed with everything from her bowel incontinence and transferring her in and out of a wheelchair to keeping their small business going. The woman had received three home care visits since she had come home from the rehab hospital. The couple had begged the agency for more help, but their insurer wouldn't pay. The head therapist had called the woman's insurer to get more care authorized, she told the group, but the insurer's gatekeeper refused, saying that because the woman was never going to regain any physical control, "all their problems are just emotional now."

The rage was palpable. The home care staff saw the insurance company as flagrantly unjust. "They paid for insurance," one person said, "and if they have insurance policies, it's their right to get help." Someone suggested that the woman "should be encouraged to call the governor." They discussed "other resources" the woman might use, ticking off federal and state government programs. They asked themselves over and over, "Is there anything?" As the talk progressed, the staff became more and more outraged. Finally, one nurse blurted out, "Well, I'm screwed. I am going to go see her as a friend. And if I happen to have some things in my pocket . . ." She let her thought trail, but the silence was quickly interrupted by a therapist: "Yeah, that's what *I* told them. 'I shop at Market Basket. You need something? Tell me. Give me your list.'"

It wasn't until I went over my notes from the meeting that I noticed the nurse's grammar. Not "*She's* screwed," but "*I'm* screwed." Each of the home care staff could have visited the paraplegic woman no more than three times, yet they had already become so tightly attached to her that they were ready to fight. From an initial therapeutic relationship with the woman and her husband, the agency staff transformed their connection into a political alliance. They fought the insurer on the couple's behalf (unsuccessfully, but they tried). They looked to government programs for other sources of assistance. They announced that they were ready to break some agency rules to continue helping the couple on their own time. (Their supervisor, the director of nursing, chaired this meeting. She didn't bat an eyelash when the staff rebelled.) These clinical caregivers saw themselves as instigators, encouraging the woman to exercise her political voice by calling the governor. What happened in that meeting can only be described as an uprising.

Everyday altruism gives helpers new glasses, so to speak. Whether as a onetime spontaneous act, as part of a job, or as volunteer work, helping places people in the midst of trouble, and although they carry their own interpretive frameworks with them, interacting with the people they help often challenges those frameworks. In Karen Olson's National Interfaith Hospitality Network, local coalitions of religious congregations take turns feeding and sheltering their community's homeless people. Within each church or synagogue, members volunteer to staff these programs. "Many of our volunteers become advocates," Olson said, continuing to explain why: "They look at the problems and begin to see causes. The program changes how they read the newspapers, how they think, how they vote." One of the local program directors elaborated on this process: "The experience of working with the homeless causes many volunteers to ask questions about why the problem exists and what can be done to get at its roots. Volunteering can have a troubling impact. It starts people thinking."[16]

Some students of democracy see a tension between personal altruism and vigorous democratic politics. Community service, they worry, focuses people on one-to-one helping as their mode of contributing to society, and misleads them into believing that if every person only did his or her part, social problems would be solved. This individual focus unwittingly masks the need for large-scale collective efforts and government action. Too much emphasis on personal helping distracts citizens' attention from the larger political and economic causes of social problems, and keeps them from challenging the status quo.[17]

Other critics say that volunteer work and community service are valuable for alleviating human suffering, but they fail to build citizenship skills or strengthen democracy. The large membership groups that once did this job have almost disappeared from the political landscape. Instead of joining the local Boy and Girl Scouts, the Grange, or fraternal organizations, Americans now participate in politics largely by writing checks to distant advocacy groups such as the Children's Defense Fund or the Sierra Club. According to political scientist Theda Skocpol, community service is no substitute for these older schools of citizenship: "Volunteer efforts . . . are usually professionally coordinated sporadic or one-shot undertakings. They involve people in 'doing for' others—feeding the needy at a church soup kitchen; tutoring children at an after-school clinic; or guiding visitors at a museum exhibit—rather than 'doing with' fellow citizens. Important as such volunteering may be, it cannot substitute for the central citizenship functions that membership federations performed." Moreover, Skocpol says, volunteers "do not form as many reciprocal ties; they are normally not elected to leadership posts"; and they do not usually experience the "sense of brotherhood or sisterhood and shared American citizenship" that older membership organizations provided.[18]

Nothing could be further from the truth of everyday altruism. When people help others, they tend to form intense ties and bonds of loyalty, often far more powerful than those they form with their fellow members of a local club. Today's everyday altruists may not speak of brotherhood and sisterhood, but they do use the language of "common humanity," and they commonly say that they feel like the people they help *are*, or *are like*, brothers, sisters, mothers, and fathers.

The intimacy of helping relationships between people who are superficially different often makes them feel their sameness viscerally, as we saw in Chapter 6. Their ties may not be reciprocal in a strict quid pro quo sense, but reciprocity rings loudly in the near-universal refrain, "I get more than I give." And although volunteers may not hold traditional leadership posts, they lead themselves by figuring it out as they go along: "We're not anyone special, but we can sing and bring cookies and read the papers."

Individual altruism has a way of growing into something more organized and, often, something more political. Individual acts often become magnets for other people, spurring a kind of spontaneous organization. A personal gesture, such as Karen Olson's buying a sandwich for a homeless women, can be the first step to building an organization. And individual altruists often come to see the individuals they help as victims of a systemic problem, prompting them to move from helping individuals to becoming advocates for an issue.

Economists are fond of saying that investment has a "multiplier effect." A loan to a start-up business creates new construction jobs, then more jobs for new employees. With paychecks in hand, these new employees can afford to buy more goods and services, stimulating growth of other local businesses (or at least so it was in the days before global outsourcing and Internet shopping).

When altruists act, they set in motion a similar multiplier effect. When one person stops to help, other people might stop in simple imitation. "Oh, yes, I should (or could) do that, too." Daniel Goleman was descending a concrete staircase at rush hour in the New York City subway. A disheveled, half-dressed man had collapsed and was lying motionless and unaware. People stepped over him, but no one stopped to help. Goleman stopped, and suddenly others, seeing him, stopped to help, too. One person fetched water, another fetched food, another summoned a subway patrol.[19]

Often people start a project to help others and then recruit help from their friends. Eddie Tuduri, the injured rock drummer who turned his passion into a rehabilitation program for people with developmental disabilities, built his program by recruiting his percussion-playing friends. "He didn't have to twist my arm," one friend said. "He just told me about it and I saw what he was doing and I said, 'Count me in.'" Pretty soon, Tuduri's former bandmates were drumming in rehab centers and fund-raisers. At age eleven, Amber Coffman started a Saturday-afternoon sandwich delivery to homeless people, with the help of her mother as a driver. Eventually, she had ten or twelve kids making bologna and cheese sandwiches in her apartment every weekend and local businesses donating drinks, fruit, and other items. Her "Happy Helpers" program, as she named it, inspired chapters in other cities.[20]

Right after September 11, Stephen Jay Gould with his wife and stepdaughter organized a makeshift supply depot "to collect and ferry needed items in short supply, including face masks and shoe inserts, to the workers at ground zero." At first, Gould felt despair at the gulf between his family's efforts and the enormity of the disaster. But the depot caught on and grew into a major distribution center: "Word spreads like a fire of goodness and people stream in, bringing gifts from a pocketful of batteries to a $10,000 purchase of hard hats, made on the spot at a local supply house and delivered right to us."[21]

Help multiplies by the power of example, of course, but there's something more than modeling or even networking going on here. The Gould family and Karen Olson, the founder of the National Interfaith Hospitality Network, all made paths for others to follow. They were altruistic entrepreneurs. They created jobs for altruists and gave them on-the-job training. They made altruism easy. "People in churches will respond if they're given a program they're comfortable with," noted one founder of a local program in Olson's network. "Most people are more comfortable on their own turf, in their own church. The volunteers can reach out in a way that is comfortable, convenient, and non-threatening."[22]

Altruistic entrepreneurs create channels and reservoirs for everyday altruism. As Karen Olson puts it, "There is a hunger in people's hearts to help others. Compassion is alive and well in America. But people are busy—they need vehicles." Dr. Jack MacConnell had no trouble staffing the free medical clinic he established in Hilton Head, South Carolina, because his clinic provided "an outlet for the reservoir of good will people have for others in need. Give people a spot where they can help and they'll come running."[23]

Organizations grow out of everyday altruism in a very different way from how political science imagines organization-building. Traditionally, political scientists have assumed that people learn to build and run organizations through civic education courses and participation in clubs and other organizations. They learn, for example, how to run a meeting according to Robert's Rules of Order, and they learn to be comfortable with organizational rituals and procedures, the rules and rigidities, the ways of divvying up tasks and following directions, delegating, coordinating, and leading.[24]

People do sometimes draw on learned skills when they wish to expand their own passion to help into something larger. But often, they wing it, approaching the problem pragmatically, step-by-step, even sometimes consciously avoiding traditional modes of organization, which they see as obstacles rather than solutions. They start with a small gesture and multiply it into something original, rather than joining an existing organization as one more pair of helping hands.

When Agnes Stevens retired from teaching, she decided to volunteer as a tutor in a public school with many homeless children. One day two brothers told her they hadn't learned to read because they were traveling so much they hadn't been able to stay in one school. That put Stevens face-to-face with a problem neither the school nor she had noticed, and gave her the idea to bring schooling to homeless children, rather than catching them hit-or-miss inside a public school. If the children were on the move, she realized, then their schooling needed to be mobile, too. She and a friend went to Memorial Park in Santa Monica, befriended a five-year-old homeless girl, and started to work with her right there on a park bench. The little girl soon brought other homeless families with her, and Stevens and her friend recruited more tutors to come with them. Eventually, out of this one-to-one beginning, "Schools on Wheels" brought hundreds of volunteer tutors to shelters in many communities.[25]

Sometimes organization grows into political advocacy. Helping people who have a particular kind of need makes people notice "that kind of problem." The more you see, the more you see, and then, as one student said of her community service experience, "Once you see the issues, you feel compelled to do something and not just be part of the system."[26] Seeing many people with the same problems again and again prompts helpers to think in terms of systemic causes rather than individual responsibility.

There has not been much research into how volunteering affects the political attitudes of adults, but among students, studies are legion and the results compelling. Young people who participate in community service are more likely to believe that changing policy is a better approach to social problems than reforming individuals, and they are more likely to think that they themselves ought to get involved in policy and politics.[27] And in fact, young people who do community service participate in politics as adults more than those without early experience in community service.[28]

Not every volunteer launches an organization or becomes an advocate. But these stories—and one can find hundreds like them—show that everyday altruism, individual volunteerism, and community service *can* inspire people into civic affairs, *can* make leaders out of them, and *can* build structures that engage ever more citizens in helping their neighbors and solving social problems. Community service *can* kindle civic engagement.

Why, then, doesn't the spark catch more often?

Barriers Between Everyday Altruism and Political Action

Finally, we come back to the first requisite of civic culture: faith in government. Democracy holds no appeal if people don't see government as an institution dedicated to helping people. The reason the Scouts, fraternal lodges, the Grange, and their ilk so successfully served as civic bridges was not because they held weekly meetings according to Robert's Rules of Order, showed members how to pull the right political levers, and educated them on issues of the day. Rather, these organizations caught members' hearts by engaging them in service to their communities. They helped members channel their moral aspirations into concrete activities, both service and civic. They allowed their members to feel they were doing something worthwhile, and they connected members not only to friends and neighbors but to the larger human community as well. Impassioned by service, members had moral motives to influence politics. These older political organizations enticed people across the bridge from private life because on the other side of the bridge, public life was a place where they could live their deepest values more fully. The old membership associations joined the heart and the ballot.

In the political climate of the past thirty years, public life is less and less a place where people can live their moral values. No matter what their civics teachers tell them, political leaders have been teaching them that "government is the problem, not the solution." President George H. W. Bush praised volunteer work to the skies—a thousand points of light and all that—but cast it as an alternative to government, a replacement for the public money Reagan spent but didn't have. "Our funds our low. We have a deficit to bring down," Bush warned in his inaugural address. "We will turn to the only resource we have that in times of need always grows—the goodness and courage of the American people." Throughout his presidency, he called on Americans to volunteer: "If you know how to read, find someone who can't. If you've got a hammer, find a nail. If you're not hungry, not lonely, not in trouble—seek out someone who is." Then he told them in so many words, "You're on your own": "The key to solving [America's problems] remains the same. It is the individual—the individual who steps forward."[29]

Sara Mosle, a white teacher and journalist, took Bush père's message to heart. She mentored a group of New York City black teenagers over many years and later wrote about her experience in the *New York Times Magazine*.[30] By her own account, she made a difference in the kids' lives. She expanded their horizons. Once she took them to an Atlantic Ocean beach, a sight none of them had ever seen, and one of the kids marveled that unlike the market economy he knew so well, nature left all those beautiful shells "for free." Mosle rescued her kids from a hundred daily troubles that afflict children who grow up poor. She taught them that somebody cared about them and was willing to pull strings for them, and, most important, that a person can sometimes get out of jams with help.

Yet Mosle chronicled her mentoring experience as if all her efforts were for naught and she were a failure. "What my kids really need, I can't give them: better housing, less crowded schools, access to affordable health care, a less punitive juvenile justice system, and for their parents, better child care . . . and a living wage." The *Times*, too, gave volunteerism bad grades. It titled the article "The Vanity of Volunteerism," and subtitled it, "Why Volunteerism Doesn't Work." Mosle didn't in any way show that volunteerism doesn't work. She showed only, as she wrote, that "it doesn't offer a systemic solution to entrenched problems," and that a thousand points of light cannot replace government altruism. Arguably, Mosle had a strong sense of efficacy, else she couldn't have written so lovingly about "her kids." But when she looked at her volunteerism in the mirror of her government's message—that individual volunteerism ought to be able to solve big social problems—she found herself coming up short.

Only a grossly distorted mirror could make Mosle's mentoring a vanity and a failure. By shirking government responsibility, conservatives set up citizens for failure and disappointment. For its part, the *Times* ought to have titled the article, "Why Compassionate Conservatism Doesn't Work," but by framing the story as it did, the paper invited readers to wallow in the futility of personal altruism.

Bill Clinton at last put public money behind individual community service by creating Americorps in 1993. The program pays minimal stipends, health insurance, and educational grants so that young people can afford to devote a year of service to nonprofits and local and state government agencies. Americorps thus links volunteerism, government, and politics—the local, community-building kind of politics—in a creative symbiosis. It is exactly the right way to harness altruism to civic engagement, but conservatives loathed it ("A $27,000-per-person boondoggle for rich kids trying to find themselves," Senator John Ashcroft sneered) and consistently tried to starve its budget.[31]

Nonprofits are places from which volunteers might move naturally into politics. Most volunteering takes place in nonprofit organizations. But thanks to conservative attacks on nonprofits as "liberal advocacy groups," they have been effectively sidelined from politics. If we wonder why more one-to-one volunteers don't become politically active, all we have to do is look at U.S. tax law. As Jeffrey Berry says, "Under the tax law governing nonprofits, lobbying is considered an unsavory and suspect activity."

A federal appeals court likened "attempting to influence legislation" to "propaganda."[32] Nonprofits deliver most of the government's helping services to poor, sick, elderly, disabled, troubled, disadvantaged citizens, yet government tightly restricts their ability to influence public policy.

The tax code forces nonprofits to make a choice: either they can have their nonprofit status and the all-important "501(c)(3)" designation that allows them to tell donors their donations are tax deductible, or they can participate in government. If they choose to be a nonprofit, they may not lobby legislators about policy changes they would like. They may not endorse political candidates who they think will support their mission. They may not encourage members or volunteers to contact their representatives and urge them to vote for or against a bill.[33]

Nonprofits are so dependent on private donations that they dare not jeopardize their tax-deductible status. Their leaders tend to be unduly cautious about exercising political muscle, and as Berry found out, they tend to believe the law restricts them more than it does. Many nonprofits, as part of staff orientation, warn their staffs about the IRS rules. When the outraged home care staff started talking politics in the case conference I described, their supervisor kept distinctly silent. I didn't think to ask her about it at the time, but I'd bet she withheld comment so as not to be seen as encouraging politics.

If political activity wafts into nonprofits in a miasma of illicitness, corruption, and danger, staff people aren't likely to encourage volunteers to press their concerns through politics. They aren't even likely to talk about politics and public policy, and perhaps they avoid political conversations when volunteers initiate them. The law discourages nonprofits from engaging in politics, so nonprofits, the only organizations that might mobilize volunteers into politics as older service organizations used to, can't and don't play that role.

Tighter restrictions on nonprofits' political engagement rolled in with the same conservative tide that has been pounding against government help. The same politicians, intellectuals, and think tanks that wanted to curtail government social assistance wanted to silence the political voices of people who represent our needy neighbors. Although these conservatives failed to pass what would have been devastating restrictions on nonprofits' political and advocacy work, the drumbeat had a chilling effect nonetheless.[34]

Everyday altruism can bring people into politics, but only if politics is worth joining. Politics is worth joining only if it connects people with their fellow citizens, enables them to make a difference, and nurtures their better selves. The only government that can make that kind of politics is one that helps your neighbor and helps you help your neighbor, too.

8

How Government Should Help Your Neighbor

Done right, government help strengthens democracy. Both the New Deal and the Great Society grew out of deep political unrest fueled by visible inequalities of wealth and power. Reformers understood, even long before the word *empowerment* came into vogue, that what the downtrodden needed most of all was more power. Redistributing power was the heart of the Great Society, captured in the phrase "maximum feasible participation." Reformers designed community agencies to give poor people a voice in policy decisions affecting their lives and their communities. Sixties liberals explicitly saw their programs as a political revolution first, an economic program second.[1]

With Ronald Reagan's presidency, the conservative remedy for poverty reversed the old liberal prescription. Instead of power, the poor needed someone to exercise strong authority over them. They needed tough discipline. Instead of assertiveness, they needed to learn submissiveness to social norms and obedience to authority. They needed helpers who would demand something of them in return for help, who would impose obligations and enforce them. The Great Society programs failed, wrote Lawrence Mead, "because they largely ignored behavioral problems among the poor. In particular, they did not tell their clients with any authority that they ought to behave differently."[2]

True help, according to self-proclaimed compassionate conservatives, comes with strings attached. It requires something of the recipients as a quid pro quo. Perhaps the recipients should have to pay back the help in some way, or reciprocate by doing work for the donor. Perhaps they should have to submit to lessons in character reform, through training programs, classes, and religious indoctrination. Or perhaps they should receive help only after they have reformed and demonstrated their compliance with the donor's wishes about the kind of person they ought to be.

Help, in this view, should be discipline first, assistance second. The quid pro quo of conservative help isn't meant to empower recipients by making them feel they have something to offer or any worth as human beings. It's meant to control people. "To offer an exchange," James Payne advises the would-be charitable helper, "you have to know what you want the needy person to accomplish."[3] Conservatives frame their help as an exchange, but there's no doubt about who sets the rules, who defines the obligations, who enforces the contract, and who holds the power.

Nor is there much doubt about what kind of service the powerful would like the needy to perform in exchange for help. Lawrence Mead's writings are a campaign to ensure that unskilled workers have to do dirty work. Work in dirty low-wage jobs (*dirty* is his word) can't be treated as a voluntary choice for unskilled workers, he says, because "they have too many other sources of income, including government benefits, for them to work reliably. . . . At least for these workers, employment must become a duty, enforced by public authority, rather than an expression of self-interest." James Payne suggests that people who get medical care courtesy of Medicaid ought to be asked to sweep the hospital floors after they recover, or at least to pay back a few cents on the dollar. Parents whose kids partake of free school lunches ought to work off their debt by volunteering in the classroom, helping in the cafeteria, or supervising the playgrounds. (Don't ask when they're supposed to volunteer around school while holding down a paying job, which they are also supposed to do.) Mickey Kaus advocates a Works Progress Administration-style public employment program in which aid recipients would maintain highways, schools, playgrounds, subways, and public libraries, and clean the city streets twice a day, for wages "slightly below the private sector minimum wage." These and other welfare-to-work reformers claim they want to redesign government help to instill the work ethic. Their real goal seems to be ensuring that society's dirty work gets done on the cheap.[4]

For all the professed concern about how help demeans, the compassionate conservative program was designed to create second-class citizenship. People who need help lose their right to the liberties other citizens deserve. Paternalistic help is usually demeaning, Mead acknowledges, but we needn't worry because chronically poor people don't have the same psychology as everyone else. They don't respond to self-interest like most people. What's the evidence? "If self-interest were a sufficient motivation, living in poverty and being on welfare should themselves motivate people to avoid or leave these conditions. Government action [read: help] would not be needed." David Kelley, whose libertarian credo resents government whenever it tells anybody what to do, applauds a Massachusetts program for teen mothers because it submits them to daily room inspections, limited telephone privileges, curfews, and signing in and out.[5] Unfortunately, the chronically poor can't have prosperity and their liberty and dignity. For them, conservatives believe, losing liberty and dignity is preferable to being poor.

Conservative "help" was meant to disempower not only the poor but the working class as well, by removing the safety net that enabled low-wage workers to hold out for higher wages and better working conditions. From the Reagan cutbacks in government assistance to the Clinton welfare reform and the Bush welfare tightening, the dismantling of government help stripped workers of their bargaining power. Conservatives wrapped their reforms in psychotherapeutic rationales—withholding help would benefit the needy by strengthening their personalities—but the conservative attack on help was an unabashed coup against the Great Society.[6]

Government help can empower citizens to care about politics and participate as equals—as long as it's the right kind of help.

Give Them Control

Anyone who wants to understand power and powerlessness should visit nursing homes. People wind up in nursing homes primarily because their life force has diminished, only secondarily because no one is willing and able to take care of them. Nursing homes mushroomed starting in the 1950s as more women joined the workforce, more families spread out around the country, and, suddenly, there was no one next door to take care of Gram and Gramp. With the growth of nursing homes, gerontologists noticed something curious. People entered debilitated and relatively incapacitated—that much was expected—but they often deteriorated unexpectedly quickly once they entered. The gerontologists began to suspect that nursing homes *taught* their residents how to be helpless.[7]

In the 1970s, two psychologists designed a clever experiment to see what would happen if nursing-home residents were given a little more control over their lives.[8] They arranged for the residents on two floors to get some perks—a plant for their rooms, and movies twice a week—but they persuaded the nursing-home director to dole out the perks quite differently on the two floors. On one floor, he called the residents together and made a long speech about all the decisions they could make, such as how to arrange their rooms, how to spend their time, whether to visit other people, and where to spend their time. He told them that the home was their home and it was their responsibility to make suggestions and complaints about changes they would like to see. Then he passed around a box of plants and told them they could decide whether they wanted a plant, select the one they wanted, and take care of their plants as they would like. He told them there would be movies two nights a week, and they could choose which night they wanted to attend, if they wanted to go at all.

On the other floor, the director gave a speech about the activities and facilities available to the residents and said that the staff "feel that it's our responsibility to make this a home you can be proud of and happy in." Then he passed around a box of plants, saying,

"They're yours to keep. The nurses will water and care for them for you." He told them about the two movie nights and promised that "we'll let you know later which day you're scheduled to see it."

After three weeks, the residents who had been given more responsibility and control were happier, more alert, and more active, as rated by both themselves and the nurses. They spent more time visiting other patients and people outside the home, and talking with the staff. They tooled around more in their wheelchairs. Remarkably, eighteen months later, the group with more control were healthier and had fewer deaths, though they had started out with similar health levels.[9]

The experiment showed that even at the extremes of physical frailty, it's possible to empower people. Give people control over something so trivial as plants and movie nights, and you stimulate their minds, boost their initiative, activate their bodies, pep up their social lives, and make them happier and healthier.

In the 1990s, political scientist Joe Soss designed a clever way to replicate the nursing-home experiment in government.[10] Well, not exactly replicate, because Soss didn't persuade government officials to treat citizens differently. He did find two government programs that helped relatively poor people, but like the two nursing-home floors, they implemented the help very differently. Aid to Families with Dependent Children, popularly known as welfare, allows its clients virtually no decisions, other than complying with caseworkers' demands. (In 1996, AFDC was changed to an even stricter program with less client autonomy, called Temporary Assistance for Needy Families, but still known as welfare.) Social Security Disability Insurance, popularly called "disability," doesn't give a lot of authority to clients, but it does treat them with great respect and offer them opportunities to express grievances and appeal if their applications are rejected.

Soss asked clients of the two programs what it was like to apply and how they felt about their caseworker and the agency. Welfare clients described the caseworker as all-powerful and arbitrary. "Your life is in their hands. Your kid's life is in that worker's hands. If that worker don't like you, if you don't smile at that worker, she'll make your check late or whatever. She can do anything she wants to. She can send you your check, or she can't." The welfare clients felt as though they received "summonses" to show up at the welfare office, and "demands" to produce documents. They felt under constant and continuous scrutiny, and compelled to answer intrusive questions about their personal relationships and sex lives. They felt disdained: "It's pretty much like they're 'up here' and you're 'down there.' And they let you know that," one woman said. For the most part, they felt powerless to influence their caseworkers. "You learn to be quiet and take whatever is dished out." Most of them wouldn't dream of expressing a grievance: "Whatever they [caseworkers] want to do, they're going to do regardless, whether I say something or not. They've got the power, so you have to listen to what they say." With few exceptions, discussion and negotiation aren't part of the welfare experience: "They don't call you and say, 'Do you mind if we change your case manager?' . . . They don't discuss with you, 'What are your feelings about this?' They just do what they do."

Disability clients described more positive experiences. They were overwhelmed by the number of program rules, but were much more confident than welfare clients that their intake workers had to abide by the rules, too. They felt their applications would be decided by the rule of law rather than personal whim. "There are rules. It either is, or it isn't. I didn't have to be especially nice to the intake person so they would write one thing instead of another. I never got the impression that speaking up would make things difficult for you. You know it will either work or not based on the formula." Disability clients generally felt less intimidated and more able to voice their concerns. "If I ever need anything, I know that's their job. They'll be there. I believe they will," said one disability recipient. They knew their intake workers were more powerful than they, but they didn't feel squelched. "Well, if there is any power, I guess they have more than I do. But I haven't come into a situation where I've seen it. I always feel like I have some say-so in the process." Only one of the twenty disability clients Soss interviewed said she would be unwilling to raise a grievance. More than two-thirds of the welfare clients said they wouldn't raise a grievance under any circumstances, and the ones who said they might raise a grievance would do so only in extreme situations.[11]

In the nursing-home experiment, the psychologists looked to see whether giving residents control over plants and movies changed the way they lived in other aspects of their lives. In his government "experiment," Soss looked to see whether the different levels of control afforded clients in two agencies changed the way they felt about government and citizenship more generally. Just as in nursing homes, clients' experiences of control in small encounters spilled over to other parts of their lives. To most welfare clients, "the government" is the welfare office writ large. "I haven't been to most of government," one welfare client said, "but I'll bet they just treat you the way the welfare office does." Another welfare client made the leap from the welfare office to election campaigns: "When they start talking about voting, I turn the TV off. I do. It's no guarantee. This person can make all these promises but that don't mean they're going to do it. The rest of the government mostly works like the AFDC office." Welfare clients didn't expect government to be any more responsive to them than their caseworker. "I don't know if people in the government would be responsive to me. If it's anything like trying to deal with the AFDC system, I don't see how."

Disability clients, too, generalize from their personal experiences with the agency that helps them. "Social Security is not different from the rest of government. When you're in something like Social Security, you learn a lot about the way the government does things. There's a lot of paper and nothing moves very fast. Everything goes slowly." But despite their appreciation for the behemoth that is government, despite their assessment that government ought to be more responsive to individuals, disability clients overwhelmingly saw the government as open and democratic. They believed that if citizens work at it, they will be heard. As Soss put it, they fully expect public officials to be more responsive to people with money, but "these doubts did not alter their fundamental expectation that even if the government is slow to act, it eventually will respond to citizens who vote, organize, and lobby public officials." In short, experience with welfare teaches citizens not to bother with government. Experience with Social Security Disability Insurance teaches citizens that they matter.

When government organizes its help to grant citizens some control over their situations, Soss found, the help also teaches important civics lessons. Help that allows clients some control teaches that all citizens are equal. Not in some clichéd, obviously false way, because the gap between someone who needs help and someone who has the power to help reeks of inequality. But, as Soss's interviews with disability clients show, when government helpers play by the rules and listen to the people who need help, citizens learn that they have some power to change their own situations merely by expressing their needs and complaints. When government listens, citizens learn that they have voices. Help offered with some degree of control teaches citizens that government is their ally and politics is a two-way street.

Why do programs like welfare and disability insurance have such a big impact on clients' ideas about government and citizenship? One reason, as Soss suggests, is that to citizens, these programs are the face of government. They are the meeting ground where one citizen comes face-to-face with one government official (or phone-to-phone, perhaps, in disability, because, unlike welfare, disability insurance doesn't require applicants to apply in person). These programs teach implicit civic lessons because in them, clients experience government with their own eyes and ears.

But there's an even more important reason for the civic impact of these programs. People apply for welfare or disability at moments when they feel especially vulnerable and desperate. We know that people's ideas and attitudes about politics take shape at times in the life course when they are particularly impressionable.[12] Research on political socialization has always focused on childhood, adolescence, and young adulthood as the most impressionable years, but age itself doesn't make people impressionable—vulnerability does. We are most impressionable when we need help and we're frightened. Asking for help means putting ourselves in someone else's hands. How they respond shapes whether we like them or not, and then, whether we view them as kind or cruel, good or bad. Whoever helps us and preserves our dignity wins our gratitude and loyalty. Whoever helps us and makes us feel small earns our anger.

Not all government helping programs are as personal as welfare and disability, and not all programs aim to help out in desperate situations. But when government offers its helping hand to vulnerable people, it hands them a civics book along with the help.

Give Them Opportunities to Serve

In the entrance lobby of a nursing home, an elderly woman sits in a wheelchair. A younger woman, probably visiting her parent, comes through the door. The elderly resident greets her and offers to warm her cold hands. The visitor holds out her hands, and the elderly woman rubs them vigorously. "Thank you so very much," the visitor says.

"Anytime!" the elder woman says. "And let me know if I can do anything else for you."

Bethany Knight tells this story to nurses' aides to illustrate a basic human instinct: "We all need to feel we make a difference."[13] Nursing-home residents, no longer in their own homes, no longer able to make a meal for someone or even take the clothes off the line, come to feel useless. Knight suggests that as aides go about helping their patients, they should consciously create "opportunities to serve." Let patients hold the comb, ask them to deliver a message to someone, ask their opinion—find ways to let them help. In a world that cherishes independence, people who need lots and lots of help also need evidence of their capacity to act autonomously. Nothing renders such proof as being able to help someone else.

Most of us know Head Start as a preschool program for poor children. Started in 1965 as part of Lyndon Johnson's War on Poverty, Head Start has the world's most appealing constituency—three- and four-year-olds. It succeeds in boosting the children's educational performance long after preschool. And unlike most War on Poverty programs, it has consistently enjoyed strong political support. What most people don't see is Head Start's mainspring—it gives *parents* opportunities to serve. Here's how a woman named Nancy described Head Start to Joe Soss: "I was impressed that when you go to orientation, they say, 'We need you to help.' And they give you an opportunity to help. They not only give you an opportunity to help with little stuff in the classroom, they give you the opportunity to go to a meeting where you are making decisions."[14]

Head Start began in the heyday of citizen participation, when every new program was designed for "maximum feasible participation." From the beginning, local centers were required to offer parents several ways to get involved, beyond merely dropping off their children. Parents can volunteer as teacher aides in a classroom, or help with special enrichment activities. When paid staff jobs open up, parent volunteers are given preference. Among the teachers, assistant teachers, social service aides, kitchen staff, and janitors who make up the paid staff of local centers nationwide, about 70 percent are former volunteers—parents who got their start helping in their children's preschools. Parents can also help run the center by becoming members of the "parent policy council" that each center must establish. These councils decide on everything from selecting and hiring teachers to classroom curriculum to the meal menus. This is what Nancy meant when she told Soss, "they give you an opportunity to go to a meeting where you are making decisions." When mothers can translate the bureaucratic mumbo jumbo of "parent policy councils" and "maximum feasible participation" into the eloquent simplicity of "an opportunity to go to a meeting where you are making decisions," we know the civics book is working.

Law professor Lucie White was representing poor clients in a legal-aid program in the 1980s when she began to hear about Head Start. Much of her work entailed helping clients restore their welfare benefits or gain access to other public programs that could help them. Her clients kept telling her that Head Start was different from the other social assistance programs they knew. They spoke of it glowingly. She knew that all those Head Start centers in church basements, storefronts, and schools were governed by a maze of federal statutes and regulations, and she wondered what was so special about this program to women who otherwise had little regard for the government and its laws. Like Soss, White was interested in how a government program could help its clients "take their place as citizens."[15]

Being a lawyer, White began by reading congressional hearings and investigations about Head Start. In what might have been deadly dull ink, she noticed something electric: hundreds of women testified that the program had transformed their lives. Head Start, they said, "made me find my place." "There's always a place for us. . . . These are the kinds of programs we need, programs that don't judge us." Head Start gave them hope and encouragement, just like a mother figure. They went from being terrified to speak to knowing that someone would "listen when you express your opinion." "If it weren't for Head Start, I might still be a maid. Head Start gave me the first job I ever had that did not include pushing a mop."

Eventually, White decided to see for herself. She took off her lawyer hat, went into some Head Start centers, got down with the crayons and the kids, hung out with the moms and the teachers. And by entering their world, she found Head Start's secret. Hidden in the maze of rules was a dense network of everyday altruism: adults helping kids, teachers helping parents, parents helping teachers, parents helping each other, and everybody helping others learn how to help others.

White spent a lot of time with a volunteer mother she calls E.M. Gradually, E.M. let on that her life had spiraled downward into paralysis, until she was able to leave her husband, father of their three children, because of domestic violence. She credited one of the teachers who had gently, wordlessly at first, sensed E.M.'s despair and supported her to fight her way out. E.M., in turn, spent a lot of time at the Head Start center with a little girl who had been emotionally paralyzed by trauma. Just as the teacher had coaxed E.M., E.M. coaxed the child, helping her to speak, express wishes, and even take simple actions like pulling a crayon from its box. In one of their conversations, E.M. told White that helping the little girl had been "therapeutic" for her, so White asked her to explain how. E.M. replied:

I mean, anybody could have done that [helped the child]. I didn't do anything that anyone couldn't have done, but it was just something at the time that I needed to do as well as needed to help her do, because it helped me, too. It made me feel so good.

That I was able to help somebody, because I, you know, the past few years it seemed like I couldn't help anybody. I couldn't help myself.

I went to this school, and these kids are having problems. I'm having problems. I'm working with them and they're making some effort, I mean some progress. At the same time, I am too, because I'm being like pumped up in a way, but it's a good pump up.

In Head Start, mothers grow into their citizenship roles as they realize that not only are they helping others, but others are counting on them. With the encouragement of her teacher-mentor, E.M. ran for secretary of the policy council and won. Keeping the minutes, she told White, had helped her come out of despair: "I had a job to do. I had duties. I had a format to follow. I had responsibilities, you know, that people were depending on me to do." Another Head Start volunteer told Joe Soss almost the same thing: "They just give you an opportunity to get involved. So, I feel like I'm wanted, like I'm needed to do something. A lot of people are depending on me to do this, and that's great."[16]

Conservatives tout personal responsibility as the highest citizen virtue. The phrase has come to mean earning a living, not being financially dependent, being a reliable employee, and not bringing children into the world without being able to support them. The Head Start mothers articulate a more generous and community-minded sense of personal responsibility: helping others and being someone others can depend on for help. Conservatives have disgraced dependence; these Head Start mothers ennoble it by holding up its other end: dependability.

When Head Start clients testified at congressional hearings, helping others was a prominent theme. Here's a sampling of their statements, all from Lucie White's research:

"You feel good because you give yourself."

"I love getting the chance to help other people the same way I was helped."

"I think the most important thing is that through the support I have received, I have learned how to support others."

"Head Start treated me with respect and provided me with opportunities to grow, through training and support. As I continue to grow, I am able to offer other low-income parents the same kind of opportunities for training, employment, and self-realization."

"It's because of Head Start that I am training other people in assertiveness, leadership, and politics. Head Start has helped me to reach people, to encourage them. It makes me feel good to help others."

More than any other kind of help Head Start gave these women, they most appreciate empowerment, and empowering others is how they in turn choose to help. Their concept of being a good person centers around helping others. They feel gratitude to this government program because it taught them how to help others and, in the process, taught them what they want to do with their lives. Their communities will be better for Head Start's help, and theirs.

If we want government help to instill civic virtue and devotion, help people by giving them opportunities to help others.

Build Webs as Well as Ladders

At Penn [University of Pennsylvania], things changed a lot once I found the Society of Black Engineers. They were always handing you off to different people who could help you, people who had been through the classes. Everybody else seemed to have some sort of group—fraternities who had study tests from older groups or whatever. So I was fortunate that the Society ended up doing this for me.

One of my former classmates is working at Penn now, and he's soliciting alumni mentors for the new students. So we're doing an alumni network over e-mail to keep in contact with new students and help them along and answer questions as they go through the process.

—Quoted in William G. Bowen and Derek Bok,
The Shape of the River: Long-Term Consequences of Considering Race in University Admissions

American mythology celebrates the lone hero—the Davy Crocketts, Abe Lincolns, and Rosa Parkses who supposedly made it on their own grit. In reality, they all had help. We all accomplish our successes by pulling on the strings of our webs.

The web became vivid for me in one of the first courses I taught, in the seventies before "the Web" meant the Internet. The course was about the welfare state, and when we came to the topic of work and labor markets, I began by asking the students what they had done during the previous summer. About half of them had held jobs as waitresses, fast food servers, or assorted lackeys at summer tourist spots. The others had worked in law offices, scientific research labs, architecture firms, or hospitals. As we went around the seminar table, I listed each student's answer on the blackboard. Without saying anything, I placed the two kinds of jobs in two separate columns. Then I went back down the lists and asked each student to tell us how he or she had landed the job. To a person, the students who had held professional-track jobs had gotten them through family connections. The others had pounded the pavement solo.

As an educator, I've staked my career on the belief that supplying people with education helps them become independent, successful, happy, and contributing members of society. Yet I also know that furnishing them with personal ladders isn't the whole story. If we want to help people and communities thrive, we have to think about weaving social webs and keeping them in good repair.

Affirmative action might be the most controversial form of help the U.S. government has ever undertaken. It aims to spin webs in a nation that believes ladders are all it takes to get ahead.[17] Affirmative action is really a collection of policies meant to integrate groups that have been systematically excluded from schools, jobs, occupations, and business opportunities. The key means are, first, to stop the stereotyping and discrimination that have barred the doors to minorities and women and, second, to bring enough members of these excluded groups into every walk of life so that they will have webs to support them.

The controversy over affirmative action turns on whether it's a good idea to favor people on the basis of the same traits (usually race or gender) that once were used to reject them. If we think of life as a game of chutes and ladders, then sending people careening downward because they happen to have the wrong skin color or gender seems unjust. Affirmative action's opponents say it's just as wrong to *favor* someone because of their skin color as it is to *reject* them, and that it's impossible to favor dark skin without disfavoring light skin. But if we think of life as an intricate web in which people move around on pathways of personal connection, then even once discrimination ends, people with the "wrong" traits in the past won't have very many pathways open to them, because so few of their group would have made it inside. It seems unfair to expect them to do as well as people who have a lot of pathways because they happen to belong to groups with the historically "right" traits.

In the 1980s, the Supreme Court began limiting affirmative action. Municipal fire and police departments, unions, and businesses had been voluntarily using affirmative action plans to reverse the effects of past discrimination. Through many decisions, the Court said that institutions could not use affirmative action policies to integrate merely for the sake of diversity, but only as after-the-fact remedies for individuals who could prove they had been victims of discrimination. Law professor Paul Spiegelman stepped right into the middle of this controversy. By mapping out the way webs work, he showed why we should think of affirmative action as constructing webs rather than handing out ladders.

Spiegelman started with a simple observation: people relate to members of the same race, gender, ethnic group, or nationality differently from how they relate to members of other groups. The observation would seem positively trite if the explosive politics of affirmative action hadn't made it seem politically incorrect. But think of your own life: shared experiences of any kind—race, gender, extended families, high schools—tend to create a comfort level and a deep sense of understanding. What would it be like, Spiegelman tried to imagine, for a person in one of these disfavored groups suddenly to find him- or herself as the lone minority member in a workplace?

Without any peers from the same group, the Lone Example wouldn't have a support system of sympathetic coworkers, people to chat with about all the normal stresses of work and all the unusual stresses of being the exotic new minority kid on the block. The Lone Example wouldn't be privy to the all-important grapevine. How would the Lone Example find out things like what sets the boss off, what new jobs are coming down the line that might be worth bidding for, or what things earn especially high or low marks at evaluation time? The Lone Example would stand out like Gulliver among the Lilliputians and feel watched, studied, scrutinized, if only out of innocent curiosity on the part of coworkers. Always on exhibit and always being judged, it would be pretty hard to concentrate on doing one's job, let alone relax.

A black woman lawyer put some of these factors in relief when she explained why she gave up working in private law firms:

> They were looking for someone who reminded them of themselves. And I do not remind the typical private practitioner of himself in any way. I think that being black had a great deal to do with it. Being a woman, I think, meant less. A white hiring partner may not have gone to law school with women, may not have partners who are women. But he had a mother and he has a wife. Women are part of his life and if they move into another dimension of his life—co-worker—at least they're familiar to him. It's amazing how color—a black face—can overwhelm them.[18]

A Lone Example often gets treated as an exemplar, a representative of something else instead of as an individual. Lone Examples get pressed into service to represent the institution's diversity to the public and to maintain the social network for members of the minority group. One frustrated young professor imagined the speech she would like to give to university hiring committees: "Look, if you want me because I'm a woman and because I'm African American and because I'm trotting along this series of degrees, don't bother. Don't think about how many diversity committees I can head up or how many admission fairs I can go to or how many times you can stick me in your yearbook to make yourself look diverse. But think about what I can really offer your community and your school and your students."[19]

Without any supervisors from the same group, Lone Examples lack supervisors who have "been there" and can offer empathic advice. Like coworkers, supervisors are apt to treat the Lone Example as a typical representative of the minority group. With only one or a few employees from a minority group under their authority, supervisors can't gain perspective on the range of talents, annoying habits, and personalities that populate any group. When the few minority group members talk quietly or animatedly among themselves, supervisors might think they're being insular or even conspiratorial, when they're only doing what's perfectly normal for the majority—talking among themselves. Perhaps hardest of all, if Lone Examples can't be sure whether a supervisor's criticism is based on stereotypes or personal assessment, they will have a hard time building rapport and accepting guidance. Without a good relationship with supervisors, Lone Examples find it harder to move up.

For all these reasons, members of minority groups who have climbed a ladder into the white male world often find themselves stuck, not fully integrated and unable to rise. A music teacher explained how this dynamic led him to active mentoring and volunteering in the black community: "I spoke recently with one of my classmates who is a lawyer in Raleigh about why we're involved in all these things. And what we realized is that we tried to do all the right things—all the 'white' things at the right 'white' schools—and took all the usual steps up the ladder. And what we found when we got there—when we got all the way up the ladder—is that there isn't a lot of difference. People still see you first of all as black."[20]

Because networks are so crucial to individual success, discrimination against a member of a victim group harms not only the victim but the victim's community as well. Had that person been given the position, he or she would have become part of a network, someone able to spread the word about openings, recommend acquaintances, and eventually mentor younger members of the group. Discrimination against one person denies his or her community a "friend in the business," a role model, and a beacon of hope signaling that other members of the victim's group can make it, too.

Quotas are anathema in American political culture. In the past, quotas set ceilings on the number of people from a disfavored group who would be allowed to enter a school or workplace. They were used to keep people out. But quotas can just as well be used as floors—a way to bring in a critical mass of people from formerly excluded groups so that they can form webs and don't have to suffer all the disadvantages of being Lone Examples.

Courts have constrained affirmative action even more drasti-
cally since Spiegelman wrote in 1985, and I have no illusions that
the courts are about to tack left. Yet we can begin to think differently about affirmative action. Once we understand how webs
work, then we must broaden the concept of personal responsibility from worrying only about yourself to taking care of others as
well. And once we have done that, we can appreciate how
stronger affirmative action helps people help each other.

The music teacher who climbed the ladder only to be seen as
"black first" explained how that experience led him to weave a
web: "Because you get that rude awakening, I think you end up
feeling that you better hold on to those things that you knew before. And some part of that is what leads us back, to make sure
that we keep roots in the community and keep this thing going.
Like the people who helped us."[21]

The lesson goes beyond affirmative action. Every kind of government help should build webs as well as ladders. Thinking of
help as webs instead of ladders reminds us that help is a relationship, not some impersonal commodity we can deliver and be
done with, like take-out pizza. Head Start transforms children
into better learners, and mothers into better parents and citizens,
not by pumping the children with so many gallons of learning
and supervision, but by embedding mothers, children, teachers,
and aides in a web of delicate relationships with each other. By
contrast, when a welfare department thinks nothing of changing
the client's case manager without discussion or choice, it ignores
the most important ingredient of help that welfare has to offer—
a personal relationship. When government bureaucracies force
elderly and chronically ill people into nursing homes far from

their communities, or convicted criminals into prisons far from theirs, they rend whatever webs might possibly have helped these people be all that they could be.

In short, we have to reconceive government help: not something to be delivered top-down from government to individuals, like a tax-rebate check left wordlessly by the mailman, but something mutual and continuous, humming through the wires of daily conversation and contact.

Help Them Care for Kin

To say that we have obligations to strangers isn't to demand that they have the same grip on our sympathies as our nearest and dearest. We'd better start with the recognition that they don't.

—Kwame Anthony Appiah,
Cosmopolitanism: Ethics in a World of Strangers

It might seem strange to recommend help with family care in a book about helping strangers. Aren't we trying to cultivate citizens who will act like the Good Samaritan in their public as well as personal lives? Yes, but charity begins at home. The old saying carries a double meaning. People care for their own first, last, and foremost; and people learn to care for others by being cared for at home.

Government should help citizens care for kin because for most people, as we saw in Chapter 4, caring for family is Higher Law. If citizens can't fulfill the yearnings and obligations they deem most important, they won't care about much else and they certainly won't value politics. A government that doesn't help them abide by Higher Law doesn't merit their respect. If that weren't reason enough, government should help citizens care for children, because without good care, children won't grow up to be caring adults, eager and able to help others. Caring for children tends the community, and a good community must help tend its children. Treating child rearing as if it were only personal fulfillment and a private responsibility undermines democracy.

Kathryn Edin, Laura Lein, and Timothy Nelson interviewed 125 poor men who had children but not custody.[22] Some of these fathers were very involved with their children, emotionally and financially; others scarcely saw their children, and provided scanty if any economic support. As a group, the men lived hand-to-mouth. Almost all of them were or had been mixed up with alcohol, drugs, or prison. The lucky ones had formal jobs with a regular paycheck, Social Security, and even some unemployment insurance, but these jobs tended not to last long. Some worked sporadically as day laborers, some in casual, off-the-books jobs, and some in the illegal underground economy selling sex, drugs, and stolen goods.

Yet when the researchers asked these men what their lives would be like without their children, they were stunned by the answers: "We had expected them to tell us they would have more money for themselves, have less hassle from child support enforcement authorities, be able to finish high school and enroll in a training program, and so on. Instead, a significant number of fathers told us, 'I'd be dead or in jail.'" Many fathers said their children were the only source of meaning in their lives. One said, "I just want to know that when I die, there will be something out there to show that I was on the planet, something that looks like me. That way, people will know that I existed." Some saw their children as their only hope for fulfilling their dreams: "Having a son is very important to me because I know that even if I don't make nothin' out of my life, he might go beyond me and make something of his life." Still others considered having children redemptive, their impetus to stop "spinning out of control," pull themselves together, and gain control of their lives.

In these men's minds, fatherhood is tightly tied to being able to provide for their children. They feel good about themselves when they can provide, terrible when they can't. They rate the jobs available to them not according to how hard the work or how high the wage, but how well the work enables them to provide for their kids. The jobs at the top of any social reformer's list—regular, legal, minimum-wage jobs in fast food, and formal, aboveground day-labor jobs—are at the bottom of fathers' lists, because those jobs seldom offer full-time work or benefits. Such jobs are "good enough for me," fathers say, "but won't do anything for my kids."

Not being able to support their children pains these men, because their shame keeps them away from their children. "That's the only reasons I won't be around them. You know, because I don't want them to see me as a low figure. I don't like to be around them because I can't do that much for them, you know— take them out, give them money, buy them clothes." If we were to ask these men how government could best help them, they'd probably all plead, "Help me provide for my children."

Poor mothers tell much the same story, except that they usually have custody of their children. Kathryn Edin and Maria Kefalas asked poor single mothers the same question Edin and her colleagues had asked fathers: What would your life be like without children? Mothers gave the same kinds of answers: my children saved me from the streets; without them I'd be dead or in jail; "I wouldn't care about anything." Children, most poor mothers say, are their reason for getting up in the morning and their motivation to better themselves. Most important, their children give them love: "My son gives me all the love I need," said one mother. Scarcely any mothers see their children as the cause of "wrecked dreams of education, career, marriage, or material success."[23]

Social reformers since Malthus have tended to see children as barriers to poor people's personal advancement. If only the poor wouldn't have so many, and when they're so young besides . . . Some state welfare regulations even define children as "barriers to employment" that mothers must overcome.[24] For that matter, most employers treat children as barriers to employee performance, and modern workplace rules convert children into barriers to employee success.[25] Much of welfare's counseling and many of its incentives seek to reduce childbearing. Yet strikingly, the mothers and fathers for whom children might seem to pose the biggest barriers to personal advancement don't see barriers when they look at their children. They see wide-open pathways and glorious vistas.

If we want government to help our neighbors, we had better get a more realistic picture of who the neighbors are. Reformers always begin by imagining the people they're trying to help. What makes them tick? What do they need? As we think about how to alleviate poverty and how to make work and family-keeping compatible, the person I would plant in the public imagination is "TJ," a thirty-year-old African American mother of three, who told Edin and Kefalas, "I don't see myself as an individual anymore, really. Everything I do is mostly centered around my children, to make their lives better."[26] The self-interest that motivates TJ reaches beyond herself, and that is why TJ is Everyone: the self-interest that motivates all of us transcends the self.

Whatever government does to and for citizens must honor our expansive, connected, loving selves. Three broad principles of public policy would help TJ and her neighbors be the caring people they aspire to be.[27] First, all jobs should pay a living wage. Government has the power to set minimum wages and should use it. Second, all jobs should allow workers to do their jobs and care for their families. Just as gruesome factory conditions once propelled government to set sanitary and safety standards, workplaces hostile to families should propel government to set work-family standards. Third, government should supplement family care with publicly supported care for children, sick and chronically ill people, elders, disabled people, and anyone who needs personal care. The demands of caregiving are greater than ever, and the burdens ought to be spread.

In middle-class America, child rearing counts as a private responsibility. Children are a private pleasure, almost a luxury good. In the stingiest conservative accounting, people shouldn't have children unless they can afford to take care of them, and they have no right to ask their fellow workers or taxpayers to help them raise families, any more than they should seek public subsidy for their yachts.[28] In low-income America, where adults understand all too well how little of their children's well-being they can control, caring for one's own children, grandchildren, nieces, and nephews counts as both personal and social responsibility. Raising children well requires monitoring neighborhood safety and the other kids and activities around your own. The distinction between child rearing and neighborhood tending blurs. A Dominican immigrant living in Manhattan explained this double-entry bookkeeping to anthropologist Katherine Newman: "Bring your children up with an education, yes, you are helping the community. Helping the society, so that the area that you live in is not so bad. Because if everyone contributes his part to do something good on their own, they are doing something for the community." Newman concluded that "men and women living in problematic neighborhoods look to the daunting task of raising their children, or tending to the safety of the streets, as both a personal task and a contribution to the well-being of society as a whole."[29]

Metaphorically, we all live in "problematic neighborhoods." All adults depend on help from their neighbors to raise their children well, and all good child rearing helps the neighbors. By helping people take care of kin, government, too, helps the neighbors, helps communities, and helps us all.

Democracy is all about helping ourselves by making our neighborhood a better place to live. Nothing does as much for the neighborhood as taking care of the neighbors.

Create Banks of Mutual Help

Late one cold November night, I stopped at a gas station just off the highway. As I was pulling out, I heard a sharp pop, then a slow hiss. Two teenagers tried to help me, but first my tire wrench and then theirs bent in the trying. Meanwhile, a man dressed in snappy office clothes was filling up at another pump.

When he was through, he asked if he could help, retrieved a megawrench from his SUV, got down on his knees on the tarmac, and pushed with his whole body. Even with the right tools, he struggled. He changed the tire, put the flat in my car, reloaded my luggage, and gave me some advice about tires and tools. At a loss to express my overflowing gratitude without gushing, I said something banal about how nice he was to take time to help me. Like all Good Samaritans, he denied his goodness. "My wife had a flat tire once about this time of night, and somebody stopped to help her. I guess it's just payback."

My Good Samaritan wasn't paying back someone who had helped him personally, nor even the person who had helped his wife. He was making a deposit into an imaginary Bank of Mutual Help, without knowing or caring who else had already deposited and who might someday withdraw.

All societies, including ours, survive by running informal and formal Banks of Mutual Help. Mutual aid transforms a random collection of people into a community, and no collection of people remains a community without it. In the current political climate, shaped by a radically skewed distribution of wealth, the Haves would persuade us that the United States was built on rugged individualism rather than mutual aid. In fact, the American tradition is rooted in mutual self-help. Think barn raisings, fraternal organizations, and immigrant-aid societies. Think unions, neighborhood associations, business chambers, and interest groups. When we mourn the loss of social capital, we miss being able to count on our friends and neighbors for help.

Social Security is our biggest and most important Bank of Mutual Help. Social Security includes old-age pensions, health insurance (Medicare and Medicaid), disability insurance, survivor's insurance, and unemployment insurance. With all those "insurances" in its stable, you get the idea that it's not really a bank. Rather, Social Security is a collection of social insurance programs. Don't worry—I didn't bring you all the way to this point in the book to tell you how to reform Social Security. A lot of experts can do that better than I.[30] I brought you here to explain why social insurance is the best way for government to help us help our neighbors and ourselves. To do that, we'll compare the Bank of Mutual Help with your commercial savings bank down the street.

The Bank of Mutual Help runs on altruism and democracy. Citizens join together to form the bank and draw up a list of purposes they want it to serve—perhaps to help people who get sick, perhaps to help people who can't work anymore, perhaps to help families raise children and care for elders. They also decide how much each person will deposit—perhaps according to how much each can afford, or perhaps they will contribute equal amounts. In the real world, outside my fanciful metaphor, Congress creates the list of purposes for social insurance and sets the contribution levels.

There's a big difference between the Bank of Mutual Help and your commercial savings bank. At your savings bank, you can withdraw only as much money as you've already put in. If you ask for a loan, you'll have to put up collateral, and if you don't pay back your loan, you'll lose the collateral. The savings bank doesn't care how badly you need money or what you need it for. That bank runs on its owners' self-interest.

The Bank of Mutual Help pays out according to need, not how much you put in. (Sound socialist? It is, and so was the

Good Samaritan—he helped according to need.) Only people who suffer one of the problems on the bank's list may make withdrawals, because this bank's purpose is to help them over specific hurdles. If you have one of the problems on the list and need more money than you deposited, you'll get it. If you don't, you won't. Naturally, some people receive much more money than they put in, but no one begrudges them the money. If people get money from the Bank of Mutual Help, either they have had a very bad thing happen to them, like sickness or disability, or they are making a sacrifice for the common good, like rearing the next generation.

Social insurance is politically ingenious, probably the greatest social invention since Ulysses had himself tied to the mast so that he couldn't give in to the Sirens of shortsighted self-interest.

Ingenuity Number One: Social insurance persuades people to act altruistically by appealing to their self-interest. Insurance contributors know that they might turn out to be the ones in trouble, so when they make deposits, they imagine that their savings will eventually come back to help themselves. Yet when people contribute to insurance, they also know that until and unless they have a big problem on the bank's list, most of their savings will go to help other people. Social insurance channels individual contributions toward the common good by fuzzying the distinction between self-help and social help.

Ingenuity Number Two: Social insurance allows people who need help to receive it while feeling they are fully independent. When the New Dealers created the Social Security system, they deliberately peddled the fiction of individual savings accounts.[31] Never mind that in a Bank of Mutual Help, withdrawals don't correspond with deposits. The sheer act of depositing into the Bank of Mutual Help makes citizens feel like depositors, as they are. If later they need help and receive it, they can tell themselves they aren't dependent on anyone else; they made deposits, after all. That is why a sixty-six-year-old man who found himself having to ask his doctor for free drug samples could tell the *New York Times*, without a trace of irony, "I feel like I'm a lowlife looking for handouts. I'm not. It's the first time in my life I have to ask for help."[32] First time in his life? He was receiving a pension through Social Security and medical care courtesy of Medicare. Social insurance allows Americans to help each other in spite of our delusional self-image as fully independent and self-reliant creatures.

Ingenuity Number Three: Social insurance allows citizens to decide democratically how they want to help their neighbors. Through representative government, they can deliberate about which kinds of individual problems merit social assistance, they can change public programs to address new kinds of problems, and they can tinker with programs to fix mistakes and deficiencies. Meanwhile, everyone is free to volunteer time and pass out charity according to personal desires, confident that, together, they have buffered themselves and their neighbors against the basic, widespread insecurities.

Ingenuity Number Four: Social insurance gives citizens the tools to put boundaries around unlimited demands for help. People know from personal experience that relatives and friends can sometimes overwhelm them with demands for help. Conservatives exploit this fear by blowing it up into a grand Malthusian parable of "nature's mighty feast": Outside "our" banquet hall clamor vast hoards of "them" who need help; inside, "we" cower, so very few of us with barely enough for ourselves, let alone extra to give. Social insurance enables all of us—those of us who might someday be lucky and those of us who might not—to set rules for redistribution ahead of time, long before we face life-or-death situations (or think we do), long before panic sets in. When people ask for our help later on, we can offer it secure in the knowledge that we have planned ahead, and that our rules will enable us to put limits around our help.

Ingenuity Number Five: Social insurance gives citizens vested interests in government helping programs. Because they have a vested interest, they fight to preserve and expand these programs. Social insurance thus stimulates political support for government to help the neighbors. Social Security gives senior citizens a direct stake in government and so mobilizes them to participate more actively in politics.[33] Social insurance programs also stimulate helping industries and professions by making markets for them, that is, consumers who can afford their services. Home health care is a good example. In 1980, Congress expanded Medicare's coverage of home health services, largely out of fiscal concerns. It was cheaper to treat people at home than in hospitals or nursing homes. But a funny thing happened on the way to the Bank of Mutual Help: Medicare became a vast source of revenue for home care agencies. They grew, and many new ones entered the field. Seventeen years later, Congress decided that home health care was costing the taxpayers too much money. By then, however, social insurance had created strong political interests ready to defend this form of help. The home health providers had formed lobbying organizations to protect their interests. Elderly people, the primary users of home health care, and their adult children, the primary backstop when parents have no other source of care, had come to believe that home health care is essential to a decent standard of living and therefore something government ought to help provide. Government auditors and fiscal conservatives look at this process and accuse government of profligacy. People who have experience with home care count their blessings and give thanks to the benefactor.

Conservatives deem social insurance just another form of pork. There's nothing particularly moral about people defending their self-interest by supporting social insurance, they say. But to see social insurance as greedy self-help is to miss its moral and political power. No other social institution merges the motives of self-interest and altruism quite so exquisitely. No other institution guides citizens so gently yet so surely toward helping their neighbors. Social insurance sets in motion a virtuous circle, creating continuous political support for a politics of generosity.[34]

Conservatives maintain that government help weakens the citizenry. It atrophies ambition, saps self-reliance, and erodes personal responsibility. Ultimately, it undermines the foundations of democracy. On this rationale, conservative elites persuaded much of the liberal elite and all-too-many voters that government ought to do less and less for ordinary citizens. Of course, there were deeper conservative motives for dismantling government help, but conservative intellectuals concealed them behind psychological theories about rearing good citizens.

The conservative diagnosis was dead wrong and the treatment noxious. Just as individuals empower themselves by helping others, democratic government empowers itself by helping its citizens. The five principles of government help outlined in this chapter foster exactly the kind of citizenry democracy needs to flourish. Government help that allows citizens some control teaches them that government is for them and that they are entitled to participate in it. Help that gives people opportunities to serve empowers them and enables them to empower others. Help that spins webs expands and fortifies mutual self-help networks. Help with kin care strengthens families, nourishes neighborhoods, and nurtures caring citizens. Social insurance channels individual insecurities into a potent system of collective security.

Good government help instills the social counterparts of conservative virtues. Instead of personal ambition, hope for a better world. Instead of self-reliance, self-confidence in one's ability to make a difference. And instead of responsibility for self, responsibility for others and for community.

Good government help can nurture exactly the kind of citizenry that democracy needs to flourish.

Epilogue: Beyond the Samaritan's Dilemma

A politics of altruism can revive democracy. Most citizens aspire to be good neighbors in their personal lives, but everyday altruism is not merely a private matter—it is the germ of political action. Cooperation, help, and care are the weapons of ordinary people against threats to well-being. Every act of altruism protests against injustice and misery and helps to end them. Every altruistic gesture is a vote against the rule of self-interest.

Everyday altruism is a school for democratic citizenship. Government should help your neighbor and encourage you to help your neighbor because giving and getting help instill the qualities of character that make democracy work. Democracy means government by the people, but the people won't even try to govern if they don't believe they can influence anybody or get anything done. Democratic citizens have to feel empowered before they can exercise power. Help gives people the experience of making a difference, whether they are on the giving end or the receiving end. No other activity—not voting, marching, writing to legislators, or listening to debates—rivals help for giving citizens a taste of efficacy.

Politics begins with alliances—uniting for a common good. Help establishes the most primal form of alliance, because people come together in help at times of vulnerability, when urgent need trumps whatever norms, stereotypes, and other barriers normally keep them apart. In helping relationships, they see through each other's skin to the universal yearnings and pangs. They learn to see each other as equal in their common humanity. On that understanding, they build bridges across social divides. And because they come together in ways that lay bare human dependence, help forges powerful bonds of gratitude and responsibility.

A politics of altruism can inspire a new social movement and mobilize people into politics. Conservatives fueled their modern movement by exploiting differences, rivalries, and fears. Progressive leaders can revive a more just and humane democracy by appealing to commonality, cooperation, and hope.

We differ in many ways, but we hold our human vulnerability in common. We all need food, water, sleep, and air—preferably clean. We need help every day and need a lot of it at certain stages of life and in crises big and small. We all feel sadness and joy, loneliness and love, shame and pride, hurt and comfort, anger and gratitude, fear and courage, despair and hope. These needs and feelings lead us to lean on one another. They make us kin—part of the metaphorical human family.

Good leaders, like good parents, should nurture our feeling of kinship. They will speak the truth about our essential dependence on one another, not fictions about our self-sufficiency or fantasies about the perfect freedom of total independence. Dependence is part of our humanity and something else we have in common. Most citizens accept the idea that all of us need help. True, most us don't want to need it and dread the day we might need a lot of it, but most couldn't manage in a world without it. And few of us would stop giving it when it is needed.

It's time to claim our dependence and stop the conservative shame game. Treating those who need help as losers and parasites arrests democratic politics. Public shaming may not keep people away from the polls or civic and social associations, but it certainly doesn't welcome them into the public sphere. The shame game undermines empathy and suppresses generosity. Denigrating people who get help tarnishes help itself, and stifles the urge to help your neighbor. The culture of shame makes people second-guess the needy (Are they malingerers or con artists?) and themselves (Am I a sucker?). The cult of self-reliance shames people into denying how much we rely on each other for our individual and collective welfare. And then, it's a short step to questioning why we need government at all.

When leaders begin to talk honestly about vulnerability, they can acknowledge that people have good reasons to be scared: not enough food and health care, income insecurity, climate change and natural disasters, economic collapse, neighborhood decay, terrorism, and—even more frightening than what is now meant by terrorism—the terror of debility and old age. Instead of whipping up fear and fomenting conflict, good leaders should elicit our empathy by expressing theirs. Then they must assuage fear, starting with the biggest bogeyman of all, scarcity.

Progressive leaders must answer Malthus's Parable of Nature's Mighty Feast and its infinite conservative variations. According to

Malthus, nature is bountiful, but also wantonly prolific. It never provides enough food for all its children. The people who are lucky enough to find a place at nature's table, Malthus warns, dare not yield to the pleas of the hungry hordes outside the feast hall, else everyone will go hungry. The infamous "Harry and Louise" ad against Bill Clinton's universal health insurance plan was pure Malthus: If we who are lucky enough to have health insurance allow everyone to have it, Harry and Louise worried, we'll have to share our medical care with so many people that we won't get all we need. "Our plan is better," the couple concluded out loud. "It's not for us to worry about anyone else," whispered the deeper message. Malthusian threats whip up the backlashes against affirmative action and immigrants. If "we" let "them" in, there will be fewer jobs, places in good schools, and opportunities for us. Better to keep what we have than to help our neighbors.

Good leaders must persuade the people inside the figurative feast halls to unlock the doors and feed their hungry neighbors. The hardest insiders to convince are those who weren't invited to sit at the grand table but who get to pick scraps as they wash the dishes (low-wage workers, perhaps?) and feel ever-so-lucky to be inside the hall at all ("I've got my piece of the pie. It's barely a forkful, but at least it's something, so I dare not risk change."). We need a story such as the one Franklin Roosevelt told the American people in the depths of the Great Depression. It was not a story about lesser creatures who deserve their fate and, besides, the rest of us are better off without them. It was a story about bad leaders who had failed the citizens, and about mutual sacrifice for the common good. Roosevelt offered hope by showing that people can pull themselves out of dire circumstances by working together and helping each other.

Progressive leaders need to reclaim moral language. Over the course of three decades, the swelling conservative tide elevated personal responsibility to the highest civic virtue and redefined it as something rather selfish. In the modern conservative lexicon, it has come to mean responsibility for one's own personal well-being or, at best, for one's family or business. No longer an obligation to help others, personal responsibility now means a duty not to need help from others. Personal responsibility is a slogan hurled at welfare recipients, exhorting them to pay for their own kids; at seniors, warning them to pay for their own retirements and care; at workers, advising them to pay for their own health insurance and pensions; at minorities, goading them to pull themselves up by their own bootstraps; at doctors and other healers, enjoining them to watch the organizational bottom line; at people in developing countries, telling them they wouldn't need our handouts if only they would copy our market economy. And ultimately, personal responsibility is the perverse moral lesson thrust upon all of us citizens, urging us to worry about ourselves and no one else.

In every moral and religious system and in the minds of ordinary people, personal responsibility means responsibility for the well-being of others. Good leaders, instead of scapegoating some group or suggesting that "we" jettison "them" from our lifeboat, should remind us that we are all brothers and sisters, and, anyway, even strangers deserve our help, and we will render it because that is who we are. We are good neighbors.

Good neighbors need leaders who will reclaim the phrase "moral hazard."[1] Conservatives have used it to spin a cautionary tale about how help harms: if people know they can count on help when they get into trouble, they'll be less careful to avoid trouble, and they will bring more trouble upon themselves. This concept of moral hazard justifies withholding help, and conservatives trot it out to fight every conceivable form of help. Should government provide health insurance for children? No, because if parents know their children's hospital care will be covered, they'll be less careful about preventing their kids from having accidents.[2] Should towns paint crosswalks to keep pedestrians safe from cars? No, because crosswalks "may cause pedestrians to have a false sense of security and place themselves in a hazardous position."[3] Should employers help their employees buy health insurance? No, because with insurance "we can just completely disregard responsibility for our own health, then rely on well-trained physicians to remedy our ills."[4] Should government help people who lose their jobs or don't make enough to feed their families? You already know the answer. The story of moral hazard transforms collective help from a safety net into the danger itself.

The moral hazard of help *isn't* the temptation to be careless about taking care of yourself or to be cavalier about burdening others with having to rescue you. The real moral hazard is the temptation to walk past someone who needs help and to be cavalier about counting on others to act decently. A government that doesn't provide safety nets creates moral hazards for its citizens, because safety nets enable us to behave like the Samaritan, even when we can't be present at the scene. Without safety nets that we maintain together, we are collectively walking right past people who need help.

Social scientists, led by economists, have infused the image of humanity with unrelieved self-interest, to the point of creating a grotesque. Because we've been educated to think that we're moved by pure self-interest, we don't look for everyday altruism or notice it when it crosses our paths. Failing to notice it, we think it's rare. The teachings of science are self-reinforcing because they blind us to things that don't fit the model. Good leaders will reconnect us with our Samaritan selves by recognizing compassion, kindness, care, and generosity.

Finding altruism is simply a matter of believing in it and looking for it. The more you see, the more you see. Most of the stories in this book came from routine daily events that struck me because I had my eyes opened for altruism, or from news articles where I delved between the lines and pulled out a different story from the one the journalist reported. This is how one makes a new way of seeing.

Leaders, then, must show citizens the world through this lens of altruism by telling stories and celebrating altruism wherever they find it. In fact, the Good Samaritan parable in Luke's Gospel is as much a story about leadership as about morality. Jesus told the story of the Samaritan to illustrate a moral principle, but Luke told the story of Jesus's sermon to illustrate how Jesus led—by telling compelling stories that inspired people to behave rightly.

This kind of leadership is open to everyone. One of my hopes for this book is that it awakens readers to the altruism in their own lives and moves them to tell their stories. We need stories about everyday help and kindness. We need stories about how deeply people care for others and how wrenchingly they suffer when they cannot take good care of each other. We need stories about how it hurts and outrages to watch others suffer needlessly. We need stories about the injustice citizens feel when they see leaders who have the capacity to help stand by and do nothing.

Leaders campaigning for office can cultivate altruism—or not—by suggesting how voters should think about candidates and policies. Conventional wisdom about elections holds that people vote primarily on bread-and-butter issues. Ronald Reagan, campaigning for the presidency, advised voters to ask themselves, "Are you better off today than you were four years ago?" Pure self-interest. In a politics of altruism, politicians would craft campaign messages that speak to care-and-compassion issues. They might ask, "Can you care for the people you love as well as you'd like?" "Are you and your neighbors better off today than you were four years ago?" "Is your community a better or worse place to live?" Or they might inquire, "Tell me what kind of help you need to be able to care for your family and help your neighbors."

Leaders can best welcome people into the public sphere by playing the virtue game instead of the shame game. Praise the poor and the near-poor for how hard they work and for the sacrifices they make to do right by their families. Instead of treating stifled Samaritans as cheaters and outlaws, see them for the altruists they are. If they have to compromise their (and our) ethical standards in order to care for their families, at least consider whether they face double binds and whether any decent person in their shoes would not act as they do. Then ask the right question: not "How can 'we' reform 'them'?" but "How might the rest of us ease those double binds?" Bad character should be the explanation of last resort, not the starting assumption.

Leaders can stimulate a politics of altruism by offering more opportunities for community service, because, as we've seen, community service moves people, enlarges the sense of social responsibility, and nurtures democratic attitudes. Government promotes these opportunities not only through its own service programs such as the Peace Corps, Senior Corps, and Americorps but also through its funding of private nonprofit programs, such as food banks and Meals on Wheels. Slashing budgets for any of these programs harms the beneficiaries of these programs by depriving them of help; that much is obvious. Good leaders should highlight how such cuts also weaken one of the best training grounds for democratic politics.

Leading with altruism means recognizing that many people are motivated into advocacy and politics on behalf of others. Child-care activist Marcy Whitebook found that she couldn't get preschool teachers to organize on behalf of themselves, but when she presented evidence that low wages cause high teacher turnover and high turnover in turn hinders children's development, suddenly the teachers were willing to organize. They felt legitimate and fired up about pressing for children's interests, but not for their own financial well-being.[5] Caregiving occupations—home health workers, personal-care attendants, child-care workers, and nurses and hospital workers—are now the main source of new union members. Like other unionized workers, these people seek better wages and working conditions, but for them better working conditions include being able to render better care. Care workers are in a sense the vanguard of altruistic politics because their self-interested and altruistic motives are hard to separate.

As the September 11 obituaries show, the Good Neighbor is a widely shared moral identity. A politics of altruism can transcend the usual demographic identity politics and help unite people around a powerful moral aspiration. This is not to say that race, religion, gender, and other identities will ever dissipate, but the aspiration to compassion cuts across these other groupings.

Calling citizens to altruism in their private and public lives enables progressive leaders to reclaim moral language and speak to people of faith. Every religion has a part that asks its adherents to believe in its God and its doctrine and to worship in its prescribed ways, but each also has a more secular part that asks its adherents to observe certain rules of daily life. In the worldly sphere, all religions command their followers to help the poor and the suffering and to do good works on behalf of others. Thus, with the theme of helping others, leaders can reach religion but transcend sectarian differences.

If government fails to keep faith with citizens' moral values, good people will drop out of politics. When people can't be good neighbors and good citizens at the same time, they go off-duty as citizens. "After 3:30, you're a private citizen," as Nina, the home health aide, said to justify her defiance of Medicare rules. If government doesn't help the neighbors, citizens will either harden themselves to suffering or break laws and rules to help the neighbors themselves. Either way, they will lose respect for government and withdraw their support.

Citizens resent being prevented from helping others, but they do not want to be compelled to help, either. Indeed, U.S. law, following its English heritage, absolves citizens from a duty to rescue strangers. Should you come upon a baby drowning in a puddle and don't stop to help, the law won't hold you responsible or punish you. It won't hold you responsible even if you could have reached down and plucked the baby out of the puddle without so much as wetting the soles of your wing tips. If you choose to help, that's your business, but no one, especially the government, can compel you to act as a Good Samaritan.[6]

There are good reasons for not compelling altruism, the same ones that give libertarians the chills. Where would it stop? With so many people who need help and so many people who could help, how would lawmakers decide who is responsible to whom?

Most thinking on this dilemma puts the question to us as individuals: How much does each of us owe to strangers? Peter Singer, a well-known ethicist, proposed an answer that makes a lot of people very nervous. With so much poverty in the world, he said, those of us who are not poor should give away most of our money down to the point where we can be just comfortable.[7] That's further than most of us would want to go, and besides, we know that however much we sacrifice, we can't do the job alone.

Good leaders should put the question to us as members of communities: What should I as a citizen encourage my government to do for strangers? How shall government gather my and other citizens' wherewithal to help strangers? What should I ask my church to do and any other community of which I am a member? Progressive leaders past and present have imagined many ways for communities to help needy strangers that don't require each of us to spend our lives on permanent rescue duty. That's the virtue of government helping programs. Through politics, we can pool our resources, divvy up responsibility, and spread the duty to help equitably.

Democracy can't work if citizens think they don't need government or each other, if they believe that they can get all they need by hustling on their own. Democracy begins when citizens come together to make a better life for everyone. Democracy is a pact to help each other. We need leaders who can remind of us of that pact in our own history and tell us the stories of how we helped each other again and again.

All the civics education in the world won't move people into politics by itself. They need a reason to go there, a reason to care. We need leaders who reach citizens through their hearts and their hopes, not their hatreds and fears. We need leaders who can show us how government can help us all by helping us help each other. We need leaders who connect democracy with the cares that make us most fully human. Let us welcome the Good Samaritan back into the public realm.

ACKNOWLEDGMENTS

I had help galore—glorious, generous, talented, earnest, honest, caring help.

Rebecca Hayden made me look good even though she didn't want to read my book. Her refusal told me why I must write it.

Lee Rosenbaum understood why I needed to write it, opened paths, and mixed metaphors with compassionate abandon so that I could.

Brettne Bloom, my agent, gave her heart to Good Sam and found him the perfect home.

Carl Bromley, my editor at Nation Books, saw "the virtue of altruism" in a pile of stories.

Josh Berman, my project editor at Perseus Books and a writer himself, has been balm to an anxious author. Annette Wenda, my copy editor, used her way with words and gift for detail to make me look good in another way. And talk about karma: Josh is a veteran of the Peace Corps and Americorps and lives a life of service; Annette was a political science major and volunteers with Meals on Wheels and her library.

The Open Society Institute gave me an Individual Project Fellowship to develop my thinking about altruism and politics. Gail Goodman, my angel of a project officer, became my angel of a friend.

The Robert Wood Johnson Foundation gave me an Individual Investigator Award in Health Policy to explore the world of caregiving.

Home health nurses, aides, therapists, and administrators shared their work and themselves, and put the heart in this book.

The Phi Beta Kappa Society made me a visiting scholar and sent me to nine vibrant liberal arts campuses to try out my ideas and, as it happened, meet Good Samaritans and hear wonderful stories.

Linda Fowler first welcomed me to Dartmouth College, where Kathy Donald, Barbara Mellert, and the Baker-Berry Library staff support my scholarship in a thousand ways.

Kathryn Edin, Robert Coles, Alfie Kohn, and Kristen Renwick Monroe (two of whom I've never even met) nourished this book with all their written works.

Tom Baker, Bob Drago, Susan Gooden, Jonathan Haidt, Susan Hasazi, Larry Jacobs, Bob Kuttner, Suzanne Mettler, Peggy Nelson, Lewis Popper, Sally Popper, Joe Rees, Sandy Schram, Joe Soss, Joan Tronto, and Jim Wolf read or listened to bits, answered my questions, plied me with challenging questions of their own, and cheered me on. Judy Stone did all of the above and kept me in chocolate as well as intangibles that only my sister knows I need.

Barbara Holden Yeomans, who, like me, lives in books and writes them, too, extricated me from my study from time to time because "We have to talk about the world."

Two teachers have been with me ever since graduate school and find their way into most of what I write. Suzanne Berger showed me how to ask big questions and taught me that you never answer them, you just do your best to craft good arguments. Michael Lipsky taught me to hunt for the political in everyday life.

Ten years ago, "The Salonistas" began meeting monthly when Lisa Dodson, Mona Harrington, Lucie White, and I were fellows at the Radcliffe Public Policy Center, all trying to connect care and justice. Each of them is part of this book, and part of me.

Sybil F. Stone, my mother, taught me about caregiving from both sides, and gave me her love of language.

Stephen A. Stone, my father, was my safe harbor and my moral beacon. He blessed everyone who knew him with his gentleness and goodness. He did what he could to mend the world, and made me want to be like him.

And James A. Morone—Jim, to me—I can't put into words exactly how his love, faith, support, and wisdom helped, but I can say this: Ours is the story I want to write forever.

NOTES

INTRODUCTION

1. Tobi Walker, "The Service/Politics Split: Rethinking Service to Teach Political Engagement," *PS: Political Science and Politics* 33, no. 2 (September 2000): 647–49.

CHAPTER 1

1. "Panhandler Concerns Residents," Newport (N.H.) Argus-Champion, March 28, 2001, 7.

2. Barbara Ehrenreich, Nickel and Dimed: On (Not) Getting by in America (New York: Metropolitan Books, 2001).

3. Economic Policy Institute, Minimum Wage Issue Guide (Washington, D.C.: Economic Policy Institute, April 2007), available at http://www.epinet.org/content .cfm/issueguides_minwage.

4. Mark Robert Rank, *Living on the Edge: The Realities of Welfare in America* (New York: Columbia University Press, 1994), 127.

5. Quoted in Paul Krugman, *The Conscience of a Liberal* (New York: W. W. Norton, 2007), 58–59.

6. See Martin Gilens, *Why Americans Hate Welfare* (Chicago: University of Chicago Press, 2000); and Krugman, *Conscience of a Liberal,* 92–96.

7. *New York Times*, November 28, 2001, B10.

8. *New York Times*, December 4, 2001, B9.

9. *New York Times,* December 5, 2001, B9.

10. *New York Times*, September 19, 2001.

11. *New York Times*, December 11, 2001, B7.

12. *New York Times*, December 18, 2001, B8.

13. *New York Times*, December 8, 2001, B9.

14. *New York Times*, October 3, 2001.

15. *New York Times*, December 8, 2001, B8.

16. *New York Times*, December 15, 2001, B8.

17. *New York Times,* October 26, 2001, B11.

18. Donna Fowler, "Democracy's Next Generation," *Educational Leadership* (November 1990): 10–15.

19. National Association of Secretaries of State, *New Millennium Project, Phase I: A Nationwide Study of 15–24 Year Old Youth* (Alexandria, Va.: Tarrance Group, 1999), cited in Joseph Kahne and Joel Westheimer, "Teaching Democracy: What Schools Need to Do," *Phi Delta Kappan* (September 2003): 34–66.

20. Panetta Institute, "Institute Poll Shows College Students Turned Off by Politics, Turned On by Other Public Service," January 13, 2000 http://www.panettainstitute .org/surveys/survey-1999.htm.

21. Walker, "Service/Politics Split," 648 (see introduction, n. 1).

22. Fowler, "Democracy's Next Generation," 10.

23. Wendy Lesser, *The Amateur* (New York: Pantheon Books, 1999), 137–38.

24. Robert Berenson, "In a Doctor's Wallet: Financial Confessions of a Sawbones," *New Republic*, May 18, 1987, 11–13.

25. David S. Cloud, "Navy Pilots Who Rescued Victims Are Reprimanded," *New York Times*, September 5, 2005, A21.

26. Ralph Waldo Emerson, "Self-Reliance," in *The Essays of Ralph Waldo Emerson* (Cambridge: Harvard University, Belknap Press, 1987), 30–31.

27. Robert J. Samuelson, *The Good Life and Its Discontents* (1995; reprint, New York: Vintage, 1997), 12, 13.

28. Eric Lipton and Scott Shane, "Leader of Federal Effort Feels the Heat," *New York Times*, September 3, 2005, A11.

29. Quoted in Kathryn Edin and Laura Lein, *Making Ends Meet: How Single Mothers Survive Welfare and Low-Wage Work* (New York: Russell Sage Foundation, 1997), 76.

30. Mickey Kaus, "Compassion, the Political Liability," *New York Times*, June 25, 1999, A23.

31. The phrase is Edward O. Wilson's, in *On Human Nature* (Cambridge: Harvard University Press, 1978), 172, cited in Alfie Kohn, *The Brighter Side of Human Nature* (New York: Basic Books, 1990), 197.

32. Jim Dwyer, "Rescue under the Rubble Helps Ease Weight of Past," *New York Times*, November 6, 2001, A1.

CHAPTER 2

1. Ronald Reagan, first inaugural address, January 20, 1981, available at http://reaganlibrary.com/reagan/speeches/first.asp.

2. Kaus, "Compassion, the Political Liability," A23 (see chap. 1, n. 30).

3. Marvin Olasky, *Renewing American Compassion: How Compassion for the Needy Can Turn Ordinary Citizens into Heroes* (Washington, D.C.: Regnery Publishing, 1996), 27.

4. Dinesh D'Souza, "Civilizing Greed," *San Diego Union-Tribune*, February 11, 2001, available at the American Enterprise Institute's Web site, http://www.aei.org/ ra/radsou010211.htm.

5. Don Feder, "Dangers Lurk in 'Compassionate Conservatism,'" *Human Events* (January 29, 1999): 9.

6. Comment in the spin room after a presidential candidates' debate in Columbia, South Carolina, May 15, 2007, quoted in Peter J. Boyer, "Mayberry 'Man,'" *New Yorker*, August 20, 2007, 56.

7. Charles Murray, *Losing Ground: American Social Policy, 1950–1980* (New York: Basic Books, 1984). For the role of conservative think tanks in shaping American policy thinking, see Jean Stefancic and Richard Delgado, *No Mercy: How Conservative Think Tanks and Foundations Changed America's Social Agenda* (Philadelphia: Temple University Press, 1996); and John Mickelthwaite and Adrian Wooldridge, *Right Nation: Conservative Power in America* (New York: Penguin, 2004), esp. chap. 3. Sidney Blumenthal describes how the Manhattan Institute funded and promoted *Losing Ground* in *The Rise of the Counter-Establishment* (New York: Harper and Row, 1988), 294–95.

8. Albert O. Hirschman, *The Rhetoric of Reaction* (Cambridge: Harvard University Press, Belknap Press, 1991).

9. Olasky, Renewing American Compassion, 26–27; Lawrence M. Mead, Beyond Entitlement: The Social Obligations of Citizenship (New York: Free Press, 1986), 67.

10. Charles Murray, *In Pursuit of Happiness and Good Government* (San Francisco: Institute for Contemporary Studies Press, 1994), 220–21.

11. James Payne, *Overcoming Welfare: Expecting More from the Poor and from Ourselves* (New York: Basic Books, 1998), 103.

12. Murray, *Losing Ground,* 212–13.

13. Ibid., 213.

14. Ibid., 162.

15. Robert Rector quoted in Jeffrey L. Katz, "Members Pushing to Retain Welfare System Control," *Congressional Quarterly,* January 28, 1995, 280–83; Heather MacDonald, "Keep Fixing Welfare," *New York Daily News,* June 24, 2001, http://www.nydailynews.com/2 . . . 06–24/News_and_Views/Opinion/a–116001.asp; MacDonald, *The Burden of Bad Ideas* (Chicago: Ivan R. Dee, 2000), x.

16. Payne, *Overcoming Welfare,* 23.

17. Joel F. Handler and Yeheskel Hasenfeld, *We the Poor People: Work, Poverty, and Welfare* (New Haven: Yale University Press, 1997), 46.

18. David Kelley, *A Life of One's Own: Individual Rights and the Welfare State* (Washington, D.C.: Cato Institute, 1998), 104.

19. Mead, *Beyond Entitlement,* 73, 72; emphases in original.

20. Ibid., 84–85.

21. Lawrence Mead, *The New Politics of Poverty: The Non-working Poor in America* (New York: Basic Books, 1992), 142.

22. Mead, *Beyond Entitlement,* 82–88, quotation on 84.

23. John Hood, "Senior Slump," *National Review*, October 23, 2000, 56; Mark Steyn, "Gray Dawn," *National Review*, October 23, 2000, 59.

24. Clarence Thomas, *My Grandfather's Son* (New York: Harper Collins, 2007), 56–57.

25. Stephan Thernstrom and Abigail Thernstrom, *America in Black and White* (New York: Simon and Schuster, 1997), 421–22.

26. Ibid., 405–12; Dinesh D'Souza, *Illiberal Education* (New York: Free Press, 1991), 43.

27. Harvey C. Mansfield Jr., "The Underhandedness of Affirmative Action," in *Racial Preference and Racial Justice*, edited by Russell Nieli (Washington, D.C.: Ethics and Public Policy Center, 1991), 130; Abigail Thernstrom, *Whose Votes Count? Affirmative Action and the Voting Rights Act* (Cambridge: Harvard University Press, 1987), 240.

28. Mansfield, "Underhandedness of Affirmative Action," 140.

29. John Feinstein, "Golfers Ambivalent about Martin Ruling," *Lebanon (N.H.) Valley News*, June 2, 2001, A8 (from the *Washington Post*).

30. Samuelson, *Good Life*, 4, xiii, and passim (see chap. 1, n. 27).

31. Gabriel A. Almond and Sidney Verba, *The Civic Culture: Political Attitudes and Democracy in Five Nations* (Princeton: Princeton University Press, 1963), 181; emphasis added.

32. Robert D. Putnam, *Bowling Alone: The Collapse and Revival of American Community* (New York: Simon and Schuster, 2000), 338.

33. MacDonald, *Burden of Bad Ideas*, 164.

34. Mead, *New Politics of Poverty*, 149 (emphasis added), 151. Mead edges around this idea in his earlier book, *Beyond Entitlement*, 43.

35. Kaus, "Compassion, the Political Liability," A23.

36. Ayn Rand, *Atlas Shrugged* (1957; reprint, New York: Signet, 1996), 523.

37. Ibid., 839.

38. Ayn Rand, *The Virtue of Selfishness* (New York: Signet, 1964), 49; Robert J. Samuelson, "The Lesson of Tough Love," *Newsweek*, September 4, 2000, 27; Payne, *Overcoming Welfare*, 140; Mead, *New Politics of Poverty*, 131; Gertrude Himmelfarb, *The De-moralization of Society: From Victorian Virtues to Modern Values* (New York: Vintage Books, 1994), 242–43; Thernstrom and Thernstrom, *America in Black and White*, 172.

39. Kelley, *A Life of One's Own*, 107.

40. Mead, *New Politics of Poverty*, 131, 144.

41. Kaus, "Compassion, the Political Liability," A23; Mickey Kaus, "Up from Altruism," *New Republic*, December 15, 1986, 17.

42. Mickey Kaus, *The End of Equality* (New York: New Republic / Basic Books, 1992), 137–39.

43. Rand, *The Virtue of Selfishness*, 36; Kelley, *A Life of One's Own*, 100.

44. Rand, *The Virtue of Selfishness*, 34–35.

45. Robert Nozick, *Anarchy, State, and Utopia* (New York: Basic Books, 1974), 155–74, quotations on 169 (emphasis added), 172 (emphasis in the original).

46. "The donor [is] free to choose": Kelley, *A Life of One's Own*, 94–97, quotation on 96; "dangerous force": Richard Epstein, *Principles for a Free Society: Reconciling Individual Liberty with the Common Good* (Reading, Mass.: Perseus Books, 1998), 138.

47. Nozick, *Anarchy, State, and Utopia*, 160; Kelley, *A Life of One's One*, 97; Rand, *The Virtue of Selfishness*, 95. For the record, Medicare never compelled doctors to treat Medicare patients, but it did become a major source of revenue for those who do want to treat elderly patients, and Medicare payments have become essential to

hospitals, nursing homes, rehabilitation centers, home health care agencies, and medical schools. Like all private health insurance, Medicare puts boundaries on what it will cover, and in that sense could be said to restrict doctors' freedom. But also like private, voluntary insurance, Medicare enables many doctors to do things for patients that they could not afford to do without it.

48. Benjamin I. Page and Robert Y. Shapiro, *The Rational Public: Fifty Years of Trends in Americans' Policy Preferences* (Chicago: University of Chicago Press, 1992). Page and Shapiro reviewed hundreds of opinion surveys from the 1930s through the late 1980s to explore changes and trends. Except where noted, the information about public opinion in this and subsequent paragraphs is based on chapters 3 and 4.

49. Ibid., 124; "Trends in Political Values and Core Attitudes, 1987–2007" (Washington, D.C.: Pew Research Center for the People and the Press, March 2007), available at http://www.people-press.org. In this same survey, 70 percent of people also agreed with this statement: "Poor people have become too dependent on government assistance." Yet almost two-thirds (63 percent) of those who think the poor are "too dependent on government" said they believe "government has a responsibility to take care of people who cannot take care of themselves." Lawrence Jacobs explains some of these seeming inconsistencies by saying that Americans are "philosophical conservatives" but "pragmatic liberals." They subscribe to conservative principles such as small government and low taxes, but they support liberal redistributive programs ("The American Public's Pragmatic Liberalism Meets Its Philosophical Conservatism," *Journal of Health Politics, Policy, and Law* 24, no. 5 [1999]: 1021–30).

50. Page and Shapiro, *Rational Public*, 127.

51. Fay Lomax Cook and Edith Barrett, *Support for the American Welfare State* (New York: Columbia University Press, 1992), 62–65.

52. Robert Coles, *The Call of Service: A Witness to Idealism* (Boston: Houghton Mifflin, 1993), 55.

53. Dan Bustard, "Town Debates Extent of Relief Effort," *Claremont (N.H.) Eagle Times,* September 9, 2005, A1.

54. The first edition (1798) was so successful that five years later, Malthus expanded it to five times its original length—he virtually wrote a new book—but kept the same title. In the notes below I indicate which version I used in parentheses. For the 1803 edition, I use T. R. Malthus, *An Essay on the Principle of Population,* 2nd ed., edited by Donald Winch (Cambridge: Cambridge University Press, 1992). For the 1798 edition, I use Thomas Malthus, *An Essay on the Principle of Population,* edited by Anthony Flew (Harmondsworth, England: Penguin Books, 1970).

55. Ibid. (1803), book 3, chap. 5, p. 98.

56. Charles Darwin, *Autobiography,* edited by Nora Barlow (London: Collins, 1958), 119–20; Darwin, *The Origin of the Species,* 6th ed. (1872; reprint, New York: Carlton House, n.d.), 13. In his book on the evolution of morality, Matt Ridley notes that John Maynard Keynes described *The Origin of the Species* as "simply Ricardian economics couched in scientific language" and Stephen Jay Gould called natural selection "Adam Smith's economics read into nature" (*The Origins of Virtue: Human Instincts and the Evolution of Cooperation* [New York: Penguin, 1996], 252).

57. Malthus, *Essay* (1798), book 1, chap. 1, p. 14.

58. Ibid. (1803), 106.

59. Ibid., book 4, chap. 6, pp. 248–49.

60. Ibid., 249.

61. Ibid., 207.

62. Amartya Sen, *Poverty and Famines: An Essay on Entitlement and Deprivation* (New York: Oxford University Press, 1981), 137–39.

63. Ibid., 49.

64. Franklin Delano Roosevelt, first inaugural address, March 4, 1933.

65. James M. Buchanan, "The Samaritan's Dilemma," in *Altruism, Morality, and Economics,* edited by Edmund Phelps (New York: Russell Sage Foundation, 1975), 71.

66. Ibid., 74.

67. Gertrude Himmelfarb, *Poverty and Compassion* (New York: Alfred A. Knopf, 1992), 6; Payne, *Overcoming Welfare,* 21–22; Susan Saulny, "New Orleans Hurt by Acute Rental Shortage," *New York Times,* December 3, 2007, A1.

68. Buchanan, "The Samaritan's Dilemma," 84.

69. Nancy Folbre, *The Invisible Heart: Economics and Family Values* (New York: New Press, 2001).

70. Charles Darwin, *The Descent of Man,* 2nd ed. (1871; reprint, New York: A. L. Burt, 1874), 151–52.

71. Ibid., 152.

72. Charles Schultze, *The Public Use of Private Interest* (Washington, D.C.: Brookings Institution Press, 1977), 21–25. Schultze approvingly characterized the market's operation as "the Darwinian selection process."

73. "Belief in the Law of Demand is the distinguishing mark of the economist," Donald McCloskey wrote in *The Rhetoric of Economics* (Madison: University of Wisconsin Press, 1985), 59.

74. David Card and Alan Krueger, *Myth and Measurement: The New Economics of the Minimum Wage* (Princeton: Princeton University Press, 1995).

75. Arthur Okun, *Equality and Efficiency: The Big Trade-Off* (Washington, D.C.: Brookings Institution Press, 1975).

76. Milton Friedman and Rose Friedman, *Free to Choose* (New York: Avon, 1990), 99.

77. Albert O. Hirschman, *Exit, Voice, and Loyalty: Responses to Decline in Firms, Organizations, and States* (Cambridge: Harvard University Press, 1970).

CHAPTER 3

1. I got the story from Kristen Renwick Monroe, *The Heart of Altruism: Perceptions of a Common Humanity* (Princeton: Princeton University Press, 1996), 143. Monroe says she got the story from Joseph Losco, "Understanding Altruism: A Comparison of Various Models," *Political Psychology* 7, no. 2 (1986): 323–48.

2. Alexis de Tocqueville, *Democracy in America,* 2 vols. (1835 and 1840; reprint, New York: Vintage Books, 1990), vol. 2, book 2, chap. 8, p. 122.

3. Jane Allyn Piliavin and Hong-Wen Charng, "Altruism: A Review of Recent Theory and Research," *Annual Review of Sociology* 16 (1990): 27.

4. To quote another research review, altruism "provides benefits to its recipients but *also provides no benefits to the actors and even incurs some costs*" (*Encyclopedia of Sociology*, edited by Edgar F. Borgatta [New York: Macmillan Reference USA, 2000], s.v. "Altruism"). Daniel Batson's work most rigorously pursues this line of inquiry. See C. Daniel Batson, *The Altruism Question: Toward a Social Psychological Answer* (Hinsdale, N.J.: Lawrence Erlbaum, 1991).

5. Piliavin and Charng, "Altruism," 28.

6. The two best reviews of this skeptical scientific literature I have found are Alfie Kohn, *The Brighter Side of Human Nature* (New York: Basic Books, 1990), chap. 7; and Monroe, *Heart of Altruism*, chaps. 7–9. Morton Hunt presents a very readable popular summary in *The Compassionate Beast: What Science Is Discovering about the Humane Side of Humankind* (New York: William Morrow, 1990), 21–26. "Scratch an altruist . . ." is from Michael T. Ghiselin, *The Economy of Nature and the Evolution of Sex* (Berkeley and Los Angeles: University of California Press, 1974).

7. One of the earliest and best popular accounts of evolutionary theory and altruism is Ridley, *Origins of Virtue* (see chap. 2, n. 56). A thorough scientific account, one that also breaks new ground, is Elliott Sober and David Sloan Wilson, *Unto Others: The Evolution and Psychology of Unselfish Behavior* (Cambridge: Harvard University Press, 1998). Lee Alan Dugatkin narrates the scientific quest to reconcile altruism and natural selection in *The Altruism Equation: Seven Scientists Search for the Origin of Goodness* (Princeton: Princeton University Press, 2007). A short up-to-date summary of the literature is Olivia Judson, "The Selfless Gene," *Atlantic,* October 2007, 90–98.

8. The altruism part of the General Social Survey has been done twice, in 2002 and 2004. Tom W. Smith, in "Altruism and Empathy in America" (Chicago: National Opinion Research Center, University of Chicago, February 2006), reports the results from the 2004 General Social Survey. They are not substantially different from the 2002 survey, reported in Tom W. Smith, "Altruism and Empathy in America: Trends and Correlates" (Chicago: National Opinion Research Center, University of Chicago), report prepared for the Fetzer Institute, release date July 25, 2003. In the text, I used the percentages from the 2004 survey and rounded up.

9. *Giving and Volunteering in the United States, 2001* (Washington, D.C.: Independent Sector, 2001). This survey included adults twenty-one years old and over. The Independent Sector's earlier surveys found higher rates of volunteering—56 percent of adults in 1999—in large part because the earlier surveys included youths aged eighteen to twenty, who tend to have higher rates.

10. Robert Wuthnow, *Acts of Compassion: Caring for Others and Helping Ourselves* (Princeton: Princeton University Press, 1991), 8.

11. Paul G. Schervish and John J. Havens, "The Boston Area Diary Study and the Moral Citizenship of Care," *Voluntas: International Journal of Voluntary and Nonprofit Organizations* 13, no. 1 (March 2002): 47–71.

12. Wuthnow, *Acts of Compassion*, 199. Kristen Renwick Monroe heard many similar demurrals when she interviewed philanthropists and altruists for *The Heart of Altruism*.

13. Patrick M. Rooney, Kathryn S. Steinberg, and Paul G. Schervish, "A Methodological Comparison of Giving Surveys: Indiana as a Test Case," *Nonprofit and Voluntary Sector Quarterly* 30, no. 1 (2001): 551–68. For the same phenomenon in volunteering, see U.S. Department of Labor, Bureau of Labor Statistics, *Volunteering in the United States, 2006* (Washington, D.C.: Department of Labor, Bureau of Labor Statistics, January 2007). If respondents didn't answer yes to certain questions, they were asked detailed prompt questions with examples, and asked to respond again. The Bureau of Labor Statistics first used prompts in its 2006 survey, and the report notes that responses to prompts yielded higher numbers of people volunteering. See the technical note on pp. 5–6. Available at http://www.bls.gov/news.release/volun.toc.htm.

14. Katherine Edin and Maria Kefalas, *Promises I Can Keep: Why Poor Women Put Motherhood before Marriage* (Berkeley and Los Angeles: University of California Press, 2007), 147–48.

15. Gary Becker, *A Treatise on the Family* (Cambridge: Harvard University Press, 1981).

16. Folbre, *Invisible Heart*, 109–10, 40 (see chap. 2, n. 69).

17. The figure for family caregivers is from Peter Arno, Carol Levine, and Margaret M. Memmot, "The Economic Value of Informal Caregiving," *Health Affairs* 18, no. 2 (1999): 182–88. Information on employed caregivers is from National Association for Home Care, *Basic Statistics about Home Care, 1999* (Washington, D.C.: National Association for Home Care, 1999), table 12, p. 13.

18. National Alliance for Caregiving and AARP, *Caregiving in the U.S.* (Washington, D.C.: National Alliance for Caregiving, April 2004), 6, available at http://www.caregiving.org/data/04finalreport.pdf. To be considered a caregiver in this survey, a person had to be providing help with at least one activity of daily living (such as dressing, walking, or going to the toilet) or one so-called instrumental activity (such as paying bills or shopping). This figure is consistent with Robert Wuthnow's findings in his survey of about twenty-one hundred adults: more than half of them had provided care to someone who was very sick, and one-quarter of them had done so in the previous year (*Acts of Compassion*, 8).

19. National Alliance for Caregiving and AARP, *Family Caregiving in the U.S.* (Washington, D.C.: National Alliance for Caregiving, 2000), 46, 62, 64, 33.

20. John Steinbeck, *Of Mice and Men* (1937; reprint, New York: Penguin Books, 1993).

21. Katherine S. Newman, *A Different Shade of Gray: Midlife and Beyond in the Inner City* (New York: New Press, 2003), 208–9.

22. Ibid., 210.

23. Nikki Silva and Davia Nelson, *Hidden Kitchens* (n.p.: Rodale, 2005), xiii–xvi.

24. Brock Rutter, "Country Kitchen Serves Its Last Birds," *Newport (N.H.) Argus-Champion*, November 26, 2003, A1.

25. Carolyn Dube, "More than Just a Ride: COA's Volunteer Driver Program Changes Lives," *Newport (N.H.) Argus-Champion,* March 1, 2006, A4.

26. Ibid.

27. All quotations in this paragraph are from Tom Gantert, "Volunteers Are Veterans in More Ways than One," *Ann Arbor News,* November 11, 2005, A1.

28. Jamie Pilarczyk, "Volunteers Are Driven to Help," *Tampa Tribune,* August 11, 2007, available at http://global.factiva.com/ha/default.aspx; Rachel Cohen, "Meals on Wheels Seeks Donations for New Digs," *Oakland Tribune,* August 25, 2007, available at http://global.factiva.com/ha/default.aspx.

29. "Senior Companion Program Keeps Older Adults Connected to Life," http://www.racinedominicans.org/pages/senior.cfm.

30. On military contractors, see Jeremy Scahill, *Blackwater: The Rise of the World's Most Powerful Mercenary Army* (New York: Nation Books, 2007).

31. *Heart Work,* video produced by the Service Employees International Union (Washington, D.C., 1999).

32. Judith Rollins, *Between Women: Domestics and Their Employers* (Philadelphia: Temple University Press, 1985), 120; Mary Romero, *Maid in the U.S.A.* (New York: Routledge, 1992), 107.

33. Coles, *Call of Service,* 86, 88 (see chap. 2, n. 52).

34. Laura Harris-Hirsch, "Looking Good, Feeling Better," *Lebanon (N.H.) Valley News,* May 4, 2003, C1.

35. http://www.lookgoodfeelbetter.org/women/explore/feature.htm; Stacy Resnikoff, "More Stories," available at http://www.lookgoodfeelbetter.org/women/explore/more_stories/volunteers.htm.

36. Ehrenreich, *Nickel and Dimed,* 37, 104–5 (see chap. 1, n. 2).

37. Patricia Siplon, professor of political science at St. Michael's College in Colchester, Vermont, personal correspondence, October 14, 1999.

38. The story was covered widely in the news, but is elegantly told by Joseph William Singer in *Edges of the Field* (Boston: Beacon Press, 2000), chap. 1. See also Lynnley Browning, "Fire Could Not Stop a Mill, but Debts May," *New York Times,* November 28, 2001, C1.

39. Jenn Abelson, "American Success Story Ends for Grocer," *Boston Globe,* January 15, 2006, A1.

40. Manny Fernandez, "Cash to Get by Is Still Pawnshop's Stock in Trade," *New York Times,* September 14, 2007, A1.

41. See note 9. A Boston College research group found similarly high rates of giving, basing their estimates on analysis of several surveys of charitable giving, which they acknowledge use different definitions and methods. See John Havens, Mary A. O'Herlihy, and Paul G. Schervish, "Charitable Giving: How Much, by Whom, to What, and How?" in *The Nonprofit Sector: A Research Handbook,* edited by Walter W. Powell and Richard Steinberg (New Haven: Yale University Press, 2006), 543.

42. Chuin-Wei Yap, "Anonymous Donor Pays Seniors' Bill," *Bethel (Maine) Morning Sentinel,* June 16, 2005, A1.

43. Carol Robidoux, "Race Car Driver Saves NH Pantry," *Manchester (N.H.) Union Leader*, January 12, 2006, B2; Adrian Walker, "An Act of Kindness," *Boston Globe*, July 31, 2006, B1.

44. Vivian S. Toy, "Teacher Donates Tiny Violins, and Himself, to Queens School," *New York Times*, January 15, 1999, A19.

45. Rachel Emma Silverman, "A New Generation Reinvents Philanthropy," *Wall Street Journal*, August 21, 2007, D1.

46. *New York Times*, October 4, 1999, A26.

47. Loretta Schwartz-Nobel, *Growing Up Empty: How Federal Policies Are Starving America's Children* (New York: Harper Perennial, 2002), 46.

48. Lars Eighner, *Travels with Lisbeth* (New York: St. Martin's, 1993), 109–10.

49. Kathleen Brehony, *Ordinary Grace: An Examination of the Roots of Compassion, Altruism, and Empathy, and the Ordinary Individuals Who Help Others in Extraordinary Ways* (New York: Riverhead Books, 1999), 178. The story was told by Genny Nelson to Brehony.

50. Julie Salamon, *Rambam's Ladder: A Meditation on Generosity and Why It Is Necessary to Give* (New York: Workman, 2003), 144–45.

51. David Abel, "'Something I Can Do': Compassion Helps Homeless Woman Get by, Earn Her Keep," *Boston Globe*, July 14, 2002, B1.

52. Newman, *Different Shade of Gray*, 141–42.

53. "Heroes: Men Pull Lady from Burning Car," *Claremont (N.H.) Eagle Times*, October 22, 2001, A14.

54. Tom Leo, "Act of Kindness Changed His Life," *Syracuse Post-Standard*, March 3, 2007, A1.

55. Judy Levine, in "Metropolitan Diary," *New York Times*, August 20, 2007, A20.

56. Bibb Latané and John Darley, *The Unresponsive Bystander: Why Doesn't He Help?* (Englewood Cliffs, N.J.: Prentice-Hall, 1970). Morton Hunt interviewed Latané about this research and provides a nontechnical description of the experiments and what motivated Latané and Darley to do them (*Compassionate Beast*, 132–35).

57. This research is nicely reviewed in Harvey Hornstein, *Cruelty and Kindness: A New Look at Aggression and Altruism* (Englewood Cliffs, N.J.: Prentice-Hall, 1976), chap. 1.

58. Maria Cramer, "EMT Off Duty Races to Shooting," *Boston Globe*, August 14, 2007, B1.

59. Maria Cramer, "'I Knew That They Would Help,'" *Boston Globe*, January 12, 2006, B1.

60. Quoted in Monroe, *Heart of Altruism*, 113, 118. From her extensive interviews Monroe concluded that people don't calculate their ethical decisions rationally; they simply do not perceive that they have a choice. See Kristen Renwick Monroe and Connie Epperson, "'But What Else Could I Do?': Choice, Identity, and a Cognitive-Perceptual Theory of Ethical Political Behavior," *Political Psychology* 15, no. 2 (1994): 201–26.

61. Katherine Marchocki, "Rescuer Beats Death This Time," *Manchester (N.H.) Union Leader*, April 30, 2001, A1.

62. . Mary Williams Walsh, "Impulse to Help Allows a Wife to Understand," *New York Times,* December 10, 2001, B1.

CHAPTER 4

1. "None shall give him": Sophocles, *Antigone, Oedipus the King, Electra,* translated by H. D. F. Kitto (1964; reprint, Oxford: Oxford University Press, 1994), 9; "I deny nothing": Sophocles, *The Antigone,* translated by Gilbert Murray (New York: Oxford University Press, 1941), 37.

2. Sophocles, *Antigone,* translated by Kitto, 4.

3. Charles Paul Segal, "Sophocles' Praise of Man and the Conflicts of *The Antigone,*" in *Sophocles: A Collection of Critical Essays,* edited by Thomas Woodard (Englewood Cliffs, N.J.: Prentice-Hall, 1966), 70.

4. My version of this story comes from Mona Harrington, *Care and Equality: Inventing a New Family Politics* (New York: Alfred A. Knopf, 1999). See also *Upton v. JWP Businessland,* 425 756 (Mass. 1997).

5. The Family and Medical Leave Act applies to employers with fifty or more employees. It provides up to twelve weeks of unpaid leave for taking care of a newborn or adopted child, sick family members, or for the employee's own illness.

6. Multistate Working Families Consortium, "Family Values at Work: It's about Time!" draft October 2006, 9, available at http://www.9to5.org.

7. *Schultz v. Advocate Health and Hospitals Corp.,* 2002 U.S. Dist. Lexis 9517 (N.D. Ill. 2002). See also Sue Schallenberger, "A Downside of Taking Family Leave: Getting Fired while You're Gone," *Wall Street Journal,* January 23, 2003, D1.

8. Joan Williams, "Gender Stereotyping: Expanding the Boundaries of Title VII," proceedings of the 2006 annual meeting of the Association of American Law Schools, section on employment discrimination law, *Employee Rights and Employment Policy Journal* 10 (2006): 271–92.

9. Joan Williams, *Unbending Gender: Why Family and Work Conflict and What to Do about It* (New York: Oxford University Press, 2000).

10. Lisa Dodson, "Wage-Poor Mothers and Moral Economy," *Social Politics: International Journal of Gender, State, and Society* 14, no. 2 (2007): 260.

11. Ibid.

12. The 11 percent figure comes from Vicky Lovell, *No Time to Be Sick: Why Everyone Suffers When Workers Don't Have Paid Sick Leave* (Washington, D.C.: Institute for Women's Policy Research, 2004), table 4, p. 11, available at http://www.iwpr.org/pdf/B242.pdf. See also S. Jody Heymann, Alison Earle, and Brian Egleston, "Parental Availability for the Care of Sick Children," *Pediatrics* 98, no. 2 (August 1996): 226–30.

13. Dodson, "Wage-Poor Mothers," 270.

14. Kathryn Edin and Laura Lein, *Making Ends Meet: How Single Mothers Survive Welfare and Low-Wage Work* (New York: Russell Sage Foundation, 1997), 136, 96–97, 95.

15. National Alliance for Caregiving and AARP, *Caregiving in the U.S.* (see chap. 3, n. 18); National Alliance for Caregiving, *Family Caregiving in the U.S.:*

Findings from a National Survey (Washington, D.C.: National Alliance for Caregiving, 1997).

16. Katherine Newman, *No Shame in My Game* (New York: Random House / Russell Sage Foundation, 1999), provides an insightful discussion of these broken bonds among the working poor on pp. 161–74.

17. Jason DeParle, "Conflicts at Home Mine the Road to Independence," *New York Times,* July 4, 1999, A1.

18. See especially Sharon Hays, *Flat Broke with Children: Women in the Age of Welfare Reform* (New York: Oxford University Press, 2003).

19. Pensions as "salaries" from a 1914 periodical, quoted in Molly Ladd-Taylor, *Mother-Work: Women, Child Welfare, and the State, 1890–1930* (Urbana: University of Illinois Press, 1994), 144; "The pension removes the mother" from "Illinois 'State Report,'" *Child-Welfare Magazine* 10, no. 7 (March 1916): 256–57, cited in Theda Skocpol, *Protecting Soldiers and Mothers* (Cambridge: Harvard University Press, 1992), 475.

20. The details of this story come from Nina Bernstein, "As Welfare Deadline Looms, Answers Don't Seem Easy," *New York Times,* June 25, 2001, A1.

21. Sherry Wexler, "To Work and to Mother: The Politics of Family Support and Family Leave" (Ph.D. diss., Brandeis University, 1997).

22. Edin and Lein, *Making Ends Meet,* 63–65, quotation on 66. See also Valerie Polakow, *Lives on the Edge: Single Mothers and Their Children in the Other America* (Chicago: University of Chicago Press, 1993).

23. For eloquent testimony, see Edin and Lein, *Making Ends Meet,* chap. 3; Rank, *Living on the Edge,* chap. 8 (see chap. 1, n. 4); and Joe Soss, *Unwanted Claims: The Politics of Participation in the U.S. Welfare System* (Ann Arbor: University of Michigan Press, 2000), chap. 3.

24. Soss, *Unwanted Claims,* 43; Karen Roberts quoted in Rank, *Living on the Edge,* 132.

25. Lisa Dodson, *Don't Call Us Out of Name: The Untold Lives of Women and Girls in Poor America* (Boston: Beacon Press, 1998), 137–38.

26. "I needed to help": Soss, *Unwanted Claims,* 44–45; "I don't care": Barry Jay Seltser and Donald E. Miller, *Homeless Families: The Struggle for Dignity* (Urbana: University of Illinois Press, 1993), 19; "I much prefer": Rank, *Living on the Edge,* 132–33.

27. Dodson, *Don't Call Us Out of Name;* Lisa Dodson, Tiffany Manuel, and Ellen Bravo, *Keeping Jobs and Raising Families in Low-Income America: It Just Doesn't Work,* report of the Across the Boundaries Project of the Radcliffe Public Policy Center and 9 to 5 National Association of Working Women (Cambridge, Mass.: Radcliffe Institute for Advanced Study, 2002); Dodson, "Wage-Poor Mothers," 258–80; Kathryn Edin, "Single Mothers and Child Support: The Possibilities and Limits of Child Support Policy," *Children and Youth Services Review* 17 (1995): 203–30.

28. Gwendolyn Mink, "Violating Women: Rights Abuses in the Welfare Police State," in *Lost Ground: Welfare Reform, Poverty, and Beyond,* edited by Randy Albelda and Ann Withorn (Cambridge, Mass.: South End Press, 2004), 94–112.

29. Edin and Lein, *Making Ends Meet;* Sudhir Alladi Venkatesh, *Off the Books: The Underground Economy of the Urban Poor* (Cambridge: Harvard University Press, 2006).

30. Edin and Lein, *Making Ends Meet;* Dodson, "Wage-Poor Mothers"; Hays, *Flat Broke with Children.*

31. Jason DeParle, "First Time Filers: On a Once Forlorn Avenue, Tax Preparers Now Flourish," *New York Times,* March 21, 1999, A1.

32. Newman, *No Shame,* 198–99.

33. Dodson, *Don't Call Us Out of Name,* 194–95.

34. Schwartz-Nobel, *Growing Up Empty,* 43, 46 (see chap. 3, n. 47).

35. Jason DeParle, "The Grandmothers: As Welfare Rolls Shrink, the Load on Relatives Grows," *New York Times,* February 21, 1999, A1.

36. Soss, *Unwanted Claims,* 97; Dodson, *Don't Call Us Out of Name,* 141.

37. Sophocles, *Antigone,* translated by Kitto, 16–17.

38. Samuel P. Oliner and Pearl M. Oliner, *The Altruistic Personality: What Led Ordinary Men and Women to Risk Their Lives on Behalf of Others?* (New York: Free Press, 1988), 187.

39. David Eddy, "Rationing Resources while Improving Quality," *Journal of the American Medical Association* 272, no. 10 (September 14, 1994): 823.

40. Ibid.

41. Cheryl Strauss Einhorn, "Prognosis Positive: Some Debilitated Nursing Home Stocks May Be on the Road to Recovery," *Barron's,* August 3, 1998, 20–21.

42. Marilyn Elias, "Doctors Say They'd Lie to Get Insurers to Pay," *USA Today,* October 25, 1999, A1. The 58 percent figure comes from a survey by Daniel Sulmasy of St. Vincent's Hospital in New York. The 48 percent figure is from a poll conducted by the Kaiser Family Foundation in 1999.

43. Laurie McGinley, "How Medicare Altered Its Rule after Hearing a Very Desperate Plea," *Wall Street Journal,* April 26, 2000, A10.

44. California and Boston doctor stories are from Katherine Eban Finkelstein, "Medical Rebels: When Caring for Patients Means Breaking the Rules," *Nation,* February 21, 2000, 11–17. In California, a court overturned the governor's order before it could be implemented.

45. "Randy Kennedy, "Desperately Ill Foreigners at U.S. Emergency Rooms," *New York Times,* July 1, 1999, 1; Julia Preston, "Texas Hospitals' Separate Paths Reflect the Debate on Immigration," *New York Times,* July 18, 2006, A1.

46. Nancy Foner, *The Caregiving Dilemma: Work in an American Nursing Home* (Berkeley and Los Angeles: University of California Press, 1994), 65, 73–74. Foner found nursing-home workers loath to put in extra time and break rules to help a patient. "Most aides would not get into trouble for a patient" (77). I think there's a lot more rule breaking than meets the eye.

47. · Agencies can also use creative coding to get rid of patients they want to shed. For example, in one conference, after much discussion of a man who'd been getting services for a long time and the team's frustration with his lack of progress, the case manager read aloud while writing on the case notes: "Services wrapping up; caregivers

are preparing for independence." There was general conspiratorial laughter, as they all delighted in the case manager's clever bureaucratic lingo for "we're cutting him off."

CHAPTER 5

1. Herbert Hoover, *American Individualism* (Garden City, N.Y.: Doubleday, Page, 1922), 16–17.

2. Ibid., 17; emphasis added.

3. Epstein, *Principles for a Free Society* (see chap. 2, n. 46).

4. James Madison, *The Federalist*, no. 10; Alexander Hamilton, *The Federalist*, no. 51.

5. Schultze, *Public Use of Private Interest*, 17–18; emphasis added (see chap. 2, n. 72).

6. Edward O. Wilson, "The Biological Basis of Morality" (excerpt from *Consilience*), *Atlantic Monthly*, April 1998, 59; Friedman and Friedman, *Free to Choose*, 108 (see chap. 2, n. 76). I paraphrased slightly. The actual sentence, discussing the weakness of public assistance programs, reads: "Only human kindness, not the much stronger and more dependable spur of self-interest, assures that [bureaucrats] will spend the money in the way most beneficial to the recipients."

7. Wuthnow, *Acts of Compassion*, 65 (see chap. 3, n. 10).

8. Ibid., 56; Tom Shea, "Volunteer Tutor Getting More than He's Giving," *Springfield (Mass.) Republican*, December 15, 2005, B1; John Kasich, *Courage Is Contagious: Ordinary People Doing Extraordinary Things to Change the Face of America* (New York: Main Street Books / Doubleday, 1998), 39.

9. Kara Carden, "A Heart for Health," *American Profile*, Sunday supplement to the *Claremont (N.H.) Eagle Times*, June 30–July 6, 2002; Kasich, *Courage Is Contagious*, 63.

10. Monroe, *Heart of Altruism*, 142. Monroe tells much of Opdyke's story on pages 126–29, but doesn't name her except by first name, "Irene." From the descriptive details, "Irene" is clearly Irene Gut Opdyke, author of *In My Hands: Memories of a Holocaust Rescuer* (New York: Random House, 1999).

11. Bethany Knight, *For Goodness' Sake: A Daily Book of Cheer for Nurses' Aides and Others Who Care*, rev. ed. (1996; reprint, Albuquerque: Hartman Publishing, 1999), January 2 (this is a daybook, so there are no page numbers, only dates).

12. Isabelle Allende, essay for *This I Believe*, a National Public Radio program. Printed in the *WVPR* (Vermont Public Radio) *Radio Flyer*, Summer 2005, 7.

13. "Game of tennis" and "energy bolt" from Allan Luks, *The Healing Power of Doing Good* (San Jose: iUniverse.com, 2001), 53, 48; "endless energy" from Kasich, *Courage Is Contagious*, 169.

14. "UT Austin Provost Lends Helping Hand through Meals on Wheels," press release, October 28, 1999, http://www.utexas.edu/opa/news/99newssreleases/nr_199910/nr_olson991028.html; emphasis added.

15. Kasich, *Courage Is Contagious*, 95–109, quotation on 107.

16. Nancy Henderson Wurst, "Rhythm Nation," *Southwest Airlines Spirit*, December 2006, 139–50. The quotation contains the author's words, not Tuduri's own.

17. Shelley Taylor, *The Tending Instinct: How Nurturing Is Essential to Who We Are* (New York: Times Books, 2002), esp. 82–83.

18. Daniel Goleman, *Social Intelligence: The Revolutionary New Science of Human Relationships* (New York: Bantam Books, 2006), chaps. 3–4, quotation on 60–61.

19. Brehony, *Ordinary Grace,* 84 (see chap. 3, n. 49).

20. Kohn, *Brighter Side* (see chap. 1, n. 31); Daniel Batson has done extensive experiments to show the empathy link, but most researchers now accept that feeling empathy for someone is a prelude to helping them (*Altruism Question* [see chap. 3, n. 4]). For an earlier review, see Bernard Weiner, "A Cognitive (Attribution)-Emotion-Action Model of Motivated Behavior: An Analysis of Judgments of Help-Giving," *Journal of Personality and Social Psychology* 39, no. 2 (1980): 186–200.

21. Joe Troise, "The Darker Side of Generosity," "My Turn" column in *Newsweek,* April 2, 2001, 10.

22. Bernard Weiner, Raymond P. Perry, and James Magusson, "An Attributional Analysis of Reactions to Stigmas," *Journal of Personality and Social Psychology* 55, no. 5 (1988): 738–48; Kohn, *Brighter Side;* Martin L. Hoffman, *Empathy and Moral Development: Implications for Caring and Justice* (New York: Cambridge University Press, 2000); Steven L. Blader and Tom R. Tyler, "Justice and Empathy: What Motivates People to Help Others?" in *The Justice Motive in Everyday Life,* edited by Michael Ross and Dale T. Miller (New York: Cambridge University Press, 2002), 226–50.

23. Cook and Barrett, *American Welfare State,* 72–73 (see chap. 2, n. 51).

24. Buchanan, "The Samaritan's Dilemma," 71–85 (see chap. 2, n. 65).

25. Carol Stack beautifully illuminates this problem in her study of helping networks in a poor black community, *All Our Kin* (New York: Pantheon Books, 1972).

26. Newman, *Different Shade of Gray,* 15 (see chap. 3, n. 21). The stories in the next two paragraphs are also from Newman, ch. 1.

27. Lawrence Kotlikoff, *The Health Care Fix* (Cambridge: MIT Press, 2007), 17. With Scott Burns, Kotlikoff wrote another book called *The Coming Generational Storm* (Cambridge: MIT Press, 2004). Driving a wedge between young and old is one of the Right's major tactics to build opposition to Social Security. See Peter G. Peterson, *Gray Dawn: How the Coming Age Wave Will Transform America and the World* (New York: Times Books, 1999).

28. Karl Kronebusch and Mark Schlesinger, "Intergenerational Transfers," in *Intergenerational Linkages: Hidden Connections in American Society,* edited by Vern L. Bengston and Robert Harootyan (New York: Springer, 1994), 148–49.

29. Stanley Milgram, "The Experience of Living in Cities," *Science* 167, no. 3924 (March 1970): 1463.

30. Vivian Paley, *The Kindness of Children* (Cambridge: Harvard University Press, 1999), 6–7.

31. Thomas Jefferson cited in Jonathan Haidt, "Elevation and the Positive Psychology of Morality," in *Flourishing: Positive Psychology and the Life Well-Lived* (Washington, D.C.: American Psychological Association, 2002), 275.

32. See ibid., 283; and Sara B. Algoe and Jonathan Haidt, "Witnessing Excellence in Action: The 'Other-Praising' Emotions of Elevation, Gratitude, and Admiration," unpublished manuscript, December 2007.

33. Dale T. Miller and Rebecca K. Ratner, "The Power of the Myth of Self-Interest," in *Current Societal Concerns about Justice,* edited by Leo Montada and Melvin J. Lerner (New York: Plenum Press, 1996), 25–48.

34. Harrington, *Care and Equality,* 121–22 (see chap. 4, n. 4).

35. When I returned home, I went looking for the starfish story. Mike's story turned out to be a parable making the rounds in self-help books, with only a faint tie to Eiseley's essay. See Loren Eiseley, "The Star Thrower," in *The Immense Journey* (New York: Random House, 1957); and the parable in Rosamund Stone Zander and Benjamin Zander, *The Art of the Possible: Transforming Professional and Personal Life* (New York: Penguin, 2002).

36. Franklin Delano Roosevelt, first inaugural address, March 4, 1933, http://www.yale.edu/lawweb/avalon/presiden/inaug/froos1.htm.

37. See the many studies cited in Kohn, *Brighter Side,* 202–3.

38. Quoted in David O. Sears and Carolyn Funk, "The Role of Self-Interest in Social and Political Attitudes," in vol. 24 of *Advances in Experimental Social Psychology* (New York: Academic Press), 1.

39. Deval Patrick, acceptance speech, November 8, 2006, available at http://www.boston.com/news/local/politics/candidates/articles/2006/11/08/transcript_of_deval_patricks_acceptance?mode=PF.

CHAPTER 6

1. Almond and Verba, *Civic Culture* (see chap. 2, n. 31).

2. William Galston, for example, writes, "Young people typically characterize their volunteering as an *alternative* to official politics, which they see as self-absorbed and unrelated to their deeper ideals. They have confidence in personalized acts with consequences they can see for themselves; they have less confidence in collective actions (especially those undertaken through public institutions), whose consequences they see as remote, opaque and impossible to control" ("Civic Education and Political Participation," *Phi Delta Kappan* [September 2003]: 30, emphasis in original). For other statements of how youth see politics and volunteerism as alternatives, see Harry Boyte, "Civic Education and the New American Patriotism Post–9/11," *Cambridge Journal of Education* 33, no. 1 (2003): 85–100; and Kahne and Westheimer, "Teaching Democracy," 34–66 (see chap. 1, n. 19).

3. Robert Putnam, "*E Pluribus Unum?* Diversity and Community in the Twenty-first Century: The 2006 Johan Skytte Prize Lecture," *Scandinavian Political Studies* 39, no. 2 (2007): 137–74. Putnam also gives a succinct review of the research about whether diversity breeds conflict or harmony. A comprehensive review of more than five hundred studies concluded from them that "intergroup contact typically reduces intergroup prejudice" (Thomas F. Pettigrew and Linda R. Tropp, "A Meta-analytic Test of Intergroup Contact Theory," *Journal of Personality and Social Psychology* 90, no. 5 [2006]: 751–83).

4. John Kasich tells the story of Karen Olson, founder of the National Interfaith Hospitality Network, *Courage Is Contagious,* quotations on 83, 84 (see chap. 5, n. 8). The phrase "Millie was much like everyone else" is Kasich's, not Olson's.

5. Volunteer searchers: Mike Recht, "More than 300 Volunteers Look for Missing 10-Year-Old," *Claremont (N.H.) Eagle Times,* October 16, 2003, A3; Habitat for Humanity: Brehony, *Ordinary Grace,* 172 (see chap. 5, n. 19); chronic-care hospital: Sholom Glouberman, *Keepers: Inside Stories from Total Institutions* (London: King's Fund, 1990), 35; Holocaust rescuer: Monroe, *Heart of Altruism,* 92 (see chap. 3, n. 1).

6. Brehony, *Ordinary Grace,* 173, 82, 75.

7. Jenna Russell, "Students Bond with Families of Fallen," *Boston Globe,* February 26, 2007, A1.

8. This story is from Sidney Milkus, when he was chair of the Politics Department at Brandeis University.

9. Salamon, *Rambam's Ladder,* 35–36; emphasis added (see chap. 3, n. 50).

10. Hornstein, *Cruelty and Kindness,* 20–22 (see chap. 3, n. 57), citing especially Ervin A. Staub, "A Child in Distress: The Effects of Focussing Responsibility on Children and Their Attempts to Help," *Developmental Psychology* 2 (1970): 152–53.

11. Hornstein, *Cruelty and Kindness,* chaps. 2 and 8; J. F. Dovidio et al., "Extending the Benefits of Re-categorization: Evaluations, Self-Disclosure, and Helping," *Journal of Experimental Social Psychology* 33 (1997): 401–20.

12. Schervish and Havens, "Boston Area Diary Study," 47–71 (see chap. 3, n. 11).

13. Two researchers spent a year with the students in this program, and also wrote to alumni of the program to ask how it had affected them. See James Youniss and Miranda Yates, *Community Service and Social Responsibility in Youth* (Chicago: University of Chicago Press, 1997). All the quotations about these students are from this book.

14. Mark H. David et al., "Effect of Perspective Taking on the Cognitive Representations of Persons: A Merging of Self and Other," *Journal of Personality and Social Psychology* 70, no. 4 (1996): 713–26; Adam D. Glainsky and Gordon B. Moskowitz, "Perspective-Taking: Decreasing Stereotype Expression, Stereotype Accessibility, and In-Group Favoritism," *Journal of Personality and Social Psychology* 78, no. 4 (2000): 708–24.

15. May Sarton's words from *As We Were,* quoted in Mary Pipher, *Another Country: Navigating the Emotional Terrain of Elders* (New York: Penguin, Riverhead, 1999), 15; Salamon, *Rambam's Ladder,* 105.

16. Coles, *Call of Service,* 49, 50 (see chap. 2, n. 52). I shortened the second quote a little.

17. Ibid., 47.

18. Ibid., 77.

19. Allen V. Koop, *Stark Decency: German Prisoners of War in a New England Village* (Hanover, N.H:. University Press of New England, 1988), 77. All the stories and quotations about Camp Stark are from this book.

20. Ibid., 76.

21. Monroe, *Heart of Altruism,* 96.

22. Lisa Wangsness and Andrea Estes, "Right of Gays to Marry Set for Years to Come: Personal Stories Swayed Stances," *Boston Globe,* June 15, 2007, A1. Technically, the state legislature voted on whether to place the constitutional amendment on the 2008 election ballot, not on the constitutional amendment itself.

CHAPTER 7

1. Esmé Raji Codell, *Educating Esmé* (New York: Workman, 2001).

2. Harvey Meyer, "Volunteer Feats," *Sky* (Delta Airlines magazine), April 2000, 112–15.

3. Coles, *Call of Service*, 47 (see chap. 2, n. 52).

4. C. Kalimah Redd, "Woman Loses Arm in Fla. Gator Attack," *Boston Globe*, February 26, 2003, B1.

5. Wuthnow, *Acts of Compassion*, 109–10 (see chap. 3, n. 10).

6. Coles, *Call of Service*, 74–77.

7. Anne Rochell Konigsmark, "Kids Trade Spring Break for a Chance to Help," *USA Today*, March 16, 2006, D9.

8. Jennifer Ferranti, "What Drives Elizabeth Dole?" *Today's Christian*, May–June 1999, available at http://www.christianitytoday.com/tc/9r3/9r3020.html.

9. Coles, *Call of Service*, 41.

10. Michael Lipsky, *Street-Level Bureaucracy: Dilemmas of the Individual in Public Services* (New York: Russell Sage Foundation, 1980).

11. Knight, *For Goodness' Sake*, January 6 (see chap. 5, n. 11).

12. Coles, *Call of Service*, 74.

13. Ibid., 69–70.

14. Sidney Verba, Kay Lehman Schlozman, and Henry E. Brady, *Voice and Equality: Civic Voluntarism in American Politics* (Cambridge: Harvard University Press, 1995); Putnam, *Bowling Alone*, 121–22 (see chap. 2, n. 32); Stephen Macedo, *Democracy at Risk* (Washington, D.C.: Brookings Institution Press, 2005), chap. 4.

15. See Verba, Schlozman, and Brady, *Voice and Equality*, chap. 11, where they consider four "skill-building activities": writing letters, going to a meeting where one takes part in making decisions, planning or chairing meetings, and giving a presentation or speech; Putnam, *Bowling Alone*, 338–39 and 66, where he writes: "Churches provide an important incubator for civic skills, civic norms, community interests, and civic recruitment. Religiously active men and women learn to give speeches, run meetings, manage disagreements, and bear administrative responsibility." See also James Youniss, Jeffrey A. McLellan, and Miranda Yates, "What We Know about Engendering Civic Identity," *American Behavioral Scientist* 40, no. 5 (March–April 1997): 620–31.

16. Kasich, *Courage Is Contagious*, 92, 93 (see chap. 5, n. 8).

17. For some of these critiques, see Boyte, "Civic Education," 85–100 (see chap. 6, n. 2); Kahne and Westheimer, "Teaching Democracy," 34–66 (see chap. 1, n. 19); Joseph Kahne and Joel Westheimer, "The Limits of Political Efficacy: Educating Citizens for a Democratic Society," *PS: Politics and Political Science* (April 2006): 289–96; Walker, "Service/Politics Split," 647–49 (see introduction, n. 1); Tony Robinson, "Dare the School Build a New Social Order?" *Michigan Journal of Community Service Learning* 17 (Fall 2000): 142–57; and Tony Robinson, "Service Learning as Justice Advocacy: Can Political Scientists Do Politics?" *PS: Politics and Political Science* 33, no. 3 (September 2000): 605–12.

18. Theda Skocpol, "Advocates without Members: The Recent Transformation of American Civic Life," in *Civic Engagement in American Democracy*, edited by Theda

Skocpol and Morris P. Fiorina (Washington, D.C.: Brookings Institution Press, 1999), 500–501.

19. Goleman, *Social Intelligence,* 51–52 (see chap. 5, n. 18).

20. Wurst, "Rhythm Nation," 146 (see chap. 5, n. 16); Kasich, *Courage Is Courageous,* 33–43.

21. Stephen Jay Gould, "A Time of Gifts," *New York Times,* September 26, 2001, A23.

22. Richard Stowell, quoted in Kasich, *Courage Is Contagious,* 90.

23. Ibid., 87, 65.

24. Youniss, McLellan, and Yates, "What We Know," 620–31, and sources in n. 15 above.

25. Kasich, *Courage Is Courageous,* 195–207.

26. Kahne and Westheimer, "Teaching Democracy," 58.

27. Janey Eyler, Dwight E. Giles Jr., and John Braxton, "The Impact of Service-Learning on College Students," *Michigan Journal of Community Service Learning* 4 (Fall 1997): 5–15; Susan Hunter and Richard A. Brisbin Jr., "The Impact of Service Learning on Democratic and Civic Values," *PS: Political Science and Politics* 33, no. 3 (September 2000): 623–26; Mary A. Hepburn, Richard G. Niemi, and Chris Chapman, "Service Learning in College Political Science: Queries and Commentary," *PS: Political Science and Politics* 33, no. 3 (September 2000): 617–22.

28. David E. Campbell, "Social Capital and Service Learning," *PS: Political Science and Politics* 33, no. 3 (September 2000): 641–45; Putnam, *Bowling Alone,* 121–22.

29. George H. W. Bush, inaugural address, January 20, 1989; Bush, State of the Union Address, January 29, 1991.

30. Sara Mosle, "The Vanity of Volunteerism: Why Volunteerism Doesn't Work," *New York Times Magazine,* July 2, 2000, 22–27, 52–55.

31. Ashcroft quoted in Woody West, "'Good' Corporation Tax Breaks Are a Bad Idea—Like Americorps," April 22, 1996, BNET Business News, available at http://findarticles.com/p/articles/mi_m1571/is_n15v12/ai_181960904. For a conservative critique, see John Walters, "Clinton's Americorps Values," *Policy Review* (January–February 1996): 42–47. For George W. Bush's ambivalence about Americorps, see Ben Fritz, "Bush's Empty Rhetoric on Americorps," http://www.salon.com/story/news/feature/2003/06/20/americorps/index.html. Some conservatives, including John McCain, have come around from their initial opposition. See Ben Fritz, "How the Right Learned to Love Clinton's Pet Program," *American Prospect Online,* February 11, 2002, http://www.prospect.org/cs/articles?article=esprit_damericorps.

32. Jeffrey M. Berry, *A Voice for Nonprofits* (Washington, D.C.: Brookings Institution Press, 2003), 4. The Supreme Court decision was *Slee v. Commissioner,* 42 F.2d 184 (2d Cir. 1930), 51.

33. When applying for 501(c)(3) status, nonprofits can choose an option, called the H election, that permits them to participate extensively in politics, but for reasons nobody seems to understand, very few nonprofit leaders know about this

option, and only about 2 percent of nonprofit organizations choose it. See Berry, *Voice for Nonprofits*.

34. Jeffrey Berry tells this story elegantly and with supporting evidence in ibid., chap. 4.

CHAPTER 8

1. Peter Marris and Martin Rein, *Dilemmas of Social Reform* (Chicago: Aldine, 1967).

2. Mead, *Beyond Entitlement*, 49 (see chap. 2, n. 9). The two most forceful spokesmen for disciplinary government help are Mead in *Beyond Entitlement* and *New Politics of Poverty* (see chap. 2, n. 21); and Marvin Olasky, *The Tragedy of American Compassion* (Washington, D.C.: Regnery Gateway, 1992) and *Renewing American Compassion* (see chap. 2, n. 3).

3. Payne, *Overcoming Welfare*, 19, 22 (see chap. 2, n. 11).

4. Mead, *Beyond Entitlement*, 13; Payne, *Overcoming Welfare*, 62; Kaus, *The End of Equality*, 125, 137 (see chap. 2, n. 42).

5. Lawrence M. Mead, "The Rise of Paternalism," in *The New Paternalism*, edited by Mead (Washington, D.C.: Brookings Institution Press, 1997), 24; Kelley, *A Life of One's Own*, 111 (see chap. 2, n. 18).

6. Frances Fox Piven and Richard Cloward, *The New Class Warfare: Reagan's Attack on the Welfare State and Its Consequences* (New York: Pantheon Books, 1982), esp. chap. 1.

7. Martin E. P. Seligman, *Helplessness* (San Francisco: Freeman, 1975).

8. Ellen J. Langer and Judith Rodin, "The Effects of Choice and Enhanced Personal Responsibility for the Aged: A Field Experiment in an Institutional Setting," *Journal of Personality and Social Psychology* 34, no. 2 (1976): 191–98.

9. Judith Rodin and Ellen J. Langer, "Long-Term Effects of a Control-Relevant Intervention with the Institutional Aged," *Journal of Personality and Social Psychology* 35, no. 12 (1977): 897–902. I'm indebted to Jonathan Haidt for bringing these two studies to my attention, in his book *The Happiness Hypothesis* (New York: Basic Books, 2006), 93.

10. Joe Soss, "Lessons of Welfare: Policy Design, Political Learning, and Political Action," *American Political Science Review* 93, no. 2 (June 1999): 363–80; Soss, *Unwanted Claims* (see chap. 4, n. 23). All the quotations from Soss's research are from *Unwanted Claims* unless noted. The nursing home analogy is my twist.

11. Soss, "Lessons of Welfare," 366.

12. Virginia Sapiro, "Political Socialization During Adulthood," *Research in Micropolitics* 4 (1994): 197–223; David O. Sears, "Whither Political Socialization Research? The Question of Persistence," in *Political Socialization, Citizenship Education, and Democracy*, edited by O. Ichilov (New York: Teachers College Press, 1990), 69–97.

13. Knight, *For Goodness' Sake*, February 25 (see chap. 5, n. 11).

14. Soss, "Lessons of Welfare," 373.

15. Lucie White, "Care at Work," in *Laboring Below the Line*, edited by Frank Munger (New York: Russell Sage Foundation, 2002), 204–44. All the quotations about Head Start in the next few paragraphs are from this article, unless noted.

16. Soss, "Lessons of Welfare," 373.

17. My inspiration for the web-and-ladder analysis is Paul Spiegelman's article, "Court-Ordered Hiring Quotas after *Stotts:* A Narrative on the Role of the Moralities of the Web and the Ladder in Employment Discrimination Doctrine," *Harvard Civil Rights–Civil Liberties Law Review* 20, no. 2 (Summer 1985): 339–424.

18. William G. Bowen and Derek Bok, *The Shape of the River: Long-Term Consequences of Considering Race in University Admissions* (Princeton: Princeton University Press, 1998), 189.

19. Ibid., 190.

20. Ibid., 172.

21. Ibid.

22. Kathryn Edin, Laura Lein, and Timothy Nelson, "Taking Care of Business: The Economic Survival Strategies of Low-Income, Noncustodial Fathers," in *Laboring Below the Line*, edited by Munger, 125–47. The quotations about fathers in this and the next three paragraphs are from this article.

23. Kathryn Edin and Maria Kefalas, *Promises I Can Keep: Why Poor Women Put Motherhood Before Marriage* (Berkeley and Los Angeles: University of California Press, 2005), 184, 175. See generally chap. 6.

24. Deborah Stone, "Welfare and the Transformation of Care," in *Remaking America: Democracy and Public Policy in an Age of Inequality*, edited by Joe Soss, Jacob S. Hacker, and Suzanne Mettler (New York: Russell Sage Foundation, 2007), 183–202.

25. Harrington, *Care and Equality* (see chap. 4, n. 4); Williams, *Unbending Gender* (see chap. 4, n. 9); Robert Drago, *Striking a Balance: Work, Family, and Life* (Boston: Dollars and Sense, 2007).

26. Edin and Kefalas, *Promises I Can Keep*, 173.

27. Readers interested in more detailed policies to support families can find plenty of ideas in Rebecca Blank, *It Takes a Nation: A New Agenda for Fighting Poverty* (Princeton: Princeton University Press, 1997); Benjamin I. Page and James R. Simmons, *What Government Can Do: Dealing with Poverty and Inequality* (Chicago: University of Chicago Press, 2000); Sar A. Levitan et al., *Programs in Aid of the Poor*, 8th ed. (Baltimore: Johns Hopkins University Press, 2003); Williams, *Unbending Gender;* and Drago, *Striking a Balance*.

28. Elinor Burkett, *The Baby Boon: How Family-Friendly America Cheats the Childless* (New York: Free Press, 2000), espouses this view of child rearing as a privilege for people who can afford it. For a critique of the conservative view, see Christopher Jencks and Kathryn Edin, "Do Poor Women Have a Right to Bear Children?" *American Prospect*, no. 20 (Winter 1995): 43–52.

29. Newman, *Different Shade of Gray*, 202, 199 (see chap. 3, n. 21).

30. If you want to know more about how Social Security works and how we can make it even better, I recommend the following: Michael J. Graetz and Jerry L.

Mashaw, *True Security: Rethinking American Social Insurance* (New Haven: Yale University Press, 1999); Theodore Marmor, Jerry Mashaw, and Philip L. Harvey, *America's Misunderstood Welfare State* (New York: Basic Books, 1990); and Joseph White, *False Alarm: Why the Greatest Threat to Social Security and Medicare Is the Campaign to "Save" Them* (Baltimore: Johns Hopkins University Press, 2001).

31. Jerry Cates, *Insuring Inequality* (Ann Arbor: University of Michigan Press, 1983).

32. Timothy Egan, "A Prescription Plan Lauded as a Model Is a Budget Casualty," *New York Times*, March 5, 2003, A1.

33. Andrea Louise Campbell, *How Policies Make Citizens: Senior Political Activism and the American Welfare State* (Princeton: Princeton University Press, 2003).

34. I elaborate this argument in Deborah Stone, "Beyond Moral Hazard: Insurance as Moral Opportunity," *Connecticut Insurance Law Journal* 6, no. 1 (1999–2000): 11–46.

EPILOGUE

1. For the history of the concept of moral hazard, see Tom Baker, "On the Genealogy of Moral Hazard," Texas Law Review 75 (1996): 237–92.

2. Richard Epstein, letter to the editor, "Health Care Law Shows Big Government Lives," *New York Times*, August 10, 1997, sec. 4, p. 14.

3. Robert N. Leaton, letter to the editor, *Lebanon (N.H.) Valley News*, June 2, 2001, A9.

4. Holly Ramer, "N.H. Health Care System Seen as Too Complicated," *Claremont (N.H.) Eagle Times*, June 15, 2001, 5, quoting Gray Somers, vice president of Anthem Blue Cross and Blue Shield of New Hampshire.

5. Deborah Stone, "Why We Need a Care Movement," *Nation*, March 13, 2000, 15.

6. Among the voluminous commentaries on the "No Duty to Rescue" principle in U.S. law, an eminently readable one is Mary Ann Glendon, *Rights Talk: The Impoverishment of Political Discourse* (New York: Free Press, 1991), chap. 4.

7. Peter Singer, "Famine, Affluence, and Morality," *Philosophy and Public Affairs* 1, no. 2 (Spring 1972): 229–43.

INDEX